D1616318

GLENDALE CALIF. PUBLIC LIBRARY
3 9010 01273729 6

NOT TO BE TAKEN FROM THE LIBRARY
U-53

The McCubbin Papers

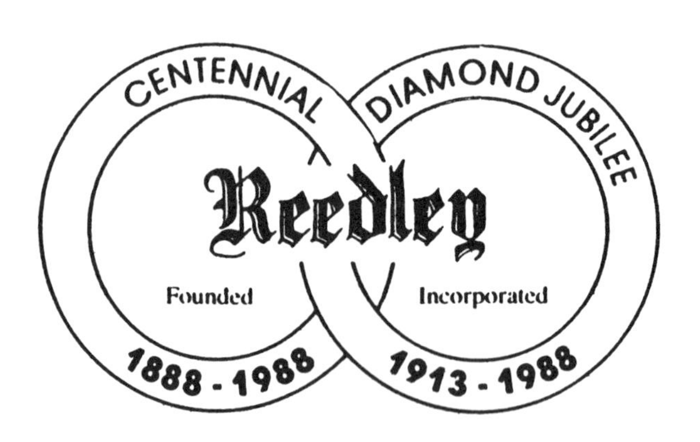
CENTENNIAL
DIAMOND JUBILEE
Reedley
Founded
Incorporated
1888 - 1988
1913 - 1988

John C. McCubbin

The McCubbin Papers

An Account of the Early History of Reedley and Vicinity

Edited, with Introduction and Notes,

by

Kenneth Zech

Reedley Historical Society

Reedley, California

1988

First Edition, 1988

Library of Congress Catalog Card Number 88-61191

ISBN 0-944194-15-X

Published by the
Reedley Historical Society
P.O. Box 877
Reedley, California 93654

Printed by
Pioneer Publishing Company
2350 E. Gettysburg
Fresno, California 93726

Contents

Maps and Drawings

Preface

I first became familiar with the writings of John C. McCubbin several years ago during the course of research on another local history project. My fascination with the writings must have been apparent, because it led my father, Norman Zech, to ask that I consider editing the papers on behalf of the Reedley Historical Society. As the long time chairman of the society's Museum Committee, he was custodian of the McCubbin archive. More important, he was the keeper of John McCubbin's dream that his collected writings would one day be published in book form.

In recognition of the importance of the McCubbin papers as a record of settlement in the Reedley district, the historical society board resolved to publish the papers as part of its contribution in commemorating the centennial of Reedley's founding and the seventy-fifth anniversary of the city's incorporation.

On behalf of the Reedley Historical Society, I would like to acknowledge the special debt that is owed to the late Oscar Noren for his role in preserving the McCubbin papers and to the Noren family for their donation of the papers to the society.

I would like to thank the staff of the Reedley Branch of the Fresno County Free Library for their courtesy and for allowing me generous access to their collection of original McCubbin papers. Thanks also to Shirley Wilder for her assistance in typing portions of the manuscript.

Most of all I owe thanks to my father for his encouragement, assistance and advice through all phases of this project; to my mother for her encouragement and support; and to my wife, Sally, for her encouragement, assistance and patience during these busy months.

— KDZ

McCubbin at his gum tree in 1916.

Introduction

When John Cameron McCubbin came to Traver, Tulare County, in August of 1886, he was following a family tradition of westward pioneering dating back to at least the mid-eighteenth century. Born twenty-three years earlier in Hancock County, Illinois, McCubbin had been raised by parents very conscious of their past and of the significance of the present. McCubbin describes his parents, Thomas B. and Martha Cameron McCubbin, as inveterate record-keepers who instilled the values of knowing one's personal history and the history of one's community. Their instruction was not without result. John Cameron became a diligent diarist who carefully recorded what he saw and heard. Coming to Traver in 1886, just two years after its establishment, and only two years before Reedley was founded, was a propitious time for the presence of a chronicler of pioneering and settlement.

When McCubbin first arrived in Traver he worked as a painter and as a hanger of wallpaper. Within a few months he changed jobs and started working for a lumber yard. A few months later he changed jobs again, this time accepting a position with the 76 Land and Water Company that would eventually lead to his becoming its Assistant Superintendent.

The 76 Company was conceived as a land and water development enterprise that would supply irrigation water to some 130,000 acres of land straddling the Tulare and Fresno County line south of the Kings River. Thirty thousand acres of land were held by the company itself for purposes of lease and sale.

McCubbin's position with the company caused him to travel widely in the "76 Country." As a consequence, he had the opportunity to meet and work with many of the people who were among the earliest settlers in the area. It was from these people, "fresh from their lips," that he learned the facts about the early days. Of course much was going on in McCubbin's own day, and this he recorded too. His writings about the 76 Country — the people, the landmarks, the old trails and river crossings, the prosperity and decline of Traver, and the rise of Reedley — are the principal, and in many cases, the only reliable accounts historians have of these places during those early times.

In late 1889, McCubbin left the 76 Company, moved to Selma, and became a beekeeper. In the years that followed he maintained his interest and activity in beekeeping, though periodically he pursued other lines of work. For a time, McCubbin returned to the lumber business as the manager of the Reedley Lumber Yard, he farmed, and appears to have been in partnership with F. S. Knauer in a firm selling real estate and insurance in Reedley. However, it was his beekeeping that occupied the greatest portion of his working life — a profession which brought him awards and widespread recognition.

McCubbin married Lucy Marie Terry, a schoolteacher, in 1892. They became the parents of a son, Bruce, in August 1894. In April 1895, the family established their residence at the ranch McCubbin had purchased in 1888, four miles south of

Reedley. McCubbin had planted a eucalyptus tree on this ranch in 1889 that eventually became so large that it became a local landmark and a source of great pride to its owner.

A daughter, Grace, was born to the McCubbins in December 1895. Sadly, Mrs. McCubbin died just seven days after Grace's birth.

In November 1899, McCubbin bought a colony lot one mile south of Reedley and moved there with his family. McCubbin remarried in 1908, but his marriage to Lottie L. Rose, a widow, did not last. They separated after three years.

McCubbin remained at the colony lot home until 1918 when he moved to Fresno. He first resided at 444 San Pablo, and later at 945 Simpson. In September 1928, McCubbin moved to Southern California. His first known address there was 1017 W. 36th Street, Los Angeles. By 1933, he was living at 2109 E. Glenoaks, Glendale, apparently with his daughter. In November 1942, McCubbin took up residence at the Hollenbeck Home for retired persons, at 573 S. Boyle, Los Angeles. He remained there until his death.

John McCubbin began compiling notes for his local histories in 1886, though it is probable that his actual writing of the articles didn't begin until sometime after the turn of the century. His historical research and writing continued for the remainder of his life. Just one year before his death at age ninety-three, McCubbin was still carrying on an active correspondence obtaining additional details about people and places, and then revising his "sketches" to be just that much more accurate or complete.

Over the years various McCubbin articles have appeared in print. Newspapers in Fresno, Reedley and Dinuba have printed his articles. The Fresno and Tulare County historical societies have published his papers in their newsletters. Katharine Nickel's book, *Beginnings in the Reedley Area* (Reedley: Nickel, 1961), contains the largest number of McCubbin's articles, but is long out-of-print and generally held in library reserve or special collections. Long excerpts from his writings appeared in Wallace Smith's book, *The Garden of the Sun* (Fresno: Hardison, 1939). More recently, two McCubbin articles appeared in *Fresno County – The Pioneer Years* (Fresno: Panorama West, 1984), by Charles W. Clough and William B. Secrest, Jr.

One of McCubbin's fondest wishes, particularly in his later years, was that someday a book of his own would be published. He realized, though, that this was unlikely to occur. A history book dealing with a comparatively small geographic area would obviously not have wide sales, and his own financial circumstances prohibited his subsidizing such a publication. Further, he doubted his own writing skills and felt that his articles would require extensive editing to be publishable in book form.

As important as his wish for a book, his greater wish seems to have been that his histories not be forgotten or lost. He sent articles to anyone who seemed the least bit interested, and to those institutions that should have been interested. He welcomed the use of his sketches in newspapers, historical society bulletins, and books.

John McCubbin at ninety years of age, 1953.

McCubbin's later years were filled with many activities aside from his history writing. He volunteered countless hours helping various groups organized for the blind, and he made regular visits (always with gifts) to a tuberculosis sanatorium. During both World Wars he wrote hundreds of letters to servicemen overseas or in hospitals.

John C. McCubbin died January 2, 1957, in Los Angeles. He is buried in the family plot at the Reedley District Cemetery — a plot on the bluff overlooking the historic Smith's Ferry site and in the very path of the "prehistoric trail" that he documented and studied.

Notes on the Editing of the Papers

Shortly after John McCubbin's death in 1957, his daughter, Grace Cheatham, sent all of his papers to Oscar Noren. Noren, raised in Reedley in the early 1900s, was a correspondent with McCubbin since at least the early 1930s, and shared McCubbin's interest in the history of the local area. Mrs. Cheatham wrote Noren saying that she was certain that there was no one more than he that her father would have wished to have his papers.

With the establishment of the Reedley Historical Society in 1976, Noren began donating selections from McCubbin's papers to the society. When Mr. Noren died in 1985, his family donated the balance of the collection to the society.

In addition to the papers on local history, the McCubbin collection includes hundreds of pages of correspondence, memorandum books, receipts, humorous newspaper clippings, extensive writings on the history and genealogy of McCubbin's ancestors, and articles on the history of Hancock County, Illinois, his birthplace.

The preparation of this book began with the assembling of the historical society's McCubbin papers into subject categories. While some initial work had been undertaken by the society to organize the archive, the process was far from complete. Several weeks were spent sorting through the approximate three linear feet of paperwork.

The next task was to complete the society's collection of McCubbin articles by locating papers not in the archive. Ironically, John McCubbin did not possess copies of all of his papers at the time of his death. His working style seems to have been to type an original and two or three carbons each time he prepared a manuscript. As he distributed his papers to correspondents and other interested persons and ran out of copies, he would simply repeat the process of typing the paper. His correspondence indicates that on occasion he would inadvertently send out his last copy, thus requiring that he write asking that his article be loaned back to him. He also writes that the storage and work space in his retirement home room was severely limited, forcing him to dispose of all but what he felt was essential.

The Reedley branch of the Fresno County Free Library has the second largest collection of McCubbin papers. In 1951 the president of the Reedley Chamber of Commerce and McCubbin discussed the publication of those papers dealing with the history of Reedley. Whatever the actual facts, it is clear from McCubbin's correspondence that he believed that a definite commitment had been made for publication in book form. He began updating his sketches and forwarding copies to the Chamber and to Neva Hunsberger, Reedley branch librarian, who apparently had offered her assistance in the project. But, in the end, no book was published.

Perhaps in consolation, Hunsberger prepared, with McCubbin's approval, a series of edited articles for publication in *The Reedley Exponent*. These ran in the paper at irregular intervals during March through June of 1955.

The Reedley library has those papers that were sent to Hunsberger and those that were sent to the Chamber, since the Chamber's copies were eventually deposited in the library. Approximately 200 pages from the Reedley library's files were photocopied for the historical society's collection.

Other area libraries and institutions were visited to determine where else McCubbin's writings were on deposit. While papers were found in other places, in no case were articles found not already in the expanded collection of the Reedley Historical Society. Based on McCubbin's correspondence and notes it is believed that the society now has all of his significant writings on the history of Tulare and Fresno Counties.

The final task was to select, arrange and edit the papers. The degree to which McCubbin's papers have been edited varies from article to article. In most cases very little was changed. Indeed, the goal was to leave the papers as close to the original as practical. Unfortunately, Mr. McCubbin's sentence construction and punctuation sometimes makes his text a real challenge to follow. His spelling is similarly problematic, particularly in the case of proper names. Changes were made in the text only when the adding of a word or two, the recasting of a sentence, the adding or deleting of a punctuation mark, or the shifting of a sentence or paragraph seemed vital to clarity. Errors, other than spelling, not seriously effecting understanding were generally left uncorrected.

Another form of revision ocurred when the editor was faced with two versions of a particular paper, each with material not found in the other. McCubbin repeatedly revised his sketches as he acquired additional information. While this results in his most recently dated versions usually being the definitive ones, this is not always the case. Many times he prepared more than one version of an article, usually doing this by altering its length so as to suit a particular purpose. Consequently, some of his more recent papers are condensations of earlier works. Solving this problem for the book meant, in some cases, merging the two texts; in other cases the material was added by way of the editor's brackets. It was a matter of doing what seemed to work best and that which was most faithful to the author's style.

McCubbin's articles were largely intended to stand on their own, the result is that they are often redundant as portions of some sketches are used in slightly altered form in others. Much of this duplicated material has been removed.

A notation at the beginning of the chapter on Reedley describes how the special problems of that material were solved.

While some of McCubbin's correspondence deals with matters of historical interest, and collectively adds much to the understanding of McCubbin and his method, no attempt has been made to include the correspondence in this book. Nevertheless, two letters of special interest have been included, and other letters are quoted or referred to in the editor's notes.

McCubbin had the foresight to use legal survey descriptions in his articles, rather than depend on road names, which often change, or man-made landmarks, which often disappear. These descriptions have been retained and the editor's brackets used to provide the reader with contemporary non-technical location descriptions. Since all survey references are to Mount Diablo Base and Meridian, this has been dropped from the end of the legal descriptions.

Not all of McCubbin's articles are dated, thus necessitating some editorial detective work (e.g., comparing typewriter fonts), and some speculation. He probably started writing his articles in earnest in the 1920s, concentrating at first on the stage roads, ferry crossings, Traver and the 76 Land and Water Company. He seems to have been quite active in the 1930s in preparing papers on these subjects that ultimately became final or near final versions. His articles on Reedley appear to have come later, with virtually all of his Reedley material undergoing final revision in the early 1950s when he thought these writings were to be published.

The maps reproduced in this book were all drawn by McCubbin.

All of the photographs appearing in the book are from the Reedley Historical Society photograph collection. The photographer's name and the date when the photograph was made is included in the caption when this information is known.

Chapter 1

The Early Years

The Prehistoric Trail

During some of my research work for the California State Historical Association, of which I have long been a member, I learned that no one had traced and located the line of travel used by the old Overland Stages passing through the San Joaquin Valley during the 1850s. I combed through the old original government surveys and located the old stage road. I also traced one of the laterals of the old stage road that formed a junction at Smith's Ferry and ran down the east side of the Kings River, in the general direction of Tulare Lake.

I located the section line crossings of that lateral, beginning at Smith's Ferry and running thence in a southeasterly direction to and across a portion of Tulare County and on into Kings County. Although the surveyors made no further record of those crossings, the trail did continue on into the Tulare Lake country. Some of the surveyors called it an "old road," while others referred to it as an "old Indian trail."

A study of my completed map of the trail, and of the early history of the territory through which it passed, led me to the conclusion that the trail had no doubt been marked out by prehistoric animals untold ages before a human being had appeared on this continent. A complete history of this old trail, beginning with its origin, would be exceedingly interesting if it were possible to obtain that valuable information. Perhaps, that history would include, among other things, an account of prehistoric animals, gigantic beasts, as well as smaller ones, that traveled over the trail in vast numbers. It would also record some of the early activities of a race of people whose first appearance on the Pacific Coast is shrouded in mystery.

A plausible theory is that at a very remote period in the past the larger migratory animals instinctively established for themselves trails connecting different localities, and when the first human beings appeared they found that some of those trails were conveniently located for their purpose. The white men in turn continued their use until the development of local conditions required different lines of travel.

This trail touched at the extreme points in the bends of the river, and its location was along the only logical route for a trail intended to reach that portion of the Tulare Lake country which it served. No animal actuated by instinct or human being prompted by reason would have marked out a trail across the dry, barren plains to the south and east, with their broad stretches of alkali, when an unobstructed route was available near a beautiful stream of pure water where food was plentiful for both man and beast, especially when that route was leading in the desired destination, as was the Kings River in this case. The west side of the river was entirely out of the question, not only because of the long detour necessary, but also because of unavoidable swamps that lay in the way.

T. H. Whitaker, who made the original survey through which this old trail ran, made his report in 1854 A portion of the report read as follows:

Facing Page

MAP
Showing Portions of both the
Stockton-Los Angeles Stage Road
and a
Prehistoric Trail.
Located in
Fresno, Tulare and Kings Counties.
Compiled and Drawn by J.C. McCubbin
From the
Original Government Survey.
Glendale, Calif. May 20, 1936.
Scale, 2 inches to the mile.
Figures along the road show the distance in chains from section corner to road crossing.

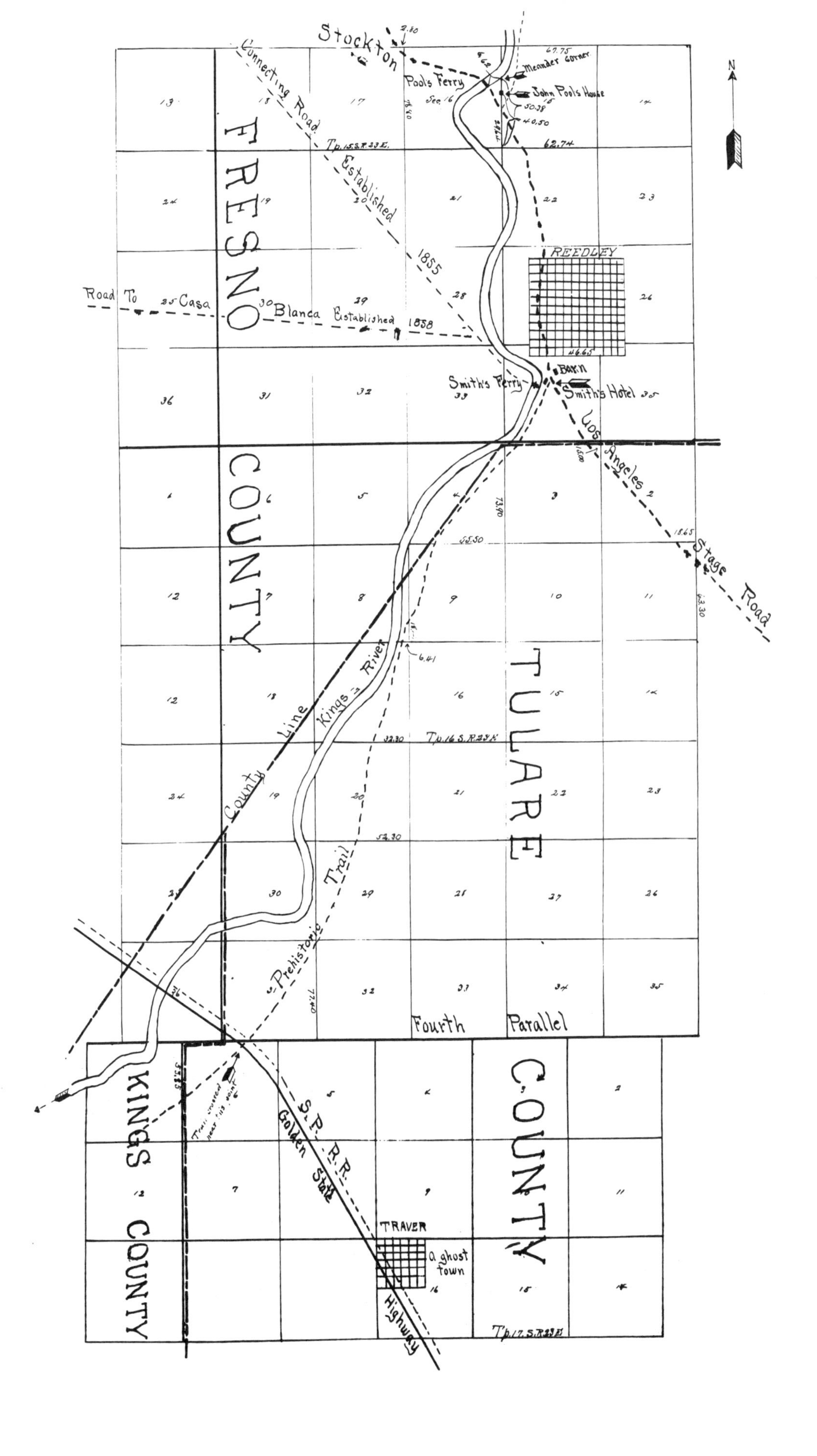
Stockton
Connecting Road
Established
1855
Pools Ferry
Meander Corner
John Pools House
FRESNO
COUNTY
REEDLEY
Road To Casa Blanca Established 1858
Smith's Ferry
Barn
Smith's Hotel
Los Angeles Stage Road
Tp. 15 S. R. 23 E.
Tp. 16 S. R. 23 E.
Tp. 17 S. R. 23 E.
TULARE
COUNTY
County Line
Kings River
Prehistoric Trail
Fourth Parallel
KINGS COUNTY
S. P. R. R.
Golden State Highway
TRAVER
a ghost town
N

> The low lands along the river are partly covered with dense willow and briar thickets, which are almost impossible to pass through by any method, and where even old bruin has to hunt his way carefully to his innumerable lairs. Any amount of antelope range in the valley, while some deer are found along the margins of the river. In the wet season geese, swans, cranes, ducks and all varieties of water fowls of California, are found in great abundance along the wet sloughs, ponds and river.

Judging from the heavy population of Indians found in the Tulare Lake country, numbering into the thousands, and the vast numbers of animals of various kinds that were roaming over the fertile plains of the San Joaquin Valley when the first white men passed that way, it is easy to believe that great multitudes of both men and beasts must have traveled over that old trail during the long ages it had probably been in use.

When this writer established his pioneer home in this portion of the San Joaquin Valley in 1886, both the old stage road and this prehistoric trail were still in use by the traveling public. This old prehistoric trail was of special interest to this writer for the reason that he had traveled over it scores of times before it was finally abandoned.

A portion of the old stage road mentioned has been declared a public highway by the board of supervisors of Tulare County. They named it the "Fremont Road" in honor of John C. Fremont, whose exploration party passed over that particular stretch of the road in the spring of 1844, when California was still a part of Old Mexico.

When the lands through which the old stage road and this lateral ran were first put into cultivation, those old road beds could be traced for miles through the grain fields by the short, stunted stalks that grew only a few inches tall over the hard packed subsoil.

In addition to my record of the section line crossings [Appendix A], there is another known point on the line of the old prehistoric trail. It is on Block 63 in the Reedley, Fresno County, cemetery, on which the three McCubbin graves are located. That point has been established, not only by the memory of this writer, but also confirmed by the sexton who dug through the hard packed subsoil of the old road bed. In addition to that block, he reported several other places in the cemetery where he contacted the same hard packed subsoil, where the old trail ran diagonally in a southwesterly direction through where the cemetery is now located.

This writer's theory of the origin of the prehistoric trail was submitted to Dr. T. T. Waterman, a prominent anthropologist. His answer was, "Your theory is well founded, and I heartily agree with it."

Librarians are the authority for the statement that the descriptive article and accompanying map of the old prehistoric trail, as prepared by this writer, are the only records of their kind to be found in any library in California.

The point where California State Highway Number 99 crosses over the old prehistoric trail bed, as indicated by this writer's map, should be permanently marked with a suitable structure.

Stockton-Los Angeles Stage Road

The old Camino Real or Kings Highway, connecting the chain of old Spanish missions that extended up and down the coastal region from San Diego to Sonoma, was the only line of travel for wheeled vehicles between the northern and southern portions of California until the early "fifties." A new road was opened up at that time extending from Los Angeles over the Tehachapi Mountains, crossing via Tejon Pass and connecting with a road already in use along the east side of the San Joaquin Valley.

Very early in the history of mining in California, prospectors pushed out from the first principal mining district, which was in the vicinity of Placerville, and established a number of mining camps in the foothills of the Sierra Nevada mountains to the south. These new camps finally extended nearly all the way down to the Tehachapi Mountains.

As a natural result of this mining activity, a wagon road was opened up, starting from Stockton and leading down near the foothills. At first the teamsters followed along in the general direction of a dim and shifting pack trail. But as travel increased, the hoofs of the oxen and the wheels of the emigrants' covered wagons marked out a roadway that was finally worn into a deep gash by the long freight teams that drew the big and heavy prairie schooners along its meandering course. Laterals, both pack trails and wagon roads, branched off to the various mining camps in the adjacent hills.

As early as 1852, or possibly the year before, intrepid emigrants made the first bold attempt to cross the Tehachapi Mountains with wagons. By working their road, and bridging chasms ahead of them as they traveled, they finally succeeded, though with great danger, in getting over the Tejon Pass and into the valley where they connected with the valley road mentioned above.

There are three members of the Akers family, still living in Fresno County (1929), who, with their parents, crossed over the Tejon Pass in 1852.

This new road over the Tehachapi Mountains provided a more direct communication between Los Angeles and the northern mines than had been possible over the old road up the coast. The new road was gradually improved and continued to grow in importance until it was handling a large share of the freight and passenger business out of Los Angeles northward.

This traffic continued until the railroad was built down the San Joaquin Valley and finally extended over the Tehachapi Mountains to Los Angeles. As the freight teams and stages were unable to compete with the railroad, the old wagon road soon began to loose its travel and it was finally abandoned. With but few exceptions, there is only a trace of the old road left. Although for about twenty years it was the only road that traversed the entire length of the San Joaquin Valley, there are but few people living who know the old thoroughfare was ever in existence.

The old stage road passed through the places where the towns of Friant,

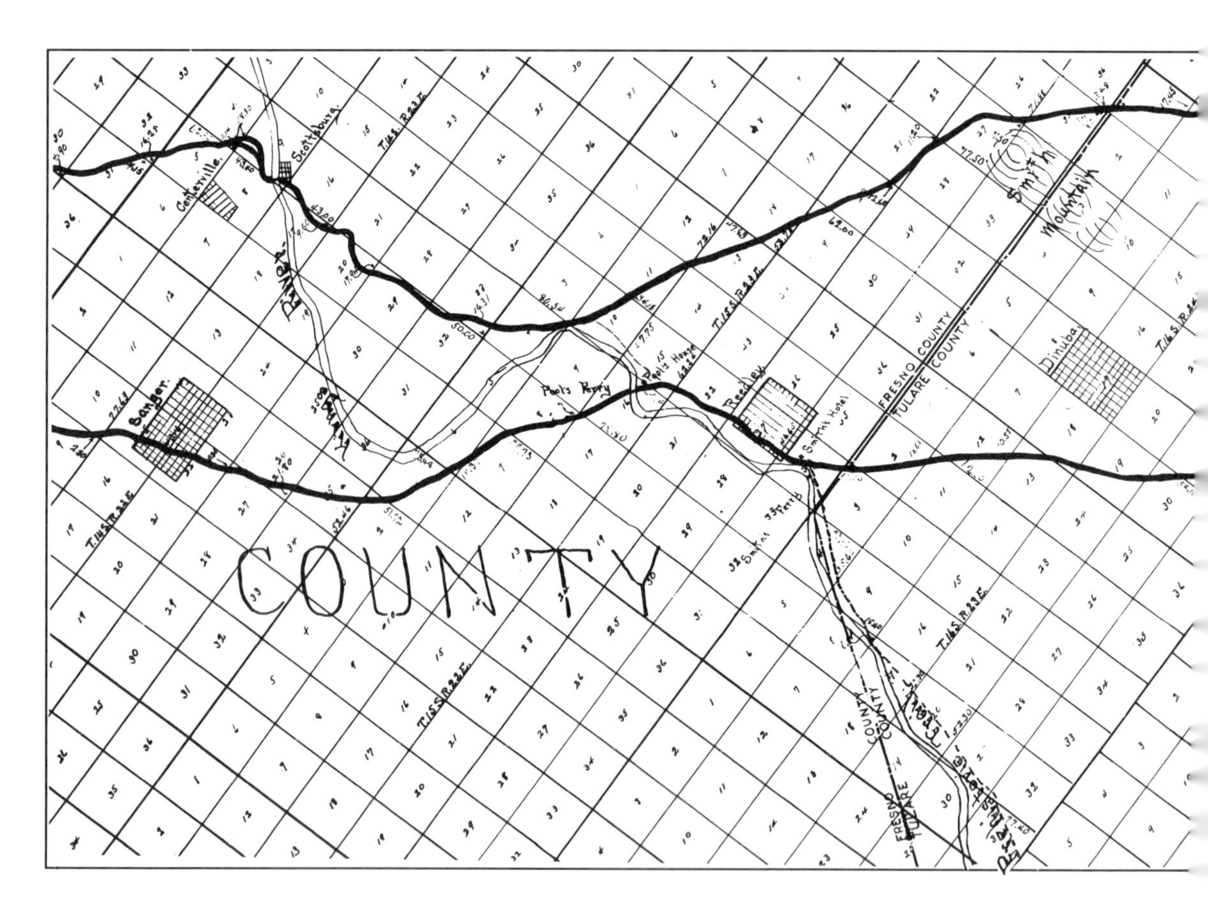

The vicinity around Reedley, from McCubbin's map entitled, "Map Showing a Portion of the Stockton-Los Angeles Stage Road." The map measures 20 inches by 11 feet and shows the route of the stage road from the Chowchilla River south to the Tulare-Kern County line.

Sanger and Reedley, in Fresno County; and Porterville and Plano, in Tulare County; are now located. Visalia and Centerville were on detours of the old road.

When this old road was serving the public, the principal streams were crossed on privately owned bridges or ferries. With the exception of a few places, such as the crossing of creeks and rivers where the banks were too steep for the teams to make the grade, there was but very little work ever done on the road in the San Joaquin Valley. Practically all the improvements in those places were made by the owners of bridges and ferries.

In 1858 the supervisors of Los Angeles County voted an outlay of $5,000 to be expended on improving the "Tejon Road." This was a special appropriation, and made in anticipation of the all-the-year-round transcontinental stage line that was established by the Butterfield Stage Company during that year. The eastern termini of that stage line were St. Louis, Missouri, and Memphis, Tennessee. The stages were routed via Los Angeles, and from there northward over the Tehachapi Mountains by the Tejon Pass. Their regular line of travel in the San

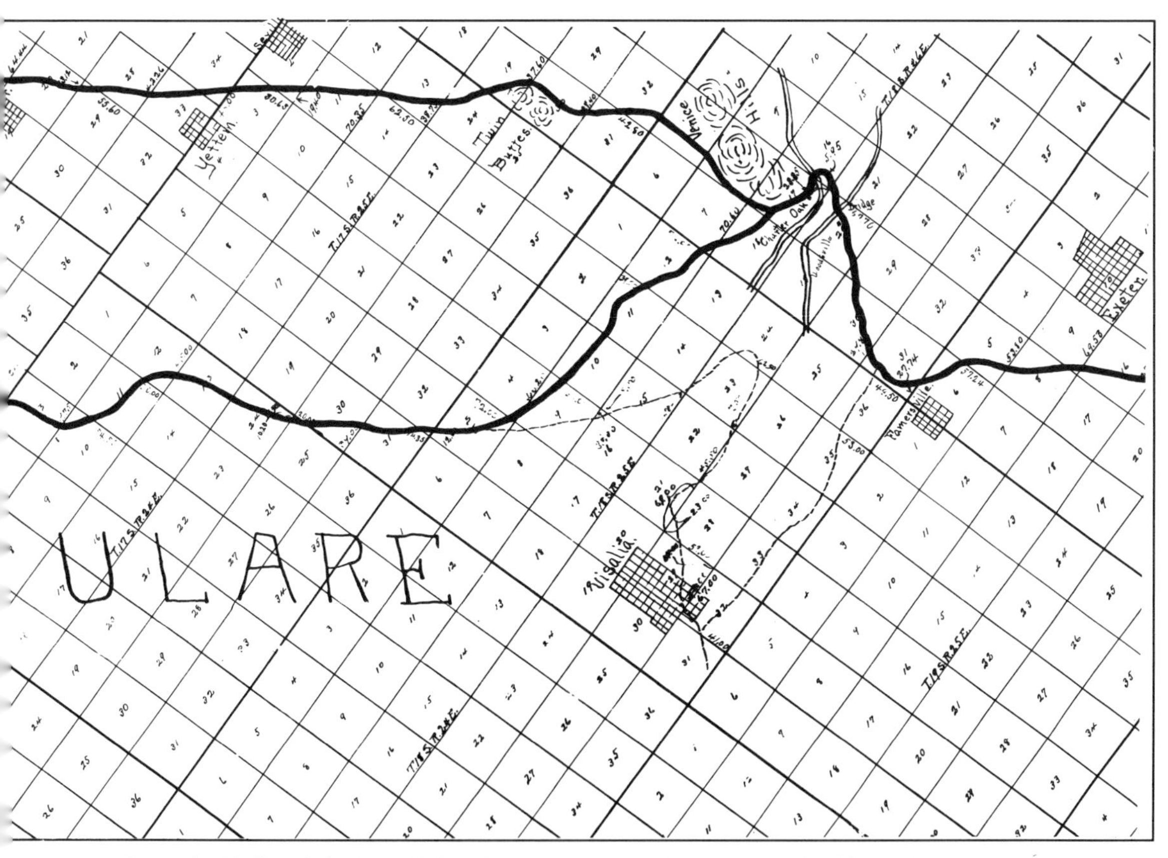

Joaquin Valley left the old Stockton-Los Angeles road at Visalia and crossed the Kings River at Kingston. The bridge piers that still stand near the river bank, about a quarter of a mile below the Santa Fe railroad bridge at Laton, mark the old Kingston ferry site.

When the river was high the stages were unable to cross at Kingston. At such times they continued on northward over the old road to Smith's Ferry, which was near where the present Reedley cemetery is located, it being the only ferry on the river that could accommodate traffic at all stages of the river. From Smith's Ferry the overland stages traveled in a westerly direction across the plains to Casa Blanca [site of present day Tranquillity], which was located at the head of Fresno Slough. There the stages formed a junction with their regular line of travel and continued their journey out of the valley via Pacheco Pass and on through the Pajaro and Santa Clara Valleys to San Francisco. The Butterfield stage line was 2,880 miles in length, and the longest continuous horse stage line ever operated in the United States.

At the present time, some of the most highly improved and attractive sections of land in the state are to be found along the line where that old stage road passed through the San Joaquin Valley. In the summer season during the time it was serving the public, there was very little along its entire length from Stockton to Los Angeles that would stir the emotions of the traveler or elicit from him a word of praise. It is true that some of the streams that were crossed in this valley were beautiful and refreshing, but these served only as a respite from the long dreary stretches of barren plains that lay spread out between them.

There is a section of the old stage road, about sixteen miles in length, running in a southerly direction from Plano (originally known as Vandalia), Tulare County, and extending over into Kern County, that is still in use. There is another small section about two miles long skirting the town of Lindsay, on the west, that is still used by the public.

When Merced County was created on April 9, 1855, that portion of the old Stockton-Los Angeles stage road extending from the San Joaquin River northwestward to the Merced River was designated as a portion of the line between the new county and its parent, Mariposa County, on the east.

When Fresno County was formed on April 19, 1856, it included the lands on both sides of that portion of the Merced-Mariposa county line extending from the San Joaquin River as far north as the Chowchilla River.

The old stage road proved to be a very unsatisfactory dividing line between the counties of Merced and Mariposa, for the reason that teamsters and stage drivers would make detours whenever conditions of the road seemed to warrant a change. This shifting of the line finally culminated in an appeal to the legislature, and as a consequence that body passed an act on March 6, 1866, ordering a survey of the north and east boundary lines of Merced County. Among other things, referring to said east boundary line, it provided that it should be marked with a permanent monument, from Phillips upper ferry, on the Merced River, along the eastern line of the old road, as traveled in 1864, to a point known as Newton's Crossing on the Chowchilla River.

This writer has definitely located some 220 points where the old Stockton-Los Angeles Stage Road, its detours, and one lateral, crossed certain section lines in what is now known as Madera, Fresno and Tulare Counties. Maps and tables have been prepared that indicate the exact distance in chains and links of each one of those crossings from a certain section corner [Appendix B]. In order to establish these points, it was necessary to go through over forty volumes of field notes that had been taken by fifteen different surveyors, while those men were making the original survey and subdividing the various townships that were traversed by that old road. These surveyors did their work separately and under contracts authorized by the legislature. Their work began in 1852 and was not completed until 1855.

From the San Joaquin River to the "Four Creeks," about fifty-five miles to the southeast, this old thoroughfare consisted of two parallel roads, running from about three to five miles apart. The northern junction was just north of the San Joaquin River and the southern junction was near the foot of Venice Hill and to the southwest. The road nearest the foothills, known as the "Upper Road," ran through a territory where much of the soil was either adobe or dry bog. The other road, known as the "Lower Road," was on land of a sandy nature. The upper road claimed nearly all the through travel during the summer season, but when the winter rains came, traffic was diverted to the lower road, which was usually free from mud.

Pool's Ferry

A Station on the Lower Detour of the Old Stockton-Los Angeles Stage Road

Three miles north of Reedley, Fresno County, and one-half mile west of the main county road, is a tract of land favored with exceptionally rich soil, and gravity water. Irrigation taxes for this land have been paid regularly since 1890, yet throughout this long period [article written in 1930], not one acre has been irrigated. All activities have been limited strictly to dry farming.

The topography of the place includes practically every surface condition found in the San Joaquin Valley. There is a high, level plain with a sheer bluff about sixty feet high on one side, and a long gentle incline extending for a quarter of a mile on the other, with all the intervening slopes between these two extremes on other parts of the tract.

The bluff mentioned is not only higher above the river at this point, but commands a more favorable view than can be obtained from any other place along the stream's seventy mile course between the foothills and Tulare Lake. When one stands at the edge of this bluff, with the river in the foreground, and nice orchards and vineyards stretching away toward the northwest and the level of the plains beyond, a magnificent panorama is spread out before him.

The water in the river first greets the eye about a half mile upstream, as it flows gently around a curve and emerges from the shadows of overhanging branches. Gracefully, it winds its way to the foot of the bluff, from where it curves toward the southwest. Continuing in that direction for about a half mile, it rounds another curve and disappears behind the same row of overhanging branches that has fringed its margin all the way down.

When the river is carrying its usual volume, there is a broad body of slowly moving water at this place. When viewed from the bluff, which is far above the tops of the trees, it has more the appearance of a long, winding lake than a section of a river.

Historical Point

Although nature in her generosity has made this place a veritable beauty spot, these gifts do not include all of its bountiful heritage. The historical associations that are closely interwoven with it are equally as interesting. John Pool's ferry, which was the first one ever operated on the Kings River, was located here. On one occasion this was the most important point (with one exception) in a territory larger in extent than the combined area of Massachusetts, Connecticut, Rhode Island, and Delaware. The time referred to was July 10, 1852, when

Tulare County was organized.

The State Legislature had passed the enabling act and created the county on the 20th of April, preceding the date mentioned, and divided it into two precincts. Pool's Ferry on the Kings River, and Woodsville on the Kaweah River, were designated as voting places [for the county's organizational election], the latter place to be the seat of the new county. A tally of the election returns showed a total of 109 votes cast, and that 58 of these, constituting a majority, were cast at Pool's Ferry. Tulare County as originally formed, included all of its present territory and parts of Fresno, Kern, Inyo, Kings and Mono Counties.

[There is some confusion as to where John Pool was actually operating his ferry at the time of the Tulare County organizational election. Since river conditions were always changing, ferryman sometimes found it necessary or desirable to move to more favorable locations. While ferry operations were supposed to be licensed, government was too distant and too new to have any effective control in these sparsely settled areas. Annie R. Mitchell, author of numerous books on Tulare County history, suggests that in 1852 there may have been as few as a dozen legitimate residents in the new 24,000 square mile county. The absence of governmental records or reliable contemporary accounts makes certainty of Pool's 1852 location a virtual impossibility.

What is known is that William J. Campbell started a ferry service on the upper Kings River about 1851. Campbell was also the sub agent responsible for the Indians at the nearby Kings River reservation. His ferry and agency headquarters were in the vicinity of where Scottsburg (about one mile southeast of Centerville) was to be unofficially established in about 1853.

John Pool is believed to have become Campbell's partner in this ferry business early in the operation. By 1852 Pool appears to have been conducting the ferry on his own, while Campbell concentrated on operating his store. It is not clear when Pool moved his ferry service to the location described by McCubbin. The earliest documentation of Pool's ferry at this second location comes from a survey conducted in 1853. The best evidence seems to suggest that in July of 1852, Pool was still operating his ferry at the first location, and that he moved to the second location sometime soon after that.

Pool continued operating at this second location until 1855, when he made plans to move his service to a place about three-quarters of a mile below where James Smith was intending to operate his ferry. Pool never did operate in this third location, instead he returned to the first location (known as Campbell's Crossing in the official Fresno County record) and operated a ferry there until 1857. He then reportedly moved to Mendocino County. W.W. Hill appears to have taken over the ferry at this location, having been granted a license in February 1858 to operate at what was now called Pool's Crossing.

The importance of knowing the exact location of Pool's Ferry in 1852 is not simply because a historic election took place there, but because it was also the place where the legendary Jim Savage was killed. Major James Savage was a successful trader and the well-known leader of the volunteer Mariposa Battalion that had fought the Indians during the uprisings of 1851. It was during one of the Battalion's forays into the Sierra that Yosemite Valley was discovered. As the commander, Savage received the historical credit for the valley's discovery. (Since Indians had been long-time residents of Yosemite Valley, this "discovery" would perhaps be more correctly described as white man's first entry into the valley.)

A raiding party of white settlers had killed several Indians from the Kings River reservation in July of 1852. Fearing renewed wars with the valley's Indians, the government persuaded Savage to see what he could do to calm the situation. Savage arrived at Pool's Ferry on August 16, 1852, and confronted Walter Harvey, the raiding party's leader. He told Harvey that there was to be an investigation and that he should surrender to authorities. A scuffle broke out, Savage's gun fell from his belt, Harvey picked it up, and shot Savage to death.

Harvey, who had been elected judge of Tulare County in the July election, was charged with murder, but the case was quickly dismissed on the basis of testimony that Savage had started the fight.

Savage's body was buried at Pool's Ferry, but three years later was moved by his friend and former business partner, Dr. Lewis Leach, to a grave near the old Savage trading post on the Fresno River.]

Ferry Site Definitely Located

Various writers of local history in attempting to locate the old site of Pool's Ferry placed it from three to seven miles from where it really was. For the purpose of correcting these errors, this writer wishes to give its true location as recorded in the original survey. It was located at a point on the Kings River nearly northwest, and about 550 feet distant from the quarter corner between Sections 15 and 16, in Township 15 South, Range 23 East.

To find the exact location of the old Pool's Ferry site, begin at the southeast corner of Section 16, Township 15 South, Range 23 East. Measure thence north along the section line 50.38 chains [one chain is equivalent to 66 feet] to the old meander corner at the edge of the bluff on the south side of the Kings River and on the line of the Swamp and Overflow survey. Measure thence downstream 6.61 chains. [The site is a half mile due west from a point on Reed Avenue six-tenths of a mile north of South Avenue.]

The point thus reached will be the place where the old Stockton-Los Angeles stage road went down the bank to Pool's Ferry. There are no surface indications to mark the spot at the present time.

John Pool's dwelling stood exactly on the section line between Sections 15 and 16, and at a point about 400 feet due south of the edge of the bluff that faces the river. He made his home at this place from the time he established his ferry, which was about 1850 or 1851, until 1855. During the latter year, James Smith established a new ferry about three miles down the river from Pool's. While Smith's boat was under construction, Pool floated his boat down the river to a point about three-quarters of a mile below the location that Smith had selected.

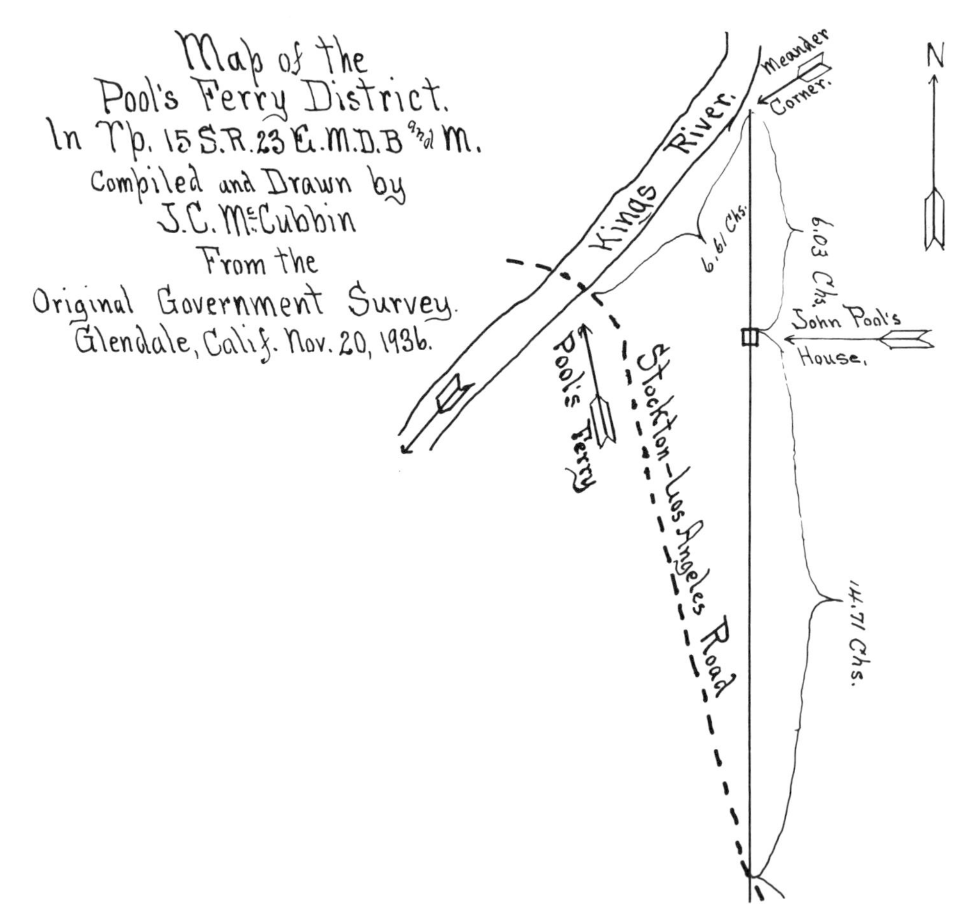

He stretched his cable across the river and installed his boat ready for service, but never operated it. As the work on Smith's boat progressed, Pool could see that his old boat could never compete with Smith's larger and up-to-date craft. He removed his cable, but left the old boat moored to the bank where it later sank. Pool moved to Scottsburg, about seven miles to the north of his original ferry site, and took charge of the ferry business at that place.

Although John Pool had enclosed a tract of land on the flat south of his ferry, and installed an irrigation system as early as 1854, he never filed on the land, or set up a claim of any kind. Being in Section 16, it was classed as State School Lands, and was sold to W. T. Cole on March 15, 1875. Cole kept it until 1887 when he sold it to the 76 Land and Water Company, and on October 9, 1891, they sold it to D. N. Hershey, and it is still in the Hershey family. Such a limited number of transfers of land of that nature and location is another very unusual thing in connection with this particular place.

The Williams Topographical Survey Party, in search of a railroad route, camped at Pool's Ferry on August 1, 1853. While there, William B. Blake, the mineralogist of the party, was prompted to write in his journal the following paragraph:

> From the banks of the river at this ferry, there is nothing to obstruct the vision across the whole breadth of the Tulare valley, and the coast mountains may be dimly seen rising above the limits of the far-stretching plains. The Sierra Nevadas

also present a magnificent spectacle from this place. The chain appears to reach a great altitude and to rise abruptly from the surrounding subordinate ridge. The outlines of the distant chain were sharply defined, and the prominent peaks showed out boldly against the clear blue sky. Snow was resting on the summits in broad white fields that glittered under the rays of the unclouded sun, and by its rapid melting kept the river well supplied with water.

Alone In Its Beauty

This place is now located a half mile from any county road, and although surrounded by highly improved farms, it has been entirely devoid of human habitation since Pool abandoned it in 1855. Neither is there a tree, vine nor shrub to be found anywhere on the tract, except those growing along the margins of the river and that were planted there by the hand of nature. The setting is one that naturally suggests quiet solitude and reverie.

Under the spell of its enchanting environment, the visitor, in his imagination, may go far back into the past and reproduce scenes that were enacted by an interesting procession that passed along over the flat below and continued their journey on across the ferry — scenes that were common at this place during the early "fifties" when the old stage road was serving the traffic of that restless period. A traffic that included, among other things, the footman, horseback rider, pack train, stage coach, emigrant train with its covered wagons and ox teams, and the big freight wagons drawn by horses or mules numbering in some cases as high as sixteen animals per team and guided by the single "jerk line." Also, as a part of that traffic were bands of loose stock of various kinds. Along with the procession, and a part of it, were men of every race, color, and creed, and from every walk of life, and representing every civilized country on the face of the earth.

After continuing but a few short years the curtain fell and closed the above described scene. All those activities permanently ended with the departure of John Pool in 1855. The visitor of today will find practically everything just as it was when the place was in its original beauty.

Woodsville

On the Old Stockton-Los Angeles Stage Road

Crossing the Kaweah River delta was a difficult task for the pioneers even with pack animals, but when wheeled vehicles were brought into service their problems were greatly increased. That portion lying to the south of Venice Hills was selected as the most feasible route by which to cross the quaggy swamps and the various units into which the river had divided itself. Very early in the history of the place, the name "Four Creeks," was applied to this particular portion of the delta, and it retained this name as long as the crossing was in use.

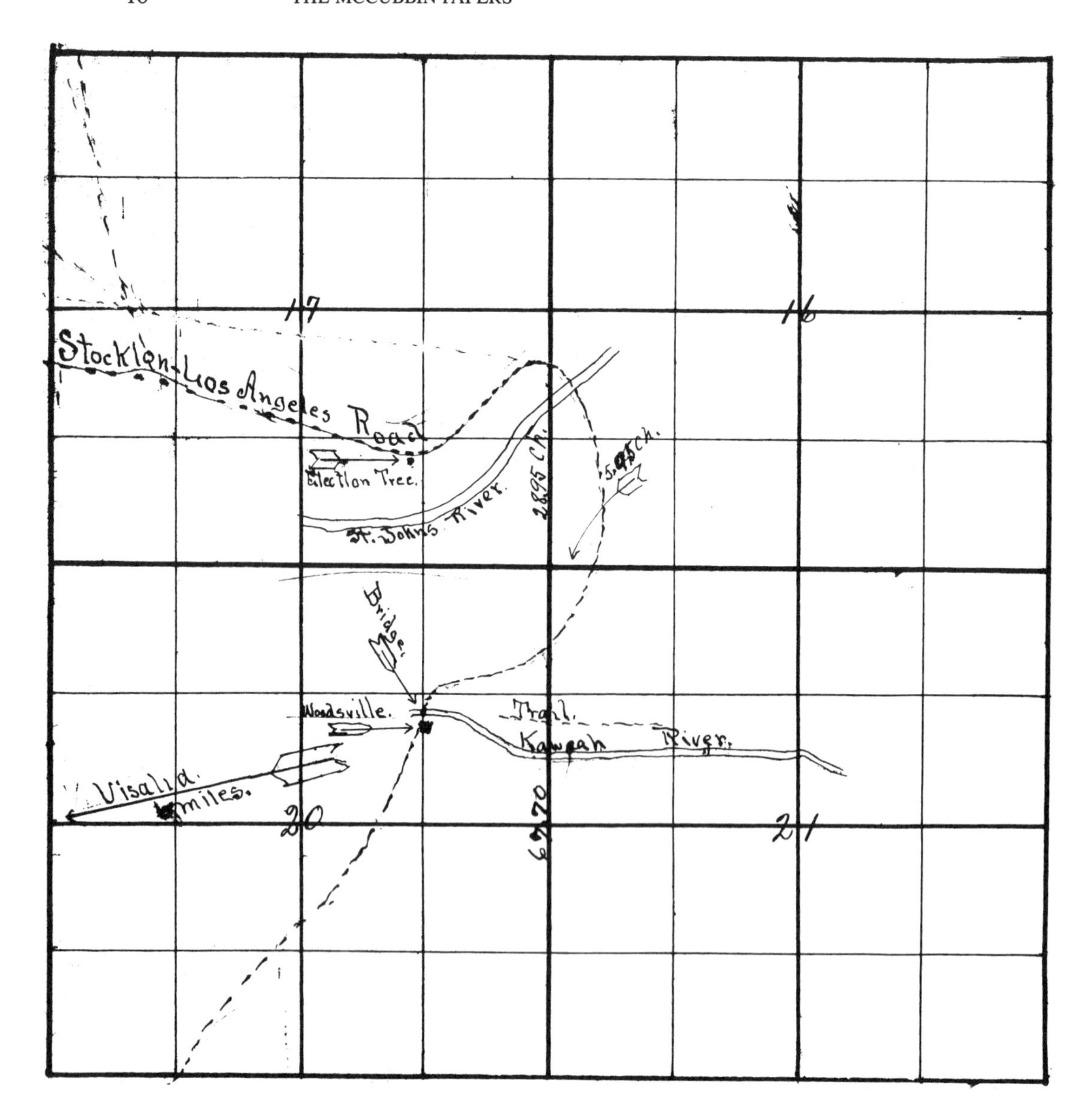

Old site of Woodsville, located in the northeast quarter of Section 20, Township 18 South, Range 26 East.

When through travel was established between Stockton and Los Angeles, the stages and freight teams were routed via Four Creeks. Connecting the Four Creeks with the ferry on the San Joaquin River near Fort Miller, a distance of about fifty-five miles, the old road was divided into the "upper and lower roads," as they were then called. The junction at the southern end of this detour was near the base and to the southwest of Venice Hills. It was near where the present Southern Pacific railroad crosses St. Johns River. The lower detour came in from the west. The upper one, after passing around to the east of the "twin buttes," skirted along the west side of Venice Hills down to the junction mentioned above. From this point the united roads followed around near the base of the Venice Hills, passing the "Charter Oak," or "Election Tree," and continued along the base of the same hills about a quarter of a mile before crossing the St. Johns River. After crossing that stream, the road ran in a southerly direction about a half mile, thence in a southwesterly direction about a quarter of a mile to where it crossed the Kaweah River. This crossing was about a half mile south of the "Election Tree."

A settlement was attempted in this portion of the delta in 1850. Loomis St. Johns, for whom St. Johns River was named, came in during that year, as did also a party of about fifteen men from Mariposa headed by a man named [John] Woods. The Woods party built a substantial log house a short distance south of the Kaweah River crossing mentioned above. St. Johns built his house about a half mile away. The Woods party brought saddle and pack horses, and arms and implements.

There are different accounts given of the fate that befell the Woods party, but the following is considered fairly correct. After being in their new location only a few months, a delegation from the Indians called upon them and demanded that they leave, but gave them ten days in which to make their departure. This the Woods men agreed to do, and began to make preparation to that end. They secretly buried their provisions and implements and proceeded to round up their loose stock. Some difficulty in getting their stock together caused a delay extending beyond the ten days of grace. Making their previous threat good, the Indians attacked and killed all but two of the party, and one of these was wounded. It is claimed that Woods was skinned alive. It appears that St. Johns was not molested at the time of the Woods party tragedy, but remained permanently.

When the news of the Woods party massacre reached Fort Miller, a detachment of troops was sent over. The troops began the construction of a fort, but were withdrawn before it was completed.

Pioneers were always persistent, and could seldom be frightened away except temporarily, from a locality where a settlement had once been attempted. The Woodsville territory was no exception to this rule. In the fall of 1851, two brothers, A. A. and C. R. Wingfield, settled near the Woods cabin and laid claim on a "squatter's right" to the land from the Kaweah River southward. During the same year (1851), the Vise brothers, Nathaniel and Abner, established a settlement a few miles to the southwest of Woodsville, and it eventually grew into a town and was named Visalia in honor of these two brothers.

The enabling act of the Legislature creating Tulare County was approved April 20, 1852. It provided, among other things, "That the seat of justice shall be at the cabin on the south side of Kaweah creek, near the bridge built by Thomas Payne, and shall be called Woodsville, until changed by the people as prescribed by law." The act also provided that during the second week in July following a set of county officers should be chosen. Major James B. Savage, M. B. Lewis, John

Howling and W. H. McMillon were appointed as commissioners to carry out the law and conduct the election.

A detachment under the command of Major Savage came to the new county and made their first camp on Grand Island believed to be near the 1852 site of Pool's Ferry on the Kings River, where they held their first meeting on July 8, 1852. At this meeting the commissioners ordered an election to be held on July 10, 1852, and appointed William J. Campbell to be inspector at Pool's Ferry and William Dill to be inspector at Woodsville. These two were the only precincts established.

Major Savage marshalled the fighting men for the advance on Four Creeks. Including the board of commissioners, the men under Major Savage were fifty-two strong. On the morning of July 9, they started from Pool's Ferry to cross the plains. Late in the afternoon they arrived at the outskirts of the timber at the foot of Venice Hills, where it is claimed they saw hostile Indians, and that Major Savage's men rode along the southeast side of these hills firing right and left at every Indian they saw.

As soon as the party arrived at their destination, the commissioners began to prepare for the election. On the morning of July 10, the polls were opened under the tree that stood furthest out on the open ground. That tree is now known as "Election Tree," also "Charter Oak" mentioned above.

On July 12, the newly elected county officers took the oath of office. The county seat remained for some time under the "Election Tree," although the Woods cabin about a half mile to the south was the legal location as designated by the Legislature. The first school in Tulare County was conducted in the old Woods cabin.

At a general election held September 7, 1853, the county seat was moved from Woodsville to Visalia, but the old Four Creeks crossing continued to serve the traveling public for many years afterwards, although a crossing lower down and nearer to Visalia could be used during a part of the year.

Scottsburg

A Station on the
Old Stockton-Los Angeles Stage Road

There are several interesting features connected with the Kings River and the territory through which it flows, that are not common to the ordinary stream. One of these is a tract of land near the foothills, about five miles wide by seven miles long, known to the early settlers as the "76 Bottom." It received its title from a stock brand used by E. C. Ferguson and Andrew Darwin during the fifties.

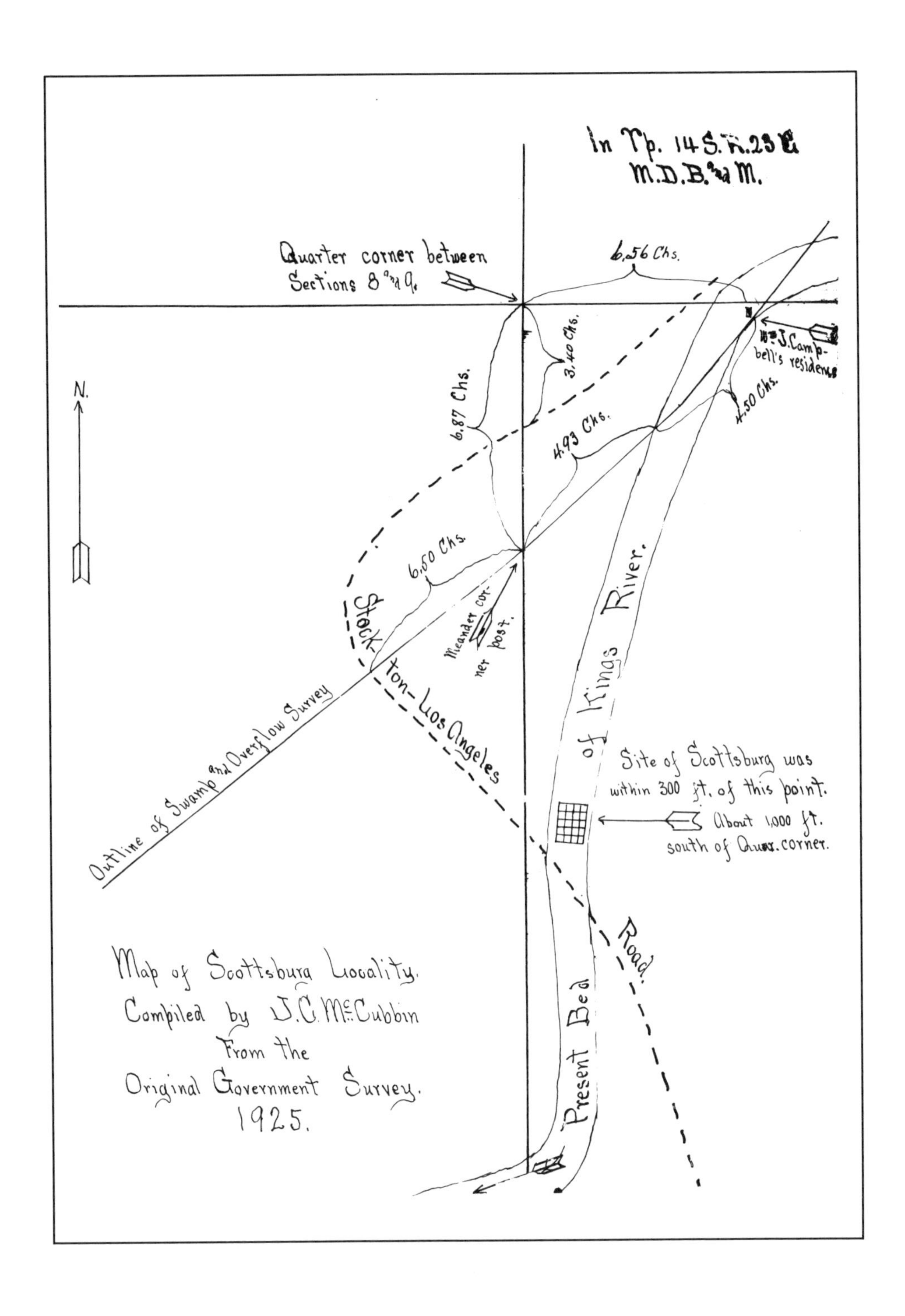
In Tp. 14 S. R. 23 E.
M.D.B.&M.
Quarter corner between
Sections 8 and 9.
6.56 Chs.
3.40 Chs.
J. Campbell's residence
6.87 Chs.
4.93 Chs.
4.50 Chs.
N.
6.50 Chs.
Meander corner post.
Stockton-Los Angeles
Road.
of Kings River.
Outline of Swamp and Overflow Survey
Site of Scottsburg was
within 300 ft. of this point.
About 1,000 ft.
south of Quar. corner.
Present Bed
Map of Scottsburg Locality.
Compiled by J. C. McCubbin
From the
Original Government Survey.
1925.

In 1856 these two gentlemen purchased a large body of land in the river bottom, east of the present location of the town of Sanger, and later on, added to their holdings by buying other lands out on the plains to the southeast. Ferguson and Darwin registered and recorded the "76" brand in Fresno County on August 4, 1857. Vast herds of their cattle wearing the "76" brand grazed far and wide, and the term "76 Country" was eventually applied to an immense territory. It embraced the present entire Alta District together with all the bottom lands that lay to the south and east of the town of Centerville.

Ferguson and Darwin sold their 76 Ranch stock and brand to Thomas Fowler and Richard Carmen about the year 1865. About ten years later, Fowler purchased his partner's entire interest in the property. After continuing the business as sole owner for about six years, Fowler turned over a large portion of his lands [in 1882] to the newly organized 76 Land and Water Company, taking in exchange therefore a large block of stock in the company.

The 76 Land and Water Company built the 76 canal system during the early eighties, and sold it to the Alta Irrigation District in 1890.

The headquarters of the old 76 Ranch was located about midway between the present Minkler depot on the Wahtoke branch of the Santa Fe Railroad and the Frankwood school house about a quarter of a mile to the southeast. The old one-story dwelling was the last of the units to disappear. It was dismantled in 1892 and the lumber was used in the construction of the buildings at the Carmelita vineyard, a half-mile to the south.

With the exception of a large mound that rears its crown to a level with the surrounding plains, the entire 76 Bottom, containing about 16,000 acres of land, is from thirty to sixty feet below the adjacent valley lands. While flowing through this depressed portion, the waters of the river are divided into over twenty different channels. Some of these unite and divide repeatedly, but their activities do not cease with those of the ordinary delta, for all are finally gathered into one solid body. The Kings River leaves this oval-shaped, sunken area as complete in volume as when it entered it. The exit is in a southerly direction and through a gorge in the plains about a quarter of a mile in width.

The 76 Bottom was also known in early days by the name of "Upper Kings River," to distinguish it from another place about twenty-five miles down stream called, "Lower Kings River." At each of these places there was eventually a white settlement, an Indian rancharia, a small town and a ferry.

First Settlers

William J. Campbell and his brother Edward were perhaps the first ones to settle in the immediate vicinity of the future site of Scottsburg. It is positively known that these two gentlemen were conducting a ferry business at that place as early as 1853 [perhaps as early as 1850 or 1851]. They had established the ferry for the accommodation of traffic over the upper detour of the old Stockton-Los Angeles stage road.

In 1854, Joseph A. Tivy, for whom Tivy Mountain to the east of the 76 Bottom was named, made the original survey and subdivided Township 14 South, Range 23 East, which includes practically all the 76 Bottom. In accordance with his contract, which had been authorized by the state legislature, Tivy classified about one-fourth of the 76 Bottom as "Swamp and Overflowed" lands, for the reason that those particular lands were subject to inundation.

The 76 Bottom being very fertile, and since many different kinds of products could be grown there to perfection without irrigation, it proved to be a very inviting place for the pioneer, and a little settlement grew up in the early fifties. The nearest trading point for these people was Fort Miller, about thirty miles to the northwest. With their slowly plodding ox teams, it required nearly two days to make the trip one way. The necessity for a local trading place was supplied just as soon as sufficient settlers in the vicinity justified such a venture.

At one place within the Swamp and Overflowed area, there was a portion where the elevation reached a little above that of the "second bottom," though separated from it by a shallow slough. This is where William J. Campbell, and his brother Edward, operated a ferry. About 1854 a little town was established at the ferry and named Scottsburg, in honor of W. Y. Scott who conducted a store and saloon in the place. Among the later residents of the town, in addition to Scott, were J. B. Sweem, W. W. Hill, John Pool, Alexander Moody, Thomas Moody, William J. Campbell, Edward Campbell, William C. Caldwell, William J. Hutchinson and Widow Flanagan.

In the immediate vicinity of Scottsburg, were the Falcon Hotel belonging to Widow Flanagan, J.B. Sweem's grist mill and residence, and the William J. Campbell residence. Scottsburg and the Falcon Hotel were on the south side of the river, while Sweem's mill and residence and William J. Campbell's residence were on the north side of the stream. The Falcon was out about a quarter of a mile from the river, and the other places mentioned were near the bank of the stream. Scottsburg, the Falcon and Campbell's residence were all located on the west half of the southwest quarter of Section 9, Township 14 South, Range 23 East. Sweem's mill and residence were less than ten rods north of this eighty acre tract. All were on soil of an unusually loose texture.

The Floods

During the winter of 1861-62 a great flood visited this portion of California and the extremely high water in the Kings River completely destroyed Scottsburg, Sweem's mill and residence, and Campbell's residence. The Falcon Hotel was undermined and so badly wrecked that it was permanently abandoned.

The peculiar actions of the river at the time of the big flood seem almost uncanny, and as though the surging waters of the angry stream were under the immediate influence of some unseen monster bent on destruction, with Sweem's mill and residence, Campbell's residence, and Scottsburg marked as special victims for its awful fury. The river channel became choked with a tangle of whole forest trees, acres of which had just been washed out by the roots far back in the mountains.

When this choking occurred the river abandoned its regular channel. The river cut a new channel, sweeping away to the right far enough to undermine Sweem's mill and residence and carry them away. Campbell's house was next in line, and it shared a like fate. From there the water changed its course again, and cutting directly across the old river bed took a straight course for Scottsburg. The swirling waters churned and bored out the loose soil on which the town had been built, until every vestige of it was washed away. Even the little burying ground where rested the remains of loved ones was not immune from the ravages of that merciless torrent. The earth was removed from that sacred spot to a depth of several feet below the beds of the graves, and the remains of those who had been laid to rest there were carried away with the great volume of debris, and reburied far below in unknown places. Not a trace of any of the bodies has ever been found.

The residents of Scottsburg and those at Sweem's and Campbell's were all transported to places of safety, but the Alexander Moody family, who were occupying the Falcon Hotel at the time, were not so fortunate. They were trapped by the water. Moody hastily built a platform on the top of some willow posts that had been used for a hog pen, and placed his wife and their four children thereon. He then managed to get ashore where he hoped to get a boat with which to rescue his family. The wife and children were compelled to remain on the platform two nights and a day before a boat could be secured to transport them to dry land.

Peter Fink, who was living in the southern part of the 76 Bottom at the time of the big flood, took his wife to the home of a neighbor who lived on high land, and then returned to make some emergency preparations for an indefinite absence. While thus engaged, the rapidly rising waters trapped him, and he was compelled to climb a tree where he remained all night before being rescued from his perilous position.

Following the disastrous flood, Scottsburg was reestablished over toward the foot of the bluff to the northwest, and below the site of the present town of Centerville. There it remained until another flood occurred on Christmas Eve, 1867. This gave the residents such a fright that they soon afterwards moved the town up on the bluff and rechristened it "Centerville." The place has always been known locally as "Centerville," but the United States Postal Department has never recognized it by any name except "King River" (The letter "s" omitted).

Original Sites Located

As near as can be ascertained, the original sites of Scottsburg, Sweem's mill and residence, and William J. Campbell's residence were as follows: Taking the big bridge that spans the river about a mile to the southeast of the present town of Centerville as a starting point and following down the north side, we find that Sweem's mill and dwelling were a short distance below that place and above the present river bed. Following on down the stream to where it changes from a southwesterly to a southerly course, we come to the site of William J. Campbell's house. It was about fifty feet from the old river bank and above the present river bed. The east wall of Campbell's house was at a point 433 feet east and 27 feet south of the quarter corner between Sections 8 and 9 in Township 14 South, Range 23 East. [McCubbin writes elsewhere that in earlier years he had placed a large concrete slab in the river bed marking the location of the east wall of the Campbell residence, but that this marker eventually washed away.] The site of Scottsburg was south and about one thousand feet down the river on the opposite side from Campbell's residence, and above the present river bed.

Usually the Kings River is as clear as crystal at the old Scottsburg site, and when shallow enough, sings merrily as it ripples peacefully along over its cobblestone bed, offering not the slightest suggestion that here on one occasion it "swallowed" an entire village.

Officers Elected from Scottsburg

Citizens who were residents of Scottsburg at various times prior to its destruction in 1867 furnished material for several of the early day officers of this part of California. The names of these men and the offices that each one filled were as follows:

William J. Campbell was sub Indian Agent and had charge of the Pasquale Indian rancharia that was located in the 76 Bottom below Scottsburg. He served as Inspector at Pool's Ferry, when Tulare County elected her first set of officers, July 10, 1852. He was Justice of the Peace at Scottsburg when that territory passed from Mariposa County to Tulare County, and this automatically made him a member of the Court of Sessions. The duties of that body were similar to those of the present Board of Supervisors.

The bold and conspicuous mountain with an altitude of about 1,750 feet, that stands about four miles to the southeast of the old Scottsburg site, was given the name of "Mount Campbell" by the early settlers of the 76 Bottom. And, it will perhaps continue to serve as a monument to the memory of William J. Campbell for all time to come.

W. Y. Scott was elected Sheriff of Fresno County. W. W. Hill was elected Treasurer of Fresno County. William J. Hutchinson was elected Assessor of Fresno County several successive terms. John Pool was elected to serve on the first Board of Supervisors of Tulare County.

In addition to the above, there were four others in the vicinity of Scottsburg, though not residents of the town proper, who filled either a county or a state office during the early days.

Peter Fink and Eliza Deakin Fink

{Peter Fink and Eliza Deakin were early settlers in the Scottsburg district. The first of the following two items is drawn from McCubbin's notes concerning Peter Fink. The second piece is from a letter McCubbin wrote to Mrs. Lilbourne Winchell in 1927.}

Peter Fink

Peter Fink was born in New York State on March 7, 1829. He was a California forty-niner. He made a fortune mining, and lost it the same way.

In the early 1850s he came to the 76 Bottom and went into the stock business. He married Miss Eliza Deakin in 1859 or 1860 when she was fifteen, and they raised quite a family.

Fink owned 1,400 acres in the bottom. Along with John Rogers he owned 1,760 acres in the hills. Fink's Bedrock ranch was 320 acres, and his 76 Bottom ranch was 1,400 acres.

Fink committed suicide on his ranch about five miles north of Reedley by hanging himself in his barn. This occurred on March 7, 1904, on his seventy-fifth birthday.

Eliza Deakin Fink

Dear Mrs. Winchell: The romantic item, connected with the experience of Peter Fink and Miss Eliza Deakin, to which I called your attention some time ago, was as follows.

William Deakin, with his wife and nine year old daughter, Eliza, settled in the Kings River bottom, south of Scottsburg, in 1855. Soon after their arrival, Jesse Morrow called and made the acquaintance of the family. A few days later, Morrow and Peter Fink were riding along on horseback near the Deakin tent. Eliza and a neighbor girl were sitting on the tongue of Deakin's ox wagon as the men rode by. Referring to the Deakins, Fink said to Morrow, "Are there any young ladies with this outfit?" Morrow replied by saying, "There are no children in the family except that biggest girl sitting on the wagon tongue." Fink in reply said, "Well then I guess I'll have to wait for her." When Eliza, who was the child referred to in his conversation reached the age of fifteen, she and Peter Fink were married.

At the time of the high water in the Kings River, when Scottsburg was washed away, the William Deakin family was living in the river bottom south of that little town. In writing about that flood and the experience of her father's family at the time, Mrs. Fink said,

> Our house was not washed away, but the water came all around it, making it unsafe to live in again. We moved out on high ground and built a temporary home. Soon we were joined by two other families making ten persons in number. Here we all lived as one in an adobe house, and as part of the outer walls had crumbled away, we had to build a new one. A party of us walked to a neighbor's a mile away to see how they had fared. We found them confined to a second story, with an angry, swift current in front of the house that threatened to start it down the river any minute. We set to work making a raft and rescued them. Father took my mother and I out to a neighbor's on high land and returned to arrange things for safety intending to join us in the evening, but the water rose so rapidly that he was forced to climb a tree and remain all night.

James Smith

Martha Lucinda Hamilton (Mrs. James) Smith

Smith's Ferry

A Station on the Lower Detour of the Old Stockton-Los Angeles Stage Road

{*Much of the information in the sketches about James Smith and the ferry was obtained by McCubbin directly from the children of James Smith. McCubbin's handwritten notes describe these meetings as follows.*

"When I learned that J. P. H. Smith, son of James Smith, was living in Monterey County, I made a special trip all the way over to his home and spent two nights and a day visiting in his home and jotting down historical items as he related them.

Later on Ham came over and I took him all over his old stamping ground when I gathered more items. Then James B. "Buck" Smith, his brother, came up from Los Angeles, and I took him on a tour similar to the one I took with his brother.

Still later, Mrs. Harriet Lucretia (nee Smith) Noonan of Stockton came down, and I took her and Mrs. E. Fink and her daughter, Mrs. Jacobs, whom Hattie hadn't seen in nearly forty years. The Smiths and Finks had been particular friends from 1855 until the Smiths moved away about 1874. I gathered much interesting and valuable information on this trip while they were talking over old times and they were visiting where many activities had been in progress during these early days."}

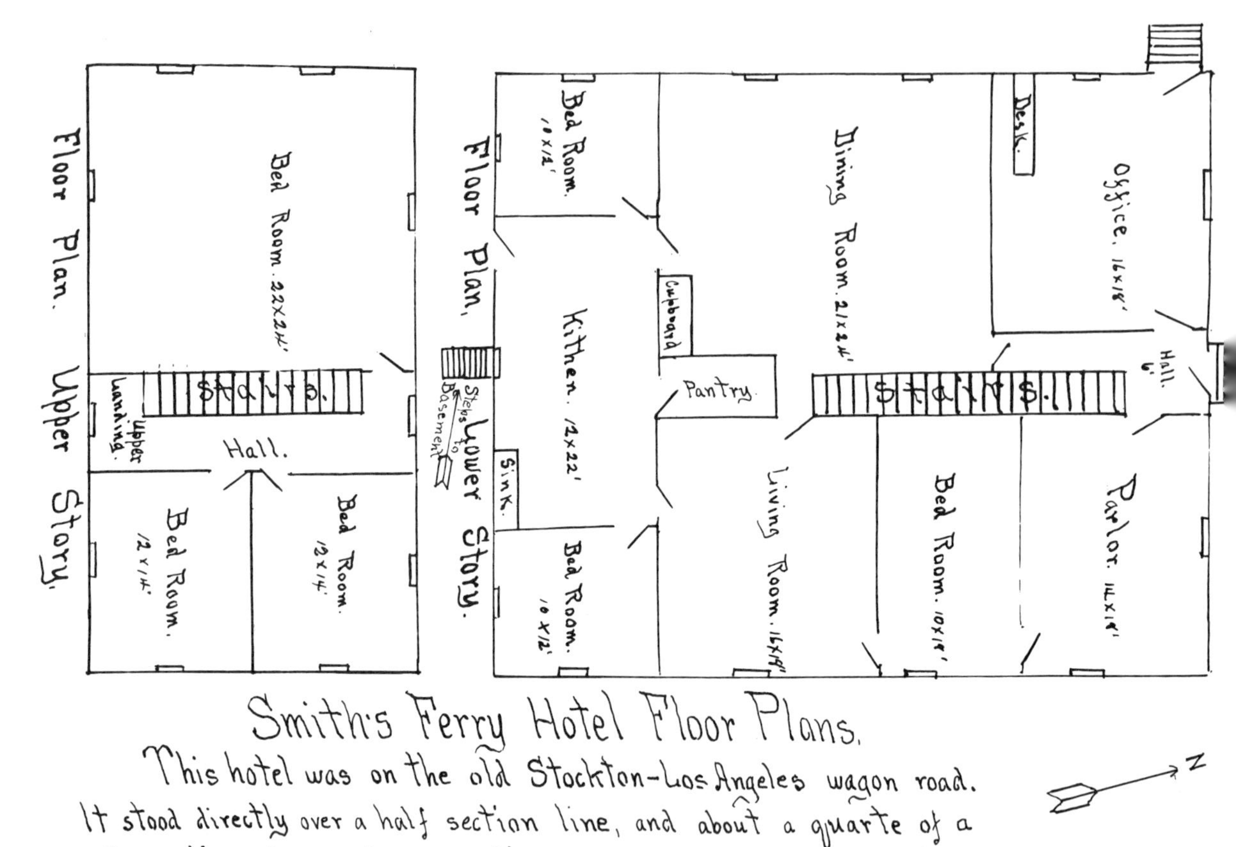

Smith's Ferry Hotel Floor Plans.
This hotel was on the old Stockton-Los Angeles wagon road. It stood directly over a half section line, and about a quarte of a mile north of the center of section 34, Tp. 15 S. R. 23 E. M.D.B.and M.
Drawn by J.C. McCubbin, Glendale, Calif. Nov. 20, 1936.

Smith's Ferry, located on the lower detour of the old Stockton-Los Angeles stage road, was established by James Smith in 1855, and for nineteen consecutive years it was the most important crossing on the Kings River. The east landing of the ferry was about a quarter of a mile from the present townsite of Reedley, Fresno County, and near the northwest corner of the Reedley cemetery. At no other place could crossings be made during high water, and for that reason it remained open to the public after all other ferries on the river had been abandoned.

The Smith's Ferry site was actually in three counties in less than four years. Prior to April 20, 1852, it was in Mariposa County. On that date Tulare County was formed, and the future site of the ferry was included in the new county. Then when Fresno County was created on April 19, 1856, the place was taken over from Tulare County.

Smith continued in charge of the hotel and ferry until the time of his death in 1862. His widow continued the business a few years until she married a man by the name of Clayborne [or Claybourne?] Wright. Wright assumed charge of the

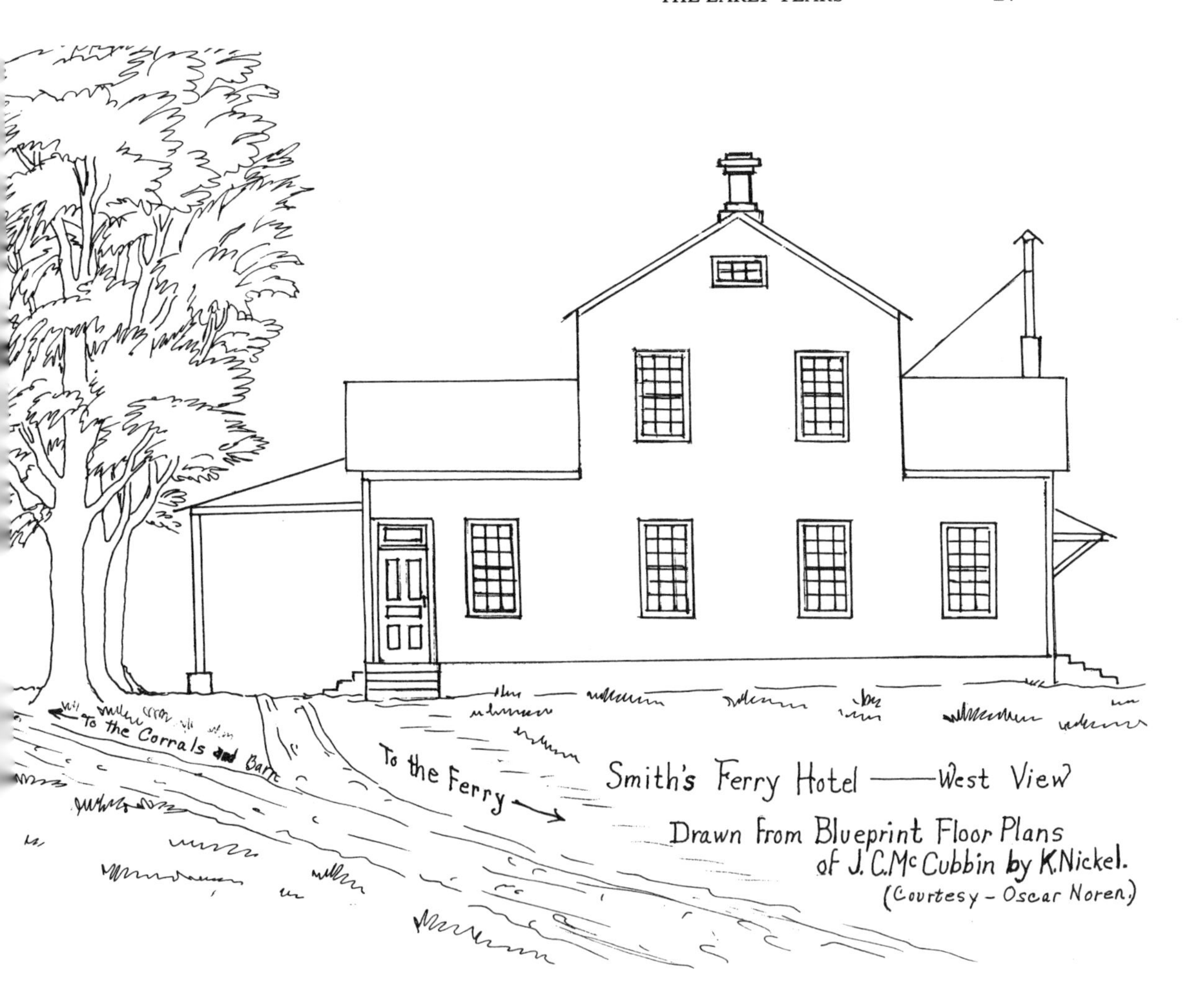

business and conducted it for a few years, until he moved to some other part of the state. Mrs. Wright again took charge, and with the assistance of her son Hamilton Smith, continued in the management of the property until 1874. During February of that year the property was deeded to J. W. Mitchell, father of the late W. D. Mitchell. Mitchell entered into a partnership with W. E. Ross for the purpose of conducting a hotel and ferry business at the old stand. Ross was the proprietor and his mother, Mrs. Lorena Hill, was landlady. The family consisted of the mother and six children. There was Ross and his three half-brothers, George, Charles and John Hill; and his two half-sisters, Sarah and Emily Hill.

The old ferry boat had been replaced with a new one, about 1865 or 1866. The new one was constructed on the same plan and dimensions as the old one, which was sixteen feet wide and sixty feet long, and provided with a landing platform at each end. These platforms were four feet wide and extended all the way across the boat, and were attached with powerful hinges.

The ends of the large stout cable that extended across the stream were attached to heavy timbers set upright on either bank. The cable was strung far enough above high water to enable driftwood to clear it at all times. The boat was attached to the cable by means of a block and tackle connection at each end of the craft. The ferry would be held at right angles to the bank while being loaded. When ready to cross, the ferryman would, by means of the block and tackle connection, bring the boat into a position pointing diagonally upstream and toward the opposite bank, and then released. The upper side of the hull would act as a rudder and the current would force the boat across the stream.

In the summer of 1860, Thomas Munn, the helper, was ferrying an emigrant wagon across. In the wagon was a family consisting of the parents and their four children. When about two-thirds of the way across, the sea grass cable broke. The river was low at the time and the current was not very strong. Munn had served as a sailor on an English ship and was used to water. He immediately jumped out, and taking the rope with him made for the shore. He succeeded in bringing the boat to the bank where he made it fast to a tree. A new steel cable was then installed replacing the rope cable.

The schedule of ferry rates was as follows:

One horse rig	$ .75
Two horse rig	1.00
Four horse rig	1.50
Six horse rig	2.00
Eight horse rig	2.50
Ten horse rig	3.00
Twelve horse rig	3.50
Fourteen horse rig	4.00
Sixteen horse rig	4.50
Footman or one horse	.50
Horse and rider	.50
Pack horse	.50
Sheep, in band, per head, each	.03
Horses or cattle, in bands,	.12
Stages, about sixty per cent of transient teams	

W. E. Ross stated that the old hotel register left by the Smiths, when he took charge, was a massive volume and showed daily cash receipts on many occasions of over $300.

In speaking of some of his guests, Ross gave the names of two "cattle kings" of the period: Henry Miller and C. W. Clarke, who took luncheon together at the hotel. After their lunch, he ferried them across the river, where they bade him "adios" and galloped off together in a cloud of dust over the old road to the northwest.

Soon after Mitchell and Ross took charge at Smith's Ferry, it became evident that the Central Pacific railroad that had recently been built through the San

Joaquin Valley, passing twelve miles to the west of the ferry, was becoming a sharp competitor in the freight and passenger business. Stages began to make trips less frequently and the number of freight teams was rapidly diminishing. Business continued to dwindle until the place could no longer be run at a profit. Finally, toward the end of the year of 1874, the partnership between Mitchell and Ross was dissolved.

The old hotel that had been open to the public continuously for the previous nineteen years was locked up and deserted. Neither the hotel nor the ferry were ever operated afterwards. During the following winter the old boat broke loose from its moorings and floated away. It lodged on an island about twelve miles below and a short distance above the present crossing of the Golden State Highway, where it was finally wrecked and hauled away, piecemeal, by the "natives."

A short section of the old Stockton-Los Angeles stage road is still plainly visible at the old Smith's Ferry site. This stretch begins near the water's edge on the east side of the river, and runs thence in a northeasterly direction toward the old hotel site at the brow of the hill.

W. E. Ross, or "Billy" as he was familiarly known, was the last man who ever operated a ferry on the Kings River. He was a veteran of the Civil War, and died at his home in Sawtelle, California, on August 21, 1927. He was never an inmate of the Old Soldier's Home at that place, but conducted a successful real estate business in the town.

With the exception of periods of flood water, rarely has there been sufficient water flowing past the old Smith's Ferry site in recent years to float even an empty boat the size of the one that plied the stream at that place during the greater portion of each year for nearly two decades. The explanation for the present condition is simple. While the old ferry was in use the entire volume of water from the Kings River drainage basin flowed past the place at all times. Neither had there been inroads made by greedy lumbermen on the magnificent mountain forests that then afforded ample protection for the vast fields of snow that lay spread out beneath their friendly shade. Instead of going off with a rush and producing a freshet, as at the present time, the snow was allowed to remain and melt gradually, thereby providing an even, prolonged and generous flow of water, that usually lasted well along toward the end of the summer season.

In July 1882, the 76 Land and Water Company acquired title to the land where the old Smith's ferry and hotel were located, and in the spring of 1886 they had the old hotel dismantled and the lumber hauled to their ditch camp at Wahtoke dam, where it was used up as junk.

The Smith's Ferry hotel was a two-story structure painted white, and faced toward the northeast. It contained eleven rooms, with a hall below and above. A row of four "Heaven Trees" (Ailanthus) grew about ten feet from the front porch. These were planted by Smith in 1861, and three of them were still standing as interesting landmarks until maliciously destroyed about 1929. They stood obliquely across the line that runs north and south through the center of Section

34, Township 15 South, Range 23 East. A peculiar coincidence relative to the locations of both the Smith's Ferry hotel and John Pool's residence at Pool's Ferry which was located three miles to the north is the fact that Smith's hotel stood exactly on a half section line and Pool's residence was located directly over a section line. Both buildings being so placed by a mere accident.

The big barn at Smith's Ferry, which stood on the opposite side of the old stage road from the hotel, and about forty yards to the northeast, was usually filled with alfilaria hay each year. This plant grew very prolific in early days, and when ripe could be raked up loose from the ground without cutting. This supply of wild hay, when exhausted, was replenished with grain hay from Smith's ranch in the 76 Bottom about seven miles to the north of his ferry.

About 1860, Smith went to the Pasquale Indian rancharia, which was near Smith's ranch in the 76 Bottom, and got an Indian boy about ten years old. He took the boy home with him. In order to destroy the vermin, Smith burned what little clothing the boy had on, and then shaved his head. After giving him a good hot bath, he put a new suit of clothes on him. They nicknamed the boy, "Muggins." Muggins made his home with the Smiths until he was grown and took him a squaw. He brought his squaw to the Ferry and both were given employment. Muggins being very skillful, learned to cook and wash and do most any kind of work around the hotel, in addition to running the ferry boat.

From Smith's hotel, stages and freight teams could be sighted far out across the dreary plains on either the road from Casa Blanca or Four Creeks. The big freight teams would be in plain sight and a half day before the melodious tones of the hame bells on the "leaders" could be heard announcing their near approach. On one occasion while the Smiths were in charge, there were seventeen freight teams of fourteen and sixteen animals each camped overnight at the ferry.

For many years Smith's Ferry was the most important crossing on the Kings River, but there was nothing else in the vicinity to attract a community. At all other public places in that portion of the San Joaquin Valley there were groups of families, forming villages or towns.

For nineteen years, one family and one only was all that occupied the place at Smith's Ferry. Sand storms, which were frequent and severe, would sweep over the dry, barren plains with great fury. Vasquez, that Mexican bandit and his group of blood-thirsty desperadoes, were committing their frightful depredations at the neighboring settlements of Millerton, Kingston and Wild Flower, and spreading terror among the inhabitants of those settlements. Knowledge of these tragedies so near by, was certainly enough to remove every assurance of safety from the minds of the isolated Smith family. Undaunted, they continued at their post of duty through all those years, ready to serve the public at any time, either day or night, with hotel, ferry or livery stable accommodations. Long may they be remembered.

James Smith

Proprietor of Smith's Ferry
A Station on the Old Stockton-Los Angeles Stage Road

The subject of this sketch was born near Little York, York County, Pennsylvania, November 26, 1821, and died at Smith's Ferry, Fresno County, California, December 17, 1862. He was of Holland Dutch extraction. When James was about ten years of age, his parents moved with their five children, three sons and two daughters, to Findlay, Ohio, where James grew to manhood.

He was an intelligent, energetic and progressive man, and among the more important activities of his life, mention might be made of the following: teaching school; on two occasions serving as captain of a company while crossing the plains; pitching the first tent in the future Columbia, a mining camp that grew to be one of the most important pioneer mining districts in California; and opening up the first line of public travel across what is now the main central body of Fresno County. As a public official, he served as the first Public Administrator of Fresno County, and later as Representative from his district [in the State Assembly].

Being of a studious nature, Smith acquired more education than the ordinary young man of his day, and at the age of eighteen we find him teaching school. After teaching in Ohio, he went to Illinois where he taught two terms in the town of Decatur.

Returning to Ohio, he engaged in the mercantile business at Findlay. In 1846 he married Miss Martha Lucinda Hamilton of that place. To Mr. and Mrs. Smith were born four children, three sons and one daughter: John Parks Hamilton, James Buchanan, Harriet Lucretia, and William B. who died at Smith's Ferry when three years of age.

The reported discovery of gold in California prompted this young man to begin at once on plans to go to the new Eldorado. Early in the spring of 1849, a party was organized at Findlay for the journey across the plains, and young Smith was unanimously chosen as captain of the expedition.

Leaving his wife and one-year-old son with relatives at Findlay, he assumed the duties assigned to him, and demonstrated his leadership during the long tedious journey by successfully managing the affairs of that motley group, and bringing them safely through to their destination.

On his first arrival in California he mined on the Feather River, but later went south, where he took up a claim and pitched the first tent in the future Columbia. This place grew to be a great mining center, and at one time boasted a population of 5,000. It aspired to be the state capitol, and is said to have lost by only a small majority to Sacramento. Though at one time of so much importance, Columbia is known now only as a "ghost city" of the west. It is located a few miles above Sonora, Tuolumne County.

Smith Grave Site

While in California on his first trip, Smith owned and operated, in addition to his mining interests, a hotel at White Rock Springs. This place is near the line between El Dorado and Sacramento Counties.

In 1851 he left the mines and started back to his old home in the east. On this return trip he took the long tedious sea voyage around Cape Horn to New York.

After spending six very busy weeks at his old home, he had everything in readiness to start again for California, this time with his family. Meantime, an emigrant train had been recruited for the west. Smith, with his previous experience and executive ability, was placed in charge of the new expedition. They traveled as far as St. Joseph, Missouri, by water, and there purchased their outfit. Late in March 1852, they started with their ox teams for California. They went via the Platte River and Salt Lake City, and arrived at Sacramento in September. Smith, with his family, continued his journey on down to Columbia where he still had his mining interests.

While at Columbia, Smith and those associated with him were very successful in their placer mining operations, and this encouraged them to branch out into quartz mining. They ran a tunnel with the full expectation of opening up a rich vein of ore, but the venture was a disappointment, and they lost heavily.

Leaving the mines early in the year 1855, Smith came down the San Joaquin Valley with his family, and "squatted" on the south side of the Kings River at a place afterwards known as "Burris Point," so named after the late David Burris, who took up the land a few years after Smith had abandoned it. The place is about five miles south of the present town of Kingsburg.

Smith remained at his first stopping place in the valley but a short time, when he moved up the river about fifteen miles, where he built a hotel and ferry boat, and established a ferry near the southwest corner of the present town of Reedley.

Martha and James Smith, with children Hariett Lucretia and John Parks Hamilton. Photograph taken in 1854 while in Columbia.

The place selected by Smith for his ferry, was the most suitable one for the purpose on the entire river.

During the first year of its operation, Aaron Crumley [or Crumbley?] was associated with Smith as part owner in the ferry boat, but at the end of that time sold his interest to Smith.

When Smith came down from Columbia, he brought seventeen yoke of oxen, besides other cattle. The oxen were divided into three teams, as follows: two teams of six yoke each and one team of five yoke.

The lumber from which Smith's hotel and ferry boat were constructed was hauled from the Thomas mill, in the Sierra Nevada mountains of Tulare County with Smith's ox teams. There was practically no road, and travel in the mountain portion was very difficult and attended with great danger.

Two carpenters, by the names of Ramblesberg [or Remblesburg] and Haskins, built Smith's hotel and ferry boat. When the two were completed and ready for service they represented an outlay of about $5600. The items segregated were about as follows: Hotel, $3000; Ferry boat, $2000; Cable, $550; two big brass shieves, $25 each.

While Smith's ferry boat was in the process of construction, his teams were hauling additional lumber to build another boat of the same design. This other lumber was for a man by the name of L. A. Whitmore. The two boats were built by the same men, the work being done on the flat below the hotel, near the river bank. When completed, the Whitmore boat was launched and with the assistance of a man by the name of George, Whitmore floated it down the river and operated it at a point about a quarter of a mile below the present Santa Fe railroad bridge that crosses near Laton.

John Pool had a small ferry boat, about ten by thirty feet in size, that he had been operating at a point about three miles north of Smith's location. He had established this ferry about 1851. Smith's boat was made of pine with the exception of such portions as the knees, which were of oak. It was sixteen by sixty feet. By thus being large and buoyant, it was capable of handling all the traffic that operated in the San Joaquin Valley at that time, a service that Pool, with his smaller and heavier boat had been unable to render.

Stages had previously been making through trips from the north via Pool's Ferry to Visalia, but they were compelled to suspend the service during extremely high water for the reason that the boat was unsafe at such times. Following the launching of Smith's boat, these stages rerouted via the new ferry and were subsequently able to maintain a regular mail, express and passenger service, which was greatly appreciated by the public.

It was the desire of James and Mrs. Smith that their children should not be continually exposed to the evil influence of a saloon, and for that reason there was never any bar at Smith's Ferry.

In the summer of 1857, a man by the name of A. C. Goodrich, who had been associated with Smith in mining operations at Columbia, came down to Smith's Ferry, and taking the two six-yoke teams of oxen and two wagons, went to Visalia where he loaded the wagons with freight and crossed over the Sierra Nevada mountains to a new mining camp near Mono Lake. There he exchanged the outfit for an interest in one of the mines, for account of himself and Smith. This mine like many others of that period, proved to be a failure, and Goodrich never returned to make a report.

During the early days of activity at Smith's Ferry, there was no line of travel extending in any direction across that broad expanse of plains lying between the San Joaquin and Kings Rivers, except near the margins of that territory. In 1858 Smith saw the necessity for a wagon road leading directly across this tract from his ferry to Casa Blanca [at the present day Tranquillity] located at the head of Fresno Slough, which was the head of navigation coming up the San Joaquin River. At that time there was no watering place or landmark of any description along the entire fifty-mile stretch of sand and alkali.

After having two wells dug, which would make the watering places about sixteen miles apart, Smith proceeded to mark out his new line of travel as follows. He had a lot of willow trees cut along the river and slough, and with the aid of one of Colberg's mule teams and "Big Jake" as driver, these trees were distributed all along the proposed route. They were then set in the ground at regular intervals, not with any thought or intention that they would grow, but to serve as temporary landmarks to guide the teamsters and stage drivers until a permanent roadbed could be sufficiently marked that the teams could follow it in foggy weather, darkness or sand storms. This cross-country road was established for the special purpose of accommodating the Butterfield overland stages when the water was too high in the river for them to cross at the Whitmore ferry.

James Smith being a very popular man and well qualified to fill the office, was elected in 1861 to represent Fresno County in the State Legislature. He was reelected in September 1862. After his reelection, he made every preparation to move, with his family, to Sacramento. There they could enjoy the social advantages to which they were entitled, a privilege that had been denied them at the ferry. He rented out his ferry and hotel, and his ranch located in the "76 Bottom" about seven miles north. Now, after thirteen years of hardship on the plains, in the mines, and at that frontier outpost, Smith's Ferry, he was ready to go and enjoy the well-earned fruits of his toil and sacrifice.

Under such promising conditions, this happy family looked forward to the approaching holidays with a feeling of assurance that a full measure of Christmas cheer and New Year happiness was in store for them. But fate decreed otherwise. Before their bright hopes could be realized, a double sorrow visited the family. Death entered the home and claimed as its victims the father and the bright little three-year-old child. The father was stricken with pneumonia and passed away December 17. One month and nine days later, the son also passed away [according to one account, the result of severe scalding in a kitchen accident]. Their remains were laid to rest, side by side, at the brow of the hill overlooking the ferry, the child's at the south side of the father's.

By the death of the Honorable James Smith, which occurred at the age of forty-one, and when he was in the prime of life, Fresno County lost one of its most valuable and highly respected citizens.

Mrs. Smith had a marble monument erected at the head of her husband's grave, and both grave and monument were enclosed within a brick wall. As a result of years of undermining of this wall by ground squirrels, and the flooding of the ground by irrigation after the Reedley cemetery was established, one end of the wall settled sufficiently to cause a wide opening in it. This wall was torn down about 1922, and instead of rebuilding it in its original location around the grave, both wall and monument were reerected about six or eight feet to the north. [According to a post card J. P. H. Smith sent to McCubbin in 1929, an ailanthus tree was planted at the James and William B. Smith gravesites in 1863. However, in a short three-paragraph caption to an old photograph of the gravesite, McCubbin writes that the tree now standing south of the grave "sprouted up from one that was planted . . . and later destroyed."]

Another and more enduring monument to the memory of the Honorable James Smith is the isolated oblong mountain that stands a few miles to the east of his old ferry site. This was designated as "Spring Mountain" by the men who made the original survey. After Smith established his ferry in 1855, the public applied his name to the age old landmark. It has since been known as "Smith Mountain."

James Smith's widow died in Kansas, in 1880, and her remains were laid to rest there.

The Honorable James Smith, whose life was marked by studious, temperate and industrious habits, always took a deep interest in the promotion of those things which made for either public or private good. The possession of such sterling qualities by this man entitles him to an enviable place on the list of those famous California pioneers of 1849.

Old brick wall once surrounding James Smith grave site, circa 1930. Note the ailanthus tree standing at the corner of the grave.

Headstone at the grave site of James Smith and son William B., Reedley Cemetery, circa 1930.

Roads Radiating From Smith's Ferry

There were six roads, including the old and "near old" roads that radiated from Smith's ferry.

When James Smith established his ferry on the Kings River in 1855, he found it necessary to make some changes in the roads already in use, as well as to establish some entirely new ones. The main lower detour, described above, that had previously crossed at Pool's Ferry, about three miles above the Smith's Ferry site, was changed to cross at Smith's Ferry. After crossing to the west side of the river, this new road ran in a northwesterly direction about six miles before connecting with the main lower detour again. The old "cut across" that had connected the upper and lower detours, near Pool's Ferry, was abandoned and a new one established about a half mile to the east and extended southward until it connected with the lower detour at Smith's Ferry.

An entirely new road was opened up on the west side of the river in 1858. It branched off about three quarters of a mile to the northwest of Smith's Ferry and ran thence in a westerly direction about fifty miles to Casa Blanca, which was at the head of Fresno Slough. This road was established for the special purpose of accommodating the Butterfield overland stages, when the river was too high for them to cross at Whitmore's Ferry, eighteen miles below Smith's. Whitmore's was their regular place of crossing.

When the Central Pacific railroad was extended from the San Joaquin River to the Kings River, in 1872, the Smith's Ferry-Casa Blanca road had been in use fourteen years. To find the place where this old road crossed the present Southern Pacific railroad, begin at the point where said railroad crosses the north line of Section 26, Township 15 South, Range 21 East, and measure thence in a southeasterly direction along said railroad track 790 feet. The point reached will be very near the intersection of the old roadbed. The place is about one and a half mile southeast of the town of Fowler.

With but few exceptions, there is nothing left in the San Joaquin Valley to show where the old roads ran, the ferries plied the streams or the bridges spanned their currents. One by one these old landmarks have gradually disappeared. This writer, who has traveled over those old roads scores of times is not alone in his regrets concerning the unnecessary destruction of some of the old landmarks that were located along their courses. Landmarks that were rich in historical associations, and had they been elsewhere, would have been considered veritable shrines and carefully preserved for the enjoyment of future generations.

Let us hope that in the future more interest will be taken in our local history, as well as the men and women, who by their noble courage and sacrifice in bygone times, helped to make that history a reality.

[In a separate, undated sketch McCubbin refers to a second "entirely new road . . . opened up on the west side of the river." This road "branched off near the ferry and ran in a southwesterly direction, about fourteen miles to Wild Flower."

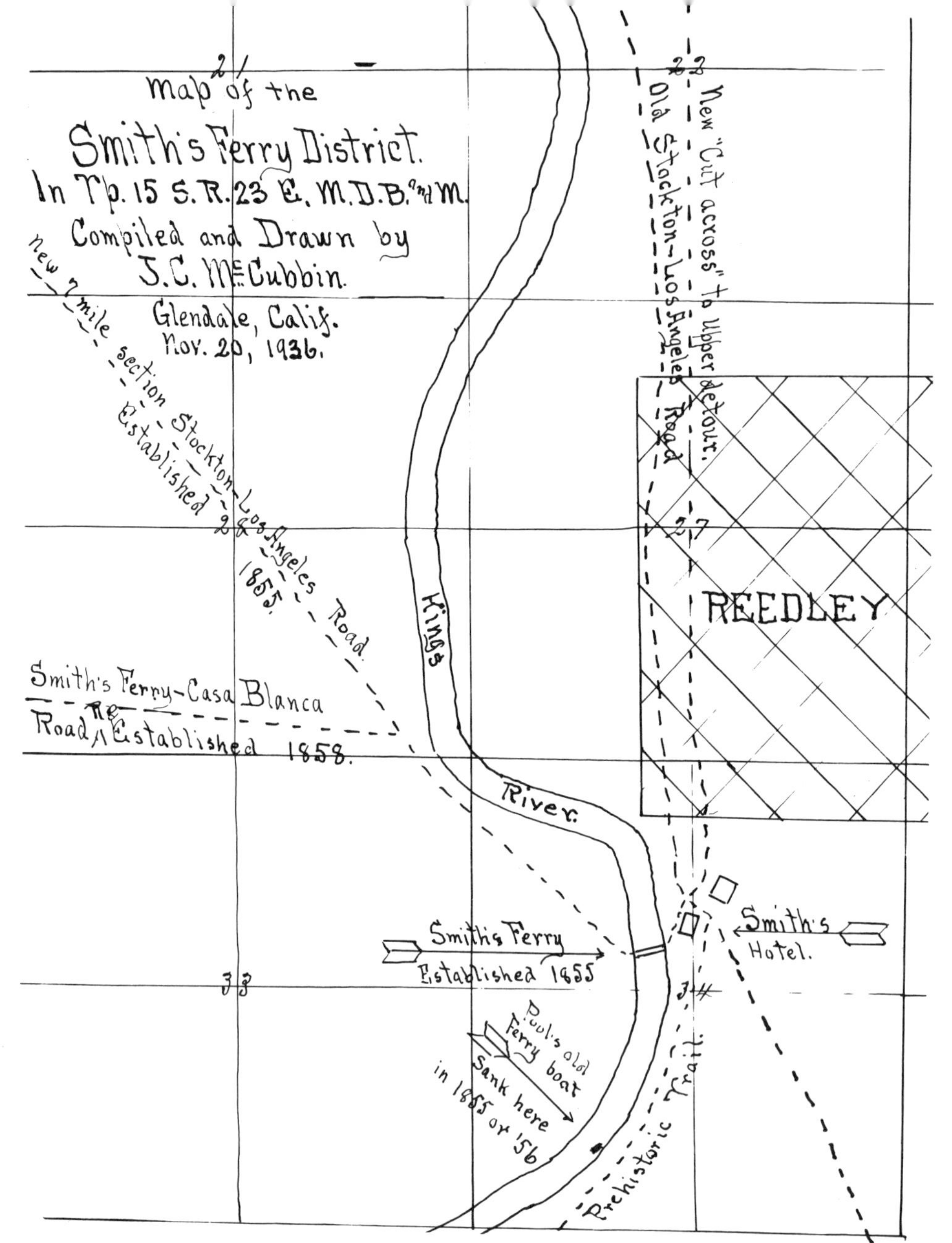

Wildflower was a settlement about eight miles west of Kingsburg. Mention of this road is made in only one other manuscript, "Reminiscences of John Parks Hamilton Smith," although in that note the road is referred to as the road to Kingston. Wildflower was in the same general direction as Kingston, but according to other sources, was not established until around 1876, two years after Smith's Ferry and Hotel were abandoned. Perhaps the road's existence preceded that of Wildflower's. In other words, Wildflower may have developed along the path of the road years after the road was established.

For the careful reader noting that McCubbin does not seem to fully account for the "six roads . . . that radiated from Smith's Ferry," they are as follows: In clockwise order, starting on the east side of the river, the old lower detour of the Stockton-Los Angeles road heading north, the new "cut across" connecting the lower and upper detours of the Stockton-Los Angeles road heading north, the lower detour of the Stockton-Los Angeles road heading southeast, and the "prehistoric trail" heading southwest to Kingston. Continuing on the west side of the river, the road James Smith established to Casa Blanca heading west, and the new six-mile section of the lower detour of the Stockton-Los Angeles road heading northwest. And, of course, if there was a road to Kingston-Wildflower, that would be number seven.]

Clemens Moore Commits a Near Murder

After the James Smith widow married Clayborne Wright he arbitrarily took entire charge of all the Smith heirs' property and handled it as if it were his own. The Smiths had a band of sheep, and the wool was handled by Wright the same as all other Smith property.

After Miss Harriet Lucinda Smith, daughter of James and Martha Lucretia Smith, married Clemens [spelled variously] Moore, Hattie decided that she and Moore would handle her own individual property. When the shearing of the sheep was nearing completion on the James Smith ranch near the Peter Fink ranch in the 76 Bottom, Hattie gave her husband a written order to go and take possession of her share of the wool.

When Moore presented his order from his wife to Wright, the latter had a "brainstorm," and among other things, stated that he would handle Hattie's wool as he had done in the past. That statement started a regular fight. It seemed that Wright, being a larger man than Moore, was going to get the best of Moore. But Moore pulled his gun and shot Wright, the bullet taking effect in Wright's side. Wright fell to the ground. Moore fearing that the bullet from his pistol would be fatal to Wright, hastened back to the ferry. Ham Smith, Moore's brother-in-law, had a very fine and fleet riding horse. Moore saddled up Ham's horse and rode south to Buzzard Roost and stayed overnight with a friend. Buzzard Roost was a small settlement, not far from the present Santa Fe Railroad which connects Tulare and Corcoran.

The next morning Moore rode across the plains to the northwest, avoiding all human habitations, fording both the San Joaquin and Kings Rivers, and went to Chowchilla, a stage station on the Stockton and Four Creeks stage line.

At Chowchilla, Moore left Ham Smith's horse and saddle in the hands of the man from whom Ham had purchased the animal. He instructed the man to notify Ham that his horse and saddle were there and to come and get it. This the man did and Ham came up on the stage and got his horse.

Clemens Moore left Chowchilla station immediately, and he has never been heard from since.

Clemens Moore was considered a fine young man, and the public was unanimous in feeling that Clayborne Wright got what was coming to him.

After his encounter with Clemens Moore, Clayborne Wright was taken over the "upper detour" of the Stockton-Four Creeks stage road, to his brother's place in Visalia where he recovered.

These are the facts as they were given to me by Hamilton Smith, Clemens Moore's brother-in-law.

For further information concerning the peculiar characteristics of Clayborne Wright, the reader is referred to the article, by this writer, on the Fleming and Bennett stage line.

Reminiscences of John Parks Hamilton Smith

{McCubbin met and interviewed John Parks Hamilton "Ham" Smith, the oldest son of James Smith, on at least two separate occasions. Much of what McCubbin gleaned from Ham Smith was incorporated into his sketches about James Smith and the ferry. Included among McCubbin's papers was a rough draft of a manuscript that detailed that information he obtained from these interviews. Since some of this information does not appear in other articles, or provides additional details about matters that are included elsewhere, an edited version of the manuscript is reproduced here.}

James Smith Establishes Ferry

When James Smith first came to the San Joaquin Valley he located on what was afterwards the David Burris place on the south side of the Kings River below Kingsburg. He built a cabin near where David Burris afterwards built his house. After remaining there about three months he abandoned the place and moved everything up to where he established the ferry.

Aaron Crumley and James Smith were in partnership in the building of the first ferry boat. Crumley had been raised by Mrs. James Smith's father (Mr. J. P. Hamilton) and came across the Plains with the Smith family and remained with them making his home there until they arrived on the Kings River. He then took up a place just about one mile below or to the west of the place where Smith first "squatted." Both of the places laid on the river.

Smith and Crumley hauled the lumber for both the ferry boat and the hotel from the Thomas Mill in the Sierra Nevada Mountains. The road to the mill ran through Drumm Valley. The lumber was hauled by ox teams owned by Smith and A. C. Goodrich.

Ramblesburg and Haskins built both the ferry boat and Smith's hotel. At the same time they were building the hotel and the ferry boat for Aaron Crumley and James Smith, they were also working on a ferry boat for Whitmore. Whitmore's original plan was to establish his ferry opposite the Van Valer house [about five miles above Kingston], but this idea was abandoned and after it was completed he had a Mr. George float it down the river from Smith's to where Kingston was afterwards established.

Both boats were built on the flat below the hotel. Getting the lumber down

The family of John Parks Hamilton "Ham" Smith, Monterey County, circa 1901.

from the mountains was a big job, and the carpenters worked on all the jobs continuously at the same time. Crumley and Smith's ferry boat was sixty feet long and sixteen feet wide. The apron of the landing platform was four feet wide and extended clear across each end.

The Smith's Ferry hotel cost about $3,000 and the ferry boat cost about $2,000. The cable and shieves cost about $600. The two solid brass shieves cost $25 each and weighed forty pounds.

John Pool's Ferry

Ham Smith says that John Pool built a ferry mostly of oak lumber about 1852. It was about ten feet wide and thirty feet long. He is quite sure that he operated it at the point of the bluff about a mile above the mouth of Wahtoke Creek.

When Smith and Crumley began building their big boat he (Pool and his brother-in-law Jack Beebe) moved his little boat down the river to a point about three-fourths mile below where Smith and Crumley planned on operating theirs. Since the law required that ferries be at least a mile apart, Crumley and Smith intended to move their boat upstream about a quarter of a mile to operate it, so they would be a mile above Pool. This was before the ferrying season began, and before fall Pool abandoned his idea. Crumley and Smith then located their ferry where it shows the old grade. Ham Smith says that Pool's old oak ferry boat was abandoned at the place above mentioned and it finally sank there.

After Pool moved his boat down to the place mentioned, Jack Beebe built a cabin on the hill above and lived there for sometime. Beebe had one daughter named Maud. She married Ross Bryson. Bryson lived about three miles southeast of Ham Smith in Monterey County. Bryson died there about 1901.

The John Pools, Jack Beebes, Bill Browns and the Humphreys all moved to Mendocino County on the Russian River about 1856. Jan Brown, Bill's daughter, married a man who ran the hotel at Point Arena about 1864.

Crumley Leaves Business

Crumley didn't care for the ferry business and sold out to Smith less than a year after the ferry boat was built. Smith and Crumley were never in partnership in any other enterprise. Crumley married a widow lady with twin girls. His wife was a daughter of Fred Smith, a farmer on the opposite side of the river. The widow's twin girls names were Arrabella and Isabella. Crumley had two children, a boy and a girl, named Douglas and Annie.

Crumley's first wife died and he later married a young lady by the name of Annie Dunn, who was working at Smith's Ferry Hotel. This young lady was from Visalia. Crumley had two children by his second wife.

After living on his ranch above Kingston for about ten years, Crumley sold it to a man by the name of Tom Thornton. It was about two or three miles above the Van Valer place.

Old Partnership with A. C. Goodrich

Smith and A. C. Goodrich had been in partnership for mining in Columbia, Tuolumne County, and also owned cattle in partnership. They had two teams of six yoke each (twenty-four head), and one team of five yoke (ten head), thirty-four head in all. They also had some cows in partnership, all of which Smith brought to the San Joaquin Valley with him early in the spring of 1855.

Goodrich abandoned the quartz mine at Columbia in 1857 and came down to Smith's Ferry. He took thirteen yoke of their oxen and two freight wagons and went to Visalia. He loaded both wagons with freight and crossed the mountains at Walker Pass and went on up to Mono Lake to a new mining camp. Goodrich exchanged his entire outfit for stock in the mines. This mine, like the one at Columbia in which Smith and Goodrich were interested, was a failure. Goodrich left there and never communicated with Smith afterwards.

Valley Stage Lines

Ham Smith says that the first stage line ever operated through the valley was started after his father started the ferry. It was a regular overland six-horse Concord Coach, and it ran through from Visalia to Stockton, via Converse Ferry and Snelling. The name of the overseer of this line was Pickley or Pixley, and a man nicknamed "Long Tom" was the first driver. This overland stage was put on immediately after the starting of this new up-to-date ferry across the Kings River. Ham thinks that his father knew this stage was to be operated when he began building his boat.

The southbound stage was scheduled to arrive at Smith's Ferry about three a.m. where all hands took breakfast. The northbound stage arrived about six a.m. All hands on this stage also took meals at Smith's hotel. No horses were changed by the overland stage drivers at Smith's.

The overland stage continued to operate via Smith's Ferry until about 1860 when the road was opened up from Visalia to Kingston. The stage route was then changed direct to Kingston from Visalia, except during high water when they came by Smith's to cross. This new route from Visalia to Stockton was via Kingston, Elkhorn, Hawthorne and Firebaugh's [Ferry?].

After the overland stage changed, its route started a two-horse three-seated stage from Visalia via Smith's Ferry to Hornitos. It would go down one day and back the next. They changed teams at Smith's Ferry. Billie Hice was one of Heston's [Thomas M. Heston, the operator of this stage] drivers in about 1860 or 1861, though Heston drove for about two years himself when the stage was first put on. Hice drove until [Amos O.] Thoms of Visalia bought it. Kit Carson's squaw came through on this stage going south on one of its trips. She was dressed in black silk or alpaca.

When Heston was running his stage from Hornitos to Visalia, [A. N.] Fisher was running a line from Stockton to Hornitos, with which Heston would connect.

Roads at Smith's Ferry

One of the regular teamsters that traveled the old road past Smith's Ferry was a man named Colberg [spelled variously]. He had three big teams of sixteen and eighteen head, all mules except the wheel animals which were big horses. Each team drew three wagons. There would be as high as seventeen of these big teams camped overnight at the ferry that would be ferried over either in the evening or the next morning.

About 1858 James Smith laid out a line of landmarks from Smith's Ferry to Casa Blanca at the head of Fresno Slough. He had his men cut a lot of willows and then "Big Jake," one of Colberg's teamsters, took one of the big teams and three wagons and distributed these small trees in a straight line across the plains, about a quarter of a mile apart. Smith's men set them in the ground so the teamsters could follow them until a road was made sufficient to follow during foggy weather or in the night. Smith had a deep-well dug on the road south of where the town of Fowler is now located. This was on the road to Casa Blanca. The water was drawn by means of a bucket and windlass.

The Centerville road took a direct line from the west side of the river at Smith's Ferry to the lone oak, about a mile to the southeast of Jimmy Kearnes place. The road forked there, one road continuing straight on to Big Dry Creek and Millerton, and the other turned to the left [right?] and went northeast to Centerville.

The road on the west side of the Kings River to Kingston left Dry Creek road about one hundred yards from the water's edge, or just as soon as it got out of the heavy sand, which Smith always kept strawed.

A Near Accident

In the spring of 1860, when the water was not overly high, the old rope broke while Tom Munn, the hired man, was ferrying a family across Smith's Ferry. The boat was a little over half way across and the momentum carried it on to the shore about two hundred yards below. Munn who had been an English sailor jumped out and tied the rope to a willow and landed the burden without much difficulty. The wagon was a light Eastern farm wagon and it contained the husband and wife and three children. At the time of this near accident James Smith was away from home. Munn spliced the old rope but it was used only a short time until it was replaced with the big new wire cable.

No tragedy ever occurred at Smith's Ferry or Hotel.

High Water

The wire cable broke in 1862 at the time of high water. The water was getting to be dangerously high and Ham and Muggins (the Indian helper) were trying to save the ferry boat from being washed away. They were at the water and had the boat fastened to the bank when the cable broke about three feet from the east end. They then kept setting posts farther up the bank and kept the boat above the high water until the limit was reached. When the water began to go down they were more careless and the boat got stranded on the bank far above the water. Peter Fink came down and helped them get it onto rollers and back into the water.

Change in Ownership

Alfred Beard rented the hotel and ferry about the year 1860 and the Smith's went up and lived on the ranch in the river bottom west of Peter Fink's old place. Beard ran the place for a year and the Smiths came back again. Smith had a spell of pneumonia while they were on the ranch.

Jesse Morrow rented the Smith's Hotel and Ferry and ran it one year. This was about 1869. The Bullards stayed there and worked for Morrow.

Ham ran a bar in the hotel one year about 1873 and the next year Mitchell and Ross took it over and their period of operations closed the year.

The property of Smith's Ferry, including the twenty-five acres and everything, passed through several hands in leaving the possession of the James Smith estate, but they got 2,100 head of sheep for it. Sheep were considered worth two dollars per head at the time.

Clayborne Wright

Clayborne Wright, who married the widow of James Smith, was a well-educated man. He came from Ohio, and had a nephew with him by the name of Jake Wright (Enos was his father) that married a Bozeman.

Clayborne Wright taught school in an adobe house that stood west on the south side of the Kings River near where the Van Valer house was afterwards built. Ham Smith went down and boarded at Crumley's and went to school to a man by the name of Brown. Each of these terms was for about three months. After this Ham went to Centerville and boarded with Dr. Ellis and attended school for three months. The school was taught at Centerville by Mr. and Mrs. Sherwood. Dr. Ellis taught a night school in Arithmetic only. Ham attended this. These schools mentioned were the extent of Ham's schooling.

Harriet Lucretia Smith, daughter of James Smith, first married Clemmons Moore. They had one child, a daughter. This daughter married Charles Runellas and died in Stockton, California.

Clemmons Moore, in about the year 1866, shot his step father-in-law, Clayborne Wright. He ran away and was never apprehended and never came back again.

The shooting occurred at the Kincaid and Jack ranch. It appears that Clayborne Wright had sold the wool from the sheep the year before and had not settled with Harriet, who owned one-third interest in the wool. Wright had his crew at Kincaid and Jack's shearing again, and Moore went down and began to make some definite inquiries about the wool. Wright told him he would attend to that himself. Moore told Wright that he guessed he would attend to his wife's business and drew out a revolver and was going to beat Wright over the head with it. Wright got hold of Moore, then Moore began shooting and one of the shots took effect, hitting Wright somewhere in the front left side below the heart and ranging through to the back and lodged there. It was never taken out.

The Mexican sheep shearers reported to Kincaid and Jack, and Tom Bates came and got Wright to the house, then went to Visalia and reported. Enos Wright, a brother, and Hoover [?] came and got him to Visalia. Moore made a getaway and came to the ferry and took Ham's racehorse and went that night to Tulare Lake and then the next night to Snelling and left the horse with Tom Patterson. Ham had traded the horse out of Tom some time before. Tom reported to Ham, and Ham then sold him back to Patterson. It was reported that Moore was afterwards elected to the Office of Sheriff at Cheyenne, Wyoming.

After being shot, Wright was taken to Visalia via Smith's Ferry road but not right by the hotel. They went out to the east of the hotel. Wright fully recovered from the effects of the shot and lived to be ninety-six years old and died in Burbank, California, about May 1, 1917. [Compare this account with "Clemens Moore Commits a Near Murder."]

Harriet afterwards married a man by the name of Noonan and her present address is 709 East Market Street, Stockton, California.

One child was born to Clayborne Wright and Mrs. Smith Wright in 1868 at Smith's Ferry. He was named William Clemmons Wright. William Clemmons Wright is a half-brother of the Smith children and he lives at Los Angeles.

Clayborne Wright and his wife, the James Smith widow, separated about 1873 when their son was about nine years old. The boy went with his father to Texas where he was put in school. The mother worried so much about the boy that it is supposed it hastened her death.

Miscellaneous Items

Clayborne and Enos Wright brought the first honey bees ever to the Kings River in about the year 1856. They were brought from San Jose and were taken to the Wright's ranch on the lower Kings River below Kingston--they owned 1,100 acres of swamp land adjoining Jack Sutherland's place on the west or down the river from Sutherland's. There were five colonies in the purchase and they cost $100 per colony in San Jose. They were located at the old adobe brick corral about ten miles below Kingston.

Dan Spangler, father of Lafe and Dan, went into the bee business about ten miles above Kingston in 1858. He had an apiary of about twenty-five colonies and sold "chunk honey."

Mrs. James Smith bought one colony from Dan Spangler in 1860 and paid $100 for it. These were the first bees on the upper Kings River. About one year afterwards, Peter Fink cut the first bee tree ever cut in that territory. He got no honey, however, but saved the bees.

The old C. W. Clarke ranch on the east side of river was first taken up by a man by the name of Hunsucker and the headquarters was known as Hunsucker Point. He had cattle there about one year and then sold it to Williams and Hawes. They had sheep and this was where they had shearing pens and dipping tanks. The old road from Smith's Ferry to Kingston ran just on the east side of the house.

Activities of Hamilton and James B. Smith

[E. C.] Ferguson and Andy Darwin established the 76 Ranch in the river bottom about 1859 and selected their noted "76" brand at that time. Tom Fowler and Dick Carmen bought Ferguson and Darwin out about 1865, including their brand. They were still in partnership in 1874.

At the time Carmen was associated with Fowler in the 76 Ranch he owned two large ranches in Nevada. One was in the Carson Valley and the other on the Walker River, about forty miles to the southeast. The Carson River ran through the upper ranch. The ranch was fenced.

Ham Smith and another man took thirty-four head of stock and started for Salt Lake with them in 18___[?]. There were three horses and one mule belonging to Ham, all the others belonged to the other fellow. They got as far as Carmen's Carson River ranch where they sold the stock, and then Ham Smith went to work for Carmen.

On their way over to Carson Valley they went to Sonora and camped there for the night. While there Ham rode back up to where their Columbia house had stood and could find no sign of habitation. The little old Catholic Church was the only building he recognized. Every foot of soil had been placered over except just where the old church stood.

The placer mine operated by James Smith and his company at Columbia was a success. When they cleaned up one Saturday night Smith came home with a gold

James Buchanan "Buck" Smith. Born at Smith's Ferry in 1857. The first white child born in the territory that would come to be Reedley.

pan almost half full of gold dust. This of course was all sunk when they ran the tunnel for quartz.

James B. Smith [Ham's younger brother] was a blacksmith by trade and went up and down the line from Smith's Ferry to Hornitos and shod the stage horses for their owner.

Whitmore's Ferry

The old site of L. A. Whitmore's ferry is about a quarter or a half of a mile down the river from the present Kings River bridge near the town of Laton. The place is permanently marked by the round cement filled columns that supported the old Kingston wagon bridge. That bridge was built on the old ferry site.

The Whitmore ferry boat was built during the summer of 1855 on the flat near the river bank just above where the Reedley cemetery is now located and near the Smith's Ferry site. Two men by the names of Ramblesberg and Haskins did the construction work. These gentlemen also built James Smith's ferry boat and hotel the same year they built the Whitmore ferry boat. The lumber for the boats and Smith's hotel was hauled from the Thomas mill in the mountains of Tulare County with James Smith's ox teams.

J. P. H. Smith, now of Pleyto, Monterey County, California, is a son of the late

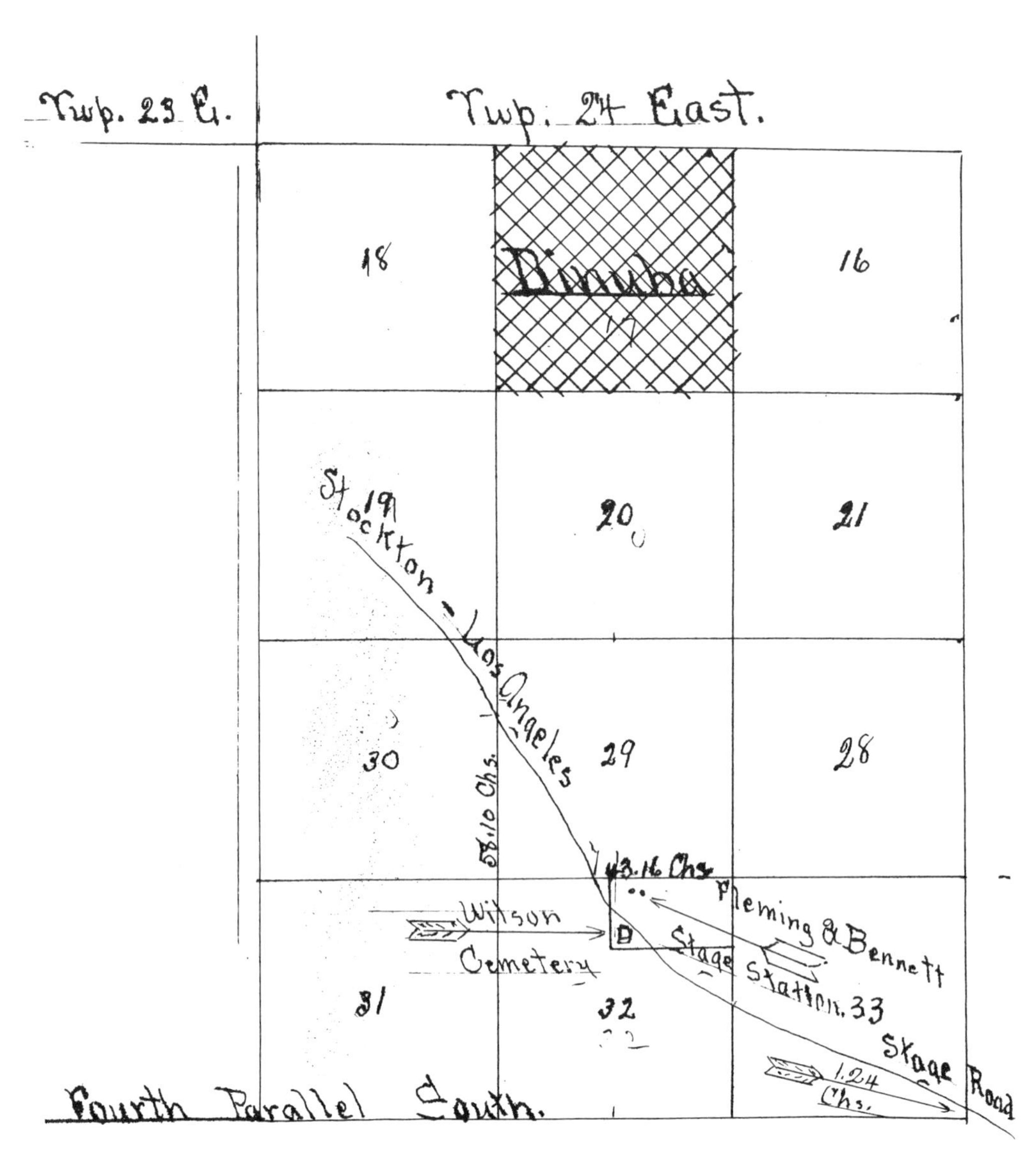

Map showing the location of the Fleming and Bennett stage station.

James Smith, who established Smith's Ferry. He saw both of the ferry boats built, and is the authority for the above items.

Fleming and Bennett Stage Line

Running from Hornitos to Visalia, via Smith's Ferry

While living at 945 Simpson Avenue, Fresno, I went over to Russell Fleming's one afternoon for a friendly call on him. During that visit he related the following story to me.

"Beginning about the year 1867, Pat Bennett and I owned and operated a stage line in partnership that connected Hornitos in the north, with Visalia in the south, running through Millerton and Smith's Ferry, which were the only places of any importance on the line.

Claybourne Wright was then in charge at Smith's Ferry, which was one of our relay stations. Wright proved to be such a very disagreeable person we soon got thoroughly 'fed up on him,' and to avoid all the contacts we could we went down the line toward Visalia and built our own relay station at a point a short distance to the north of where the Wilson Cemetery was established. We then transferred all our relay equipment to our own plant. I drove one of the stages and Charlie DeLong drove the other one for Bennett."

Fleming said that he and Bennett cleared over $30,000 in two years on their passenger, mail and express business on that line. He also told me that prior to the forming of the Fleming and Bennett partnership, that he had conducted a pack train among the mines in the Mother Lode territory.

Russell Fleming owned and operated the first livery stable in Fresno. It was located on the northeast corner of "H" and Mariposa Streets.

Charlie DeLong owned his own store and conducted a clothing and men's furnishing business on the northwest corner of "I" and Mariposa Streets, directly across the alley from the Fleming Livery Stable.

My only contact with Charlie DeLong was when I purchased a suit of clothes in his store in 1887, and Charlie waited on me personally. I was very favorably impressed with him, and the suit gave perfect satisfaction. That same corner has had a clothing store in it ever since Charlie DeLong started in business there.

In June 1887, when W. E. "Billy" Ross and I were going to the mountains together, Billy pointed out the old Fleming and Bennett relay station and gave me its history. I had been by the old building when going along the old Stockton-Los Angeles stage road the year before, but knew nothing of its history at the time.

Chapter 2

The 76 Country

The 76 Land and Water Company

Forerunner of the Alta Irrigation District

In 1882, P. Y. Baker, a civil engineer, who was then associated with C. F. J. Kitchener in the real estate business in Visalia, California, conceived the idea of a vast irrigation project to supply water from the Kings River to a body of land comprising about 130,000 acres that laid across the line in both Tulare and Fresno Counties.

Baker took a few capitalists into his confidence and laid his plan before them. After careful consideration, they decided that his scheme was feasible. Options were then secured on some 30,000 acres of land in the above territory. After organizing "The 76 Land and Water Company," and filing their certificate with the Secretary of State, the lands under option were purchased by the new company.

The six separate documents that have been filed with the Secretary of State in Sacramento, relative to the 76 Company, show some rather queer as well as interesting items in connection with its history.

On May 15, 1882, articles of incorporation were filed setting forth the following: Name, "The 76 Land and Water Company"; Place of business, Visalia, California; Capital stock, $280,000 divided into fourteen shares of the par value of $20,000 each. On June 7, 1882, articles of incorporation were filed with the Secretary of State, which were an exact duplicate of those filed twenty-three days prior to that date. There is nothing of record to show why those duplicate articles were filed.

On May 12, 1900, amended articles of incorporation were filed setting forth that the 76 Company's capital stock was $280,000, and that the number of shares were changed at that time, from the original 14 to 5,600, and that their par value was reduced from $20,000 each to $5,000 each.

On March 3, 1908, a certificate of dimunition of capital stock was filed, reducing the amount from the original $280,000 to $10,000, and reducing the par value from $50,000 each to $1 each. It also set forth that its principal place of business was San Francisco.

On February 10, 1932, an amendment was filed setting forth that the term of existence of this corporation, which was originally fifty years, was changed and made perpetual; and also adding the following provision: "That the capital stock of this corporation shall be assessable and that the liability for all assessments shall attach and become a lien upon the shares assessed, from the time of the levying of the assessment."

On October 1, 1945, a certificate of dissolution was filed with the Secretary of State.

When this sixth and last certificate was recorded, "The 76 Land and Water Company," after over fifty-three years of activity, passed into history.

1886.

THE 76 LAND AND WATER CO.

Alfalfa, Fruit, and Grain Lands

FOR SALE!

TRAVER, TULARE COUNTY, CAL.

S. F. EARL, Secretary.

Advertising card for the 76 Land and Water Company, circa 1886.

The names of the original stockholders of the 76 Land and Water Company and the amounts of stock for which each one subscribed were as follows:

H. P. Merritt	$40,000
Francis Bullard	$40,000
Charles Traver	$40,000
Thomas Fowler	$40,000
I. H. Jacobs	$40,000
C. F. J. Kitchener	$40,000
D. K. Zumwalt	$20,000
P. Y. Baker	$20,000

C. F. J. Kitchener, who was the first president, served until 1887, when failing health compelled him to retire from active business. He was succeeded by I. H. Jacobs, who was popularly known as "Big Foot Jake."

D. K. Zumwalt served as secretary from the date of the organization until March 1, 1884, when he was succeeded by S. F. Earl, who retained the office until the time of his sudden death in the spring of 1916.

H. P. Merritt, who was elected as the first treasurer, had charge of the funds until July 1888 when he was succeeded by Jacob Levi, Sr.

P. Y. Baker was appointed Superintendent of construction work, and had charge of all the outside activities until January 1, 1884, when he was succeeded by Joseph Peacock, who remained in charge until their irrigation system was sold to the Alta Irrigation District, which transfer took place on July 1, 1890.

The number "76" used as a portion of the corporate name of the new company, had, on August 4, 1857, been recorded as their brand in the office of the County Recorder of Fresno County by E. C. Ferguson and Andrew Darwin. About ten years later these men sold all their holdings, including livestock, brand and real estate to Thomas Fowler and Richard Carmen. A few years later,

Fowler purchased his partner's interest and conducted the business alone until the 76 Company was organized. He then sold the main portion of his real estate to the new company, taking in exchange therefor, $40,000 worth of their capital stock. For twenty-five years, cattle wearing the brand "76" had been roaming far and wide over a vast territory, of which the Alta Irrigation District now occupies the main portion. The name "76 Country" had been applied to that vast territory.

The first preliminary survey for the "76 Canal" was run through Dunnegan Gap, following closely the line now used by the Friant-Kern Canal.

An assessment of $5,000 per share was levied by the 76 Company, and with the $70,000 obtained, work was begun on the canal in October 1882, and continued until that money was exhausted, when they secured a loan of $150,000 from the San Francisco Saving Union, and the excavation work continued without interruption. A blanket mortgage on all the company's lands was given as security. The interest on the loan was eight percent per annum, payable semi-annually. The interest payments amounted to $1,000 per month.

The first water turned into the canal on about December 1, 1883, when Superintendent Baker, with the assistance of William "Flap Jack" Smith, opened the head gate and turned in a small head. About the time the water reached Wahtoke Dam, a bad break occurred in the west bank of the canal, opposite Dunnegan Gap, and the head was immediately closed.

No more water was turned in until about April 1, 1884, when Joseph Peacock, the new Superintendent, turned in a moderate head. This water reached the new townsite of Traver and was flowing past the place when the big crowd assembled for the first sale of town lots.

In February 1884 an unusually heavy rain storm in Clark's Valley came down Wahtoke Creek and filled the reservoir formed by the Wahtoke Dam, but the waste way took care of the excess water, and it flowed on down the creek. As a result of that same storm, a large volume of water came down Button Willow slough and emptied into the canal, but the Kennedy Slough took care of that. When the water reached the Kennedy wasteway and turned west, it broke the north bank of the canal and flooded a large portion in the south part of Sections 11 and 12 in Township 16 South, Range 23 East [north of Avenue 416, between Roads 56 and 72].

Traver was located on a portion of the 76 Company's lands in Tulare County, that lay on the Southern Pacific railroad which at that time was the only railroad running through the San Joaquin Valley. The town was named in honor of Charles Traver, one of the original stockholders and a member of the first board of directors of the company.

Traver started off with a boom, but it was short-lived. By the fall 1887, the town had grown to a population of about 1,000, while today, not one of them nor any of their descendents remain. Neither is there a vestige of a building of that period left, except the old calaboose.

Destructive fires in the town, the rise of alkali in the colonies adjoining, and the establishing of the new towns of Reedley and Dinuba, about 12 miles to the northeast, and in the heart of the 76 Country that had been the main feeder for Traver, sealed the doom of the latter.

The first land sale made by the 76 Company was on December 31, 1883. Emil Tretten was the purchaser, and the land was described as the southeast quarter of the southwest quarter of Section 18, Township 15 South, Range 24 East [northwest corner of South and Pedersen Avenues]. That forty-acre tract was located about three miles northeast of where the town of Reedley was afterwards established. The price was $20 per acre, which price included a water right of $5 per acre, leaving $15 per acre for the land.

The next sale of land was to Samuel Theal, and consisted of a ten-acre colony lot adjoining the new town of Traver. The price was $50 per acre. For several months thereafter, all land sales were colony lots, and in the vicinity of Traver.

Prior to the launching of the 76 Company's irrigation project, only small and isolated portions of the 76 Country had ever known the touch of a plowshare. In order to attract tenants who would come and farm their lands, they advertised special inducements. Those inducements were incorporated in their first leases and consisted of the following: Lease to cover a number of years, rental to be one-fifth of the crop, rental to be delivered on the land (the company to haul it to the warehouse), tenant to retain all the sheep feed (stubble), and more important than all the others--the privilege of purchase of all the lands described in the lease at a stipulated price, the option to cover the entire term of the lease.

Thousands of the company's lands, still in the virgin state, were tenanted on the conditions above mentioned, and a large portion of the rich territory was soon changed into one continuous stretch of beautiful waving grain.

Before these original leases expired, all the lands in that portion of the state had made a substantial increase in price. This unexpected advance in value made the 76 Company loath to part with the lands at the figures mentioned in the "privilege of purchase" clause in their leases. P. D. Wigginton of San Francisco, who was Attorney for the 76 Company at the time, rendered an opinion, based on certain technicalities, to the effect that the "privilege of purchase" clause could be avoided, but advised that a compromise be effected with tenants where possible.

Rather than enter into litigation, nearly all the tenants interested accepted the compromise offered. By its terms, the tenant could purchase certain portions of the land under controversy, at prices fixed in the leases, but were required to relinquish all claims to the remainder. A few of the tenants refused to compromise and brought suit for "specific performance of contract," and finally won their suits. Some of the tenants who compromised and executed new leases covering those lands formerly under dispute were "advised" that their compromises could be set aside and that the company could be forced to convey all lands that were formerly under dispute. All those who brought suit on that "advice" lost their cases.

Out of the litigation where the tenants were successful, grew other troubles for the 76 Company. On the advice of Attorney Wigginton, collections of rentals had been forced as per the terms of the lease. The final ruling of the court held the company liable for damages for all such collections.

The company succeeded in making a satisfactory settlement for all those after claims with one exception, and that case was taken into court. It was a case where the company's representative had made a forced collection of rental in the amount of thirty-five sacks of wheat, and that of inferior quality, on August 15, 1888. By a long chain of "reasoning" it was alleged that the plaintiff had been damaged to the amount of $10,000. Disregarding the Court's instructions, a jury awarded the plaintiff $2,319.94. Legal sparring continued until August 12, 1896, just three days less than eight years after the wheat had been taken, when at the end of that long period, the plaintiff accepted $75 in full for the claims, and the case was closed.

After the first batch of leases was executed, each succeeding year more and more was required of the tenant. The rate of rental was increased from one-fifth (to be delivered on the land) to one-fourth, and in some cases to one-third. All the rental was to be delivered to the warehouse by the tenant, at his own expense. The tenant was required to poison the ground squirrels, and also furnish the poison. And, the company reserved to itself all the sheep feed.

The breaking of faith with their tenants by the 76 Company, the years of litigation that followed, the exacting conditions under which the tenants farmed a succession of short crops, and the depression which brought about a decline in the price of all products and real estate, not only hampered development, but resulted in financial ruin for many of the early settlers of the 76 Country.

With justice to the memory of C. F. J. Kitchener, P. Y. Baker, D. K. Zumwalt and Senator Thomas Fowler, it should be stated that those four gentlemen had disposed of their stock in the corporation before the question of abrogating the "privilege of purchase" clause in the leases ever came up for discussion. They were, therefore, not responsible for any of the grief that followed that fatal mistake.

During those troublesome times, I was intimately associated with Joseph Peacock, who was the Superintendent of the 76 Land and Water Company. Peacock had charge of the canals while the collection of the grain rentals devolved upon me. Mine was a very disagreeable task, for in some cases it required the forceful collection of those rentals from lands under dispute, which collections formed the basis for the long drawn out litigation. Peacock and I passed through the "76 Turmoil" and came out without either one of us having known a personal enemy.

At the time the last case pending between the 76 Land and Water Company and a tenant was stricken from the court calendar, lands in that locality had declined in market value to a level of the price mentioned in the "privilege of purchase" clause in the leases. After it was too late, both sides to that bitter controversy learned that they had been lawing over something that neither side really wanted.

First Water Rights Sold by the 76 Land and Water Company

The 76 Company's first sale of water rights was made on October 1, 1884, when three water rights were sold at the same time for contiguous lands, and to members of the same family. The purchasers were : E[merson] Bloyd, his son L. J[efferson] Bloyd, and his son-in-law A. E. McClanahan. Those water rights were described as follows:

Water Right No. 1 to A. E. McClanahan for the southeast quarter of the northeast quarter of Section 33, Township 16 South, Range 23 East [on the west side of Road 48, one-quarter mile south of Avenue 392].

Water Right No. 2 to E. Bloyd for the northeast quarter of the northeast quarter of Section 33, Township 16 South, Range 23 East [on the southwest corner of Avenue 392 and Road 48, north of A. E. McClanahan's property].

Water Right No. 3 to L. J. Bloyd for the southwest quarter of the southwest quarter of Section 27, Township 16 South, Range 23 East [on the northeast corner of Avenue 392 and Road 48].

Allen Ensley McClanahan

The next sale was made one month later on November 1, and was described as follows: Water Right No. 4 to G. W. Barnes for northwest quarter of the northeast quarter of Section 22, Township 16 South, Range 23 East [southeast of the intersection of Avenue 408 and Road 52].

In March 1888, I purchased from G. W. Barnes the forty acres covered by this water right, and the original water right document was transferred to me along with the deed. The McCubbin gum tree is growing on this same forty-acre tract.

The 76 Land and Water Company sold their water rights for $5 per acre, and the annual assessment thereafter was to be fifty cents per acre.

When the Alta Irrigation District purchased the 76 Company's canal system, all the water rights were taken up by the 76 Company, paying the holders of such rights their original cost. There was one exception however. In mapping the outlines of the Alta Irrigation District, it was evidently the intention to include all the lands covered by the 76 Company's water rights. There was a 160-acre tract located one mile east of the Wahtoke switch on the Wahtoke branch of the Santa Fe Railroad omitted by mistake. L. Semorile had purchased this land from the 76 Land Company in 1888. All 76 land sales included water rights. Semorile was a non-resident when the Alta District took over the 76 canal system. How the matter was adjusted with Semorile, I don't remember.

Some of the 76 Company lands, including water rights, had been sold prior to the above four water right sales. But all such sales had been made on time. No water right was considered complete, nor any water right document executed or number given, until entirely paid for. The four water right sales listed above had been paid for in cash. Water right documents were executed immediately, and recorded in the water right book in the order named above.

Thomas Fowler

Thomas Fowler owned the 76 Ranch in Fresno County and the Mineral King mine in Tulare County. The town of Fowler in Fresno County was so named on account of the switch having been built there by the Central Pacific Railroad Company at the request of Fowler, and for the special purpose of loading cattle wearing his "76" brand. He served as State Senator from Tulare County, and died in that county about 1884.

Joseph Peacock

Joseph Peacock was born in Oneida County, New York, on January 11, 1830, and passed away in Hanford, Kings County, California, on February 11, 1910, at the age of eighty years and one month.

In 1852, at the age of twenty-two, he crossed the plains to California and located in a mining camp in Siskiyou County. During one of the severe winters in that northern mining camp, young Peacock was in charge of the commissary. Flour was selling at one dollar a pound, but no one was allowed to purchase it (even at *that* price), except where someone was under the doctor's care or where there were children.

On one occasion when Peacock was making a trip to another mining camp, he carried a written communication to a young lady from her boy friend in the camp where Peacock was located. The young lady was Hannah Bonham, who had crossed the plains with her parents from Iowa in 1855. About the year 1860 Peacock moved from Siskiyou County to Solano County where he again met Miss Bonham merely by accident. This second meeting developed into a romance that finally climaxed in their marriage in 1864.

The Peacocks made their home in Napa County until 1873 when they moved to Tulare County and purchased 160 acres of land from the railroad company. The land was located a few miles to the south of where Hanford, the present seat of Kings County, was afterwards established.

Harrison Peacock, a brother of Joseph, moved with his family from Wayne County, New York, and settled near where Joseph was already living in Napa County. In 1875, he followed Joseph to Tulare County and also purchased railroad land there.

Fortunately, neither Joseph nor Harrison Peacock were involved in the serious land troubles with the railroad company that finally resulted in the bloody "Mussel Slough Tragedy," a conflict between purchasers of railroad lands and peace officers representing the company, in which eight men were killed.

Joseph Peacock was a progressive citizen and a main leader in promoting the very first irrigation projects that diverted water from the south side of the Kings River. While serving as Superintendent of the People's Ditch Company, that was supplying water to the main portion of the Mussel Slough District, he was offered a similar position with the newly organized 76 Land and Water Company. He accepted the offer and resigned his position with the People's Ditch Company. His new position consisted of broader activities and increased responsibilities as well as a better salary.

His new position included, among other things, supervision of the canal system and the construction work of the main laterals. He also had charge of the rentals of their 20,000 acres of land that was just being brought under cultivation from its raw state.

These combined duties proved to be too heavy for one man to handle

Joseph Peacock

efficiently. Supervision of the lands, with their various tenants, was turned over to me. I was given a written commission to which was attached the company's official seal. This enabled Peacock to devote his entire time to the management of the vast canal system. That close business relationship coupled with a warm cordiality between us afforded me an exceptional opportunity for knowing the man more intimately, perhaps, than did any other one at the time.

During the six and one half years that Joseph Peacock served as Superintendent of the 76 Land and Water Company, he was the best known man perhaps in the entire territory now known as the Alta District. One of our tenants who farmed several thousand acres of the company's lands once remarked to me, "The 76 should feel themselves extremely fortunate in having you and Peacock in such important positions at this time." This tenant had in mind the company's land troubles. He was involved in those same troubles.

The 76 canal system was sold to the newly organized Alta Irrigation District in 1890. On July 1 of that year the entire canal system was officially transferred to the new purchaser.

When the above important transaction took place, Joseph Peacock was well past sixty years of age. After having spent forty years of his life in aiding the development of California, he felt that he had earned a good rest. He tendered his resignation to the 76 Land and Water Company, sold his ranch, and purchased a nice, comfortable home in Hanford, into which he moved with his family and where he spent the remainder of his life in quiet retirement.

Intelligence, personality, and natural executive ability, as well as an entire absence of everything in the way of arrogance, endeared Joseph Peacock to all of those who were under his supervision. When he was spending the night at any of the camps, a stranger would never have picked him out, either by dress or demeanor, as being the Superintendent of that vast corporation. These admirable characteristics made him a welcome visitor in either the humble cabin of the homesteader out on the plains, or in the palatial residence of the city dweller. He was equally at home in both places.

Joseph Peacock had clear blue eyes. His black hair that grayed very early in life, rapidly became perfectly white, though it never thinned.

Mr. and Mrs. Joseph Peacock were the proud parents of ten fine, healthy children, five sons and five daughters, whose names in the order of their births were as follows: Harrison Ross, Clara Irene, Mary Ellen, Leonard Elisha, Frank James, Walter Scott, Belle Rebecca, George Allen, Myrtle Idell, and Edna Vivian.

The memory of Joseph Peacock was held in high esteem by all those who were fortunate enough to come within the circle of his vast acquaintance.

The Bloyds and Their Pioneering Activities

{In 1806, members of the Bloyd and McCubbin families, residents of Rockingham County, North Carolina, moved their families to Green County, Kentucky, in what was to be the first of several individual and joint pioneering efforts. Twenty-four years later members of these two families moved once again, this time to what is now Hancock County, Illinois, arriving in the spring of 1831. From here, members of both families eventually moved to California, and eventually to the same parts of Tulare and Fresno Counties. The following, excerpted from a longer piece, details the Bloyd's pioneering activities upon leaving Illinois.}

Early in the year 1861, William R. Bloyd organized a company to cross the plains to California. The principal members of the party were the four children of Levi and Barbara Bloyd. The elder Bloyds, and their parents, had come to Illinois from Kentucky some thirty years before.

Just as soon as it was safe to travel, members of the emigrant party starting from Illinois gathered at the home of Joseph and Nancy F. (Bloyd) Goodell. The party drove as far as Centerville, Iowa, where William R. Bloyd and his son, William Washington Bloyd, and family, joined them. After continuing their westward journey for about a day, the company was increased by three families of Gumms, who had come up from Missouri by previous arrangement. The

Bloyds, Gumms and McCubbins were old friends when they had lived in Kentucky. The complete caravan included about thirty-five persons.

Three men in this train had crossed the plains before. They were William R. Bloyd, his brother Benjamin Bloyd, and his nephew Frank Bloyd. In 1852, the men had traveled to Siskiyou County, California. There they engaged in the business of preparing and selling mining and building timbers. They returned to their old home in 1855 via the Isthmus of Panama and New York. Benjamin had originally traveled to California for his health, and was returning to California — this time with his family — for the same reason. He had returned to New York after his first stay in California fully restored in health.

The Bloyd train traveled as a unit until they got well out onto the plains. There they joined another small train under the direction of a Captain Gillis. When this augmented train neared the Rocky Mountains, they felt they would be safer with more men for defense, and they joined with a larger train.

This combined train of about one hundred wagons remained as a unit until they got well into Nevada. There the combined train with which the Bloyd section had first united branched off and went north. They passed through the Honey Lake Valley and camped at Susanville, California. At Susanville, the two small groups divided and the Bloyd section drove over the mountains to the McCloud River, and from there to Red Bluff, Tehama County, their destination. It was now September 1861, and the train had been on the road nearly six months.

On one occasion during this trip a band of Indians stole about a dozen of their horses, including two fine horses that belonged to Benjamin Bloyd. A detachment of men went in hot pursuit as soon as the stock was missed. They soon overtook the Indians as the stock they had stolen were all slow moving. The Indians had to abandon their loot in order to make good their own escape.

Pioneering in the West

William R. Bloyd continued to make his home with his son, William Washington Bloyd, and the younger man's family. They and the Emerson Bloyd family remained near each other until 1869. The two families lived in Tehama County one year, in Sutter County six years, and in the vicinity of Corvalis, Oregon, one year (about 1864), after which they moved back to Sutter County.

During the winter of 1869-70, William R. Bloyd and Washington Bloyd moved to Hills Ferry, Merced County. The next spring they moved to Tulare County and filed homesteads on land a few miles northwest of where the city of Hanford was later established. That was a very dry year and as no water was available for irrigation, they went down near Tulare Lake where the land was moist enough to grow crops. There they constructed temporary shelters of brush and tules and raised corn, pumpkins, sweet and Irish potatoes, melons, etc. When early fall rains came they left their camps and went back to their lands out on the plains.

With the exception of one year near Asotin, Washington, William R. Bloyd and Washington Bloyd spent the remainder of their days near where they had settled in Tulare County (now Kings County) in 1871.

After living in Sutter County for about twenty years, Emerson Bloyd sold out all his holdings. Bloyd, along with his son, Jefferson, and son-in-law A. E. McClanahan, moved with their families to Tulare County. They purchased a body of land containing 480 acres and divided it equally between themselves. This land was about twenty miles to the northeast of where William R. Bloyd and Washington Bloyd were living. It was far out on the dry plains in what was then known as the 76 Country.

The 76 Land and Water Company had already begun excavation work on their canal system, but it was nearly two years later before water was available for irrigation. These three men, like William R. Bloyd and Washington Bloyd, were not only pioneers, but progressive people as well. They purchased the first water rights ever sold under the 76 canal system. That same system now irrigates 130,000 acres of land. These three water rights covered 40 acres each, and were all dated October 1, 1884. (The next water right sold under that same system was for the 40-acre tract where the famous McCubbin gum tree is growing. It was dated November 1, 1884.)

Joseph and Nancy Goodell lived in Tehama County one year and then moved along with the Bloyds to Sutter County. After one year in Sutter County, the Goodells moved to Butte County, where Mrs. Goodell died on December 27, 1876.

Robert W. and Levi C. Goodell, sons of Joseph and Nancy, married sisters. Robert married Mariah Loshbaugh, and Levi married Florence Loshbaugh. In April 1881, the two men moved, with their families, to Fresno County. Each family bought 160 acres of land about four miles west of where the town of Selma is now located.

The Goodell children were compelled to travel about four miles to the south to attend school until the Terry School District was organized in their neighborhood.

Robert Willis Goodell died in Selma, and his brother Levi Calvin died in Fresno.

At a Bloyd-McCubbin reunion held in Dinuba, on August 21, 1927, there were four generations of Bloyds, and three generations of McCubbins represented. Those in attendance had come from four counties in California and three counties in Oregon. Present were quite a number of great great great great grandchildren of John Bloyd, and one great great great grandchild of James McCubbin. The hearty greetings and good cheer, as shown by the many smiling faces in that group, indicated that the fraternal feelings that have existed between the descendants of those two men continually since the revolutionary period, still exists.

John Mathews

John Mathews was born in Iowa, where he grew to manhood. After he had finished grammar school he accepted a position in a local store in which he clerked for some time before coming to California in 1867.

Mathews settled in Woodland, Yolo County, where in 1869 he married Miss Gertrude Latham, a native of New York state who had come to California with her parents and who had settled in Yolo County. After their marriage, John and his wife moved to Colusa County, California, where he rented 2,000 acres of land from E. C. Hunter and farmed it all to wheat.

When the 76 Land and Water Company was offering special inducements to those who would come and farm their raw lands located in what is now the Alta Irrigation District, John Mathews was one of those in the Sacramento Valley who transferred their farming operations to the 76 Country. He already had stock and equipment of his own sufficient to farm about 2,000 acres.

The lands he rented were the following: 400 acres in Clarks Valley, belonging to Mrs. Hebro; 480 acres in Clarks Valley, belonging to C. W. Clark; and 1,020 acres in the 76 Country, belonging to the 76 Land and Water Company. These 1,900 acres of leased land together with the 160 acres of his own land in Clarks Valley gave him 2,060 acres of land under his control. Only limited portions of this land had ever been plowed.

John owned from 60 to 100 head of work stock, including both horses and mules. These were taken direct from the range, and had never had a halter on them. They were broken to work by his own men. His was the second combined harvester imported into the 76 Country, T. L. Reed's being the first one brought in.

The 1,020 acres of land that John had leased from the 76 Company were rented with a privilege of purchase clause stipulating the amount at which he could purchase the land. Later, the 76 Company refused to honor the clause. Rather than fight the case through the court, Mathews accepted a compromise of a half-section of land (320 acres), at the stipulated price of $20 per acre. When broken down, this $20 included $15 for the land and $5 for the water right.

This 320 acres lay a quarter of a mile east of where the new town of Reedley was soon afterwards located. It was described as the east half of Section 26, Township 15 South, Range 23 East [this half section is bounded by Manning Avenue on the north, Buttonwillow Avenue on the east, Dinuba Avenue on the south, and the extension of Columbia Avenue on the west]. The tract now joins the Morning Dawn subdivision, now a part of the City of Reedley.

During these land transactions, I was employed in the office of the 76 Land and Water Company in Traver, and I wrote the Mathews-76 Company Compromise, on July 28, 1888, to purchase the half-section and the eight forty-acre water rights that went with the land. I was also the subscribing witness to the compromise.

John Mathews was one of the best farmers in the 76 Country. He tilled the lands thoroughly and his superior crops showed the result of his special work. When he sold his half-section of land at Reedley, he moved to Visalia.

Pitts Linsenbigler, Alias Robert P. Sanford

{In February 1924, Eugene Ralston sent a letter to McCubbin notifying him of the death of Pitts Linsenbigler, and requesting information about Linsenbigler's activities in the West. Ralston wrote to McCubbin apparently after having found his article, "The Rise and Fall of Traver," among Linsenbigler's personal effects. McCubbin sent a reply and then prepared the following article for the Fresno Morning Republican. *It was published in their April 27, 1924, issue.}*

A recent communication from Elderton, Pennsylvania read in part as follows [as edited by McCubbin]: "I am writing to let you know that your friend Pitts Linsenbigler, or perhaps better known to you as 'Bob Sanford' is dead. He died Thursday, February 21 [1924] and was 87 years old. He had gone to California, overland, in 1861 and after writing home a few times, discontinued communications, and for nearly sixty years his folks knew nothing about him. When he left Pennsylvania there were fourteen children in his father's family, and when he wrote again there was just one sister and one brother living. He never told them much about himself or his affairs in the west, and now that he is gone, they are anxious to know something about him. Anything you can write about him or his affairs will be much appreciated."

My Reply: During the early operation of the 76 Canal System, now known as the Alta Canal, the water was all diverted from the main channel of the Kings River at the head of the Dennis Slough. In due time, however, a cut was opened some distance further up the river. This new opening was called the "Upper Head." It was about seven miles above the head gate proper, and can be seen a short distance below the town of Piedra, which is the terminus of the Wahtoke Branch of the Santa Fe Railroad.

While the 76 Land and Water Company was in charge of the irrigation system, it was necessary to keep a watchman at the "Upper Head." The place was twenty-seven miles to the north and east of Traver, which was then the "point of contact" with the outside world. It took nearly a half day to make the trip from Traver, and with the exception of one residence, no dwelling would be passed after leaving the new colonies near Traver.

The 76 Company had built a wagon road as far up as the Upper Head, but beyond that place there was nothing except an old Indian trail that extended up to an Indian Rancharia.

Aside from some visit of an employee of the Company, who would go up about once a month to replenish the watchman's supplies, rarely would he see a white man, though small bands of Indians would occasionally straggle by. Fish and game were plentiful and a short climb to any of the vantage points near by would reward the lover of nature with a view of unusual scenic beauty, but no sign of a human habitation was in sight, save the modest cabin of the watchman that nestled close to the foot of Tivy Mountain that grudgingly gave it a foothold near the bank of the river.

As the days would lengthen into weeks, the lonely watchman would tire of the scene, and its charm gradually disappear. He knew that down in Traver there was plenty of excitement of various kinds. With plenty of time for meditation he grew restless and longed for companionship. The inevitable result was a message to be relieved, brought back by any of us who went up with supplies. To keep a watchman at the Upper Head was a source of no little anxiety for Superintendent Peacock.

Early in 1886 a man known as Bob Sanford, one of the new employees of the Company, volunteered to take charge at the Upper Head. Pleased with the proposition, yet with misgivings, Peacock took the man up and installed him on the job. This man proved to be the first and only person who ever gave entire satisfaction at that place. With the exception of a few times when he was relieved temporarily, Bob remained faithful to his trust nearly two years, until he was transferred to the head gate where he took over when "Uncle" Charlie Mau had suffered a stroke and had to be relieved. Bob Sanford remained in charge of the head gate until the irrigation system was sold to the Alta Irrigation District on July 1, 1890.

On April 29, 1889, Robert P. Sanford filed a Preemption Declaratory statement on the north half of the northeast quarter and the north half of the northwest quarter of Section 24, Township 14 South, Range 23 East [on the north slope of Campbell Mountain]. The final certificate was issued to him on May 5, 1890, when he paid the United States Government $1.25 per acre for the quarter section. Bob sold the above land to the 76 Company for a consideration of $800. All those transactions were in the name of Robert P. Sanford.

Practically all the time for about thirty years, beginning when Bob went to work for the 76 Company in 1896, he remained near the same locality. The last seventeen years he was in California he served successfully as foreman of the Janowits Vineyard Company and night watchman at the Wahtoke Winery. This latter position was held until he voluntarily resigned on account of advanced age.

When he began to feel the weight of years resting heavily upon his shoulders, he longed to reestablish the family ties that had been severed for nearly three score years. He addressed a communication to "Any Survivor" of his father's family at the old home address. His letter received a prompt and affectionate reply. The correspondence that followed resulted in his going back and spending the remainder of his days with his sister, where, after rounding out eighty-seven full years he crossed "The Great Divide."

From the time that Bob Sanford made his first appearance in Traver, in 1886, until he started back to his old childhood home in Pennsylvania thirty years later, his record was that of a man always faithful to a trust, and well liked by his associates. Preceding that time, there was a period in his life covering about a quarter of a century, that for reasons best known to himself, he preferred to keep hidden from the eyes of the world. That portion of his life will perhaps remain forever shrouded in mystery since he has taken their secrets with him on into the eternal silence.

That Bob Sanford was unable to successfully resist the varied temptations that were constantly being thrown in his way during the early days in the West will not be denied. But, for the benefit of anyone who may be inclined to assume that this man, who was going under a fictitious name had ever committed a serious crime, let such a one be reminded of the two years of solitude during his two years stay at the Upper Head followed by many at the head gate. No man of Bob's intelligence could have endured those four years with a heavy load on his conscience.

It can be truthfully said to the credit of Bob Sanford that for about eight years while he was night watchman at the Wahtoke Winery, he made the lonely and hourly beats through the long, weary nights without taking a drink, either on or off duty, with thousands of gallons of intoxicants with nothing between him and the spigot. Not only did he absolutely abstain from drink, but every dollar of his wages was saved except what was spent for actual living expenses.

Now that Bob Sanford is gone, let the living "No further seek his merits disclosed, Or draw his frailties from their dread abode."

Albert K. Smith

Albert K. "Bert" Smith was one of Thomas Fowler's vaqueros when rodeos were held at Smith's Ferry. Fowler's cattle brand was, "76." Since large numbers of cattle wearing that brand had roamed over what is now called the Alta District since the 1850s, the name "76 Country" was naturally affixed to the territory.

On one occasion when they were rounding up the cattle for the rodeo, Bert Smith broke one of the old established rules. That rule was, "No shot should be fired during a round up." A coyote had gotten in the herd and Bert couldn't resist the temptation to shoot it. Fortunately, there was no stampede. Nevertheless, Tom Fowler proceeded to curse in his usual broad Irish brogue, using all of the fancy oaths that came to mind, and fired Bert. Two days later Fowler sent for Bert and put him back to work.

In 1886, William "Flap Jack" Smith, Bert's father, was threshing grain all over the 76 Country. When I first saw Flap Jack his long heavy beard was matted like several ropes, filled with ambeer from his chewing tobacco, and dust from the machines. He left it that way until the end of his threshing season. Bert eventually took over his father's threshing outfit and continued to operate it over the same territory that his father had formerly covered.

Albert "Bert" Smith was the father of Coila (Mrs. William Kerr), Nettie (Mrs. M. W. Gregg), Bert, and Clarence, all of Reedley.

Draft Animals for Ranchers in the 76 Country

H. P. Merritt, a capitalist of Yolo County, California, was one of the original stockholders in the 76 Land and Water Company. He also served as its Treasurer from the time it was incorporated in 1882, until July 1888, when he was succeeded by Jacob Levi, Sr. of San Francisco.

One of Merritt's activities was breeding vast herds of mules and horses on his acreage in the foothills of the Coast Range mountains of Yolo County.

Some of the early tenants of the 76 Company land had formerly been wheat growers in the Sacramento Valley. These men had been offered special inducements to transfer their operations to Tulare and Fresno Counties and especially to the 76 Company's lands that had never been plowed.

In their new and larger ventures, they would require many additional work animals. Merritt had the stock these men needed but it consisted of animals running wild on his range and none of them had ever felt the touch of a human hand except when they had been branded and the males castrated.

Merritt being interested in getting the 76 Company land under cultivation entered into a rather unique arrangement with these men which was mutually beneficial. The men were to take the mature mules and horses from their range, drive them to the 76 Country, break them, use them one year and bring back well broken and gentle stock to Yolo County.

These new tenants would have their men select suitable stock, and drive a herd of them to the ranch headquarters in the 76 Country where a regular horse breaker would take over. He would soon have them harness broken so they could be distributed among the broken stock in the long twelve-animal teams. Those "long strings" would be handled entirely with the single "jerk line." With a "buck strap" and "jockey stick" they could neither harm themselves nor any of the other animals in the plow team. They were well bred and not "broncos" in any sense of the word, and would soon become used to the teamsters who handled them gently.

The farmers took good care of the Merritt stock, fed them well and at the end of the season after the crop was all stored in the warehouses, these gentle, well broken stock would be driven back in a herd to Yolo County where they were turned over to their owner. They were then ready to be put onto the market where they would command good prices. The ranch hands rather liked the novelty of "breaking in" those green animals.

Another drove of raw animals would be gathered up from the range, driven down to the 76 Country to go through the same routine of the herd of the previous year.

This plan furnished the ranchers with good well bred stock that would have cost them thousands of dollars to purchase, and Merritt had the stock taken care of for a year and worked over into marketable stock at no expense whatever.

San Joaquin Valley Pests

During the pioneer days in the 76 Country there were a great many pests that harassed the settler, but fortunately these are now entirely gone with perhaps one or two exceptions. In one class of these pests we might mention coyotes, foxes, wildcats, coons, skunks, civet cats, badgers, ground squirrels, jack rabbits, etc. Strange to say there were no rats, and but very few mice. In another group of pests there were rattlesnakes, tarantulas, centipedes, scorpions, large yellow wasps, black widow spiders, etc.

When we began to irrigate and thoroughly flood the land, many of the pests were permanently routed. Included among these were the rattlesnakes, tarantulas, centipedes, scorpions, skunks, civet cats, badgers, ground squirrels, etc.

Ground Squirrels

One of the very aggravating pests that plagued the rancher in his dry farming operations was the ground squirrel. They would select a slightly elevated portion of land, underneath which a cavernous burrow would be excavated large enough to accommodate a colony of a dozen or more individuals. For quite a distance surrounding these colonies the land would be entirely devoid of any kind of vegetation. If a colony were destroyed, the burrow would be reoccupied by other squirrel tenants in due time.

By thoroughly flooding the land, the squirrels were permanently routed from their homes that had been used and occupied by their ancestors perhaps for thousands of years. They left in their wake, however, large dens that would cave in and leave large pits on the surface that would require from two to four cubic yards of dirt to bring the surface to the level of the surrounding soil. This settling and releveling procedure was absolutely necessary before any permanent planting could take place, and if not thoroughly done beforehand, a tree or vine would occasionally sink down into the pit along with the dirt.

The flesh of the ground squirrel was not edible, nor did they possess any redeeming qualities whatever. Yet, their destructive capacity was quite well developed.

Jack Rabbits

Another pest that was the source of much grief for the early day farmer was the long-eared, fleet-footed jack rabbit, sometimes referred to as the "narrow gauge mule." Guns and greyhounds seemed to make no impression upon their vast numbers. The problem was eventually solved by employing the rabbit drives.

These drives would be advertised well in advance. Two meeting places would be established miles apart where large crowds of men and boys would congregate. Under the direction of the marshals, who were on horseback, these groups would stretch out in long curved lines and move toward each other until the ends of the two lines would meet and encircle 100,000 acres or more.

This large circle would move toward the common center, at which a large corral with a partition across it was located. On opposite sides of this corral were long wings. The rabbits would be forced into these enclosures. After the gates were closed, one end of the partition would be opened and all the rabbits crowded into the still smaller enclosure.

Armed with stout clubs, the men and older boys would begin the slaughter. Some of the men were assigned to the duty of removing all the freshly killed rabbits. They would place them in piles on either side, leaving the ground free from obstruction for the killers. This would hasten the slaughter of the helpless victims.

Perhaps the greatest rabbit drive in the history of California was the one staged in Fresno County in the year 1892, when Governor Henry W. Markham was a specially invited guest. It was estimated that about 20,000 rabbits were corralled. One coyote was also killed. This drive was centered about fifteen miles southwest of Selma, Fresno County.

The drives left but very few rabbits. Greyhounds and men with shotguns made it so very uncomfortable for them that they finally disappeared.

The "Billy" Owl

The little saucy, harmless cuckoo or "Billy" owl was very beneficial in destroying mice and vermin. Sitting at the entrance to the burrow, they with their little brood, they would utter a shrill, defiant screech at the approach of all intruders. If pressed too closely they would quickly disappear into the burrow. Also, they would occasionally fly away instead of entering the burrow.

Chapter 3

Traver

The Rise and Fall of Traver

There are several cases on record where a town has suddenly come into prominence as the result of a mining boom, and after growing into the size of a city and enjoying a brief period of prosperity, declined within a few years almost to the point of oblivion. But for a town based on agriculture to have had such a remarkable experience, there is probably but one noted example in the entire state of California.

This exception is in the San Joaquin Valley, and located on U.S. Highway No. 99 midway between San Francisco and Los Angeles. The place is not of sufficient importance now to demand more than a casual glance from travelers, but if only a small portion of the exciting incidents of its early history could be dramatized, the show would be sufficiently thrilling to satisfy the most exacting.

In March 1884, the 76 Land and Water Company had completed the construction work on their main canal to a point on the Southern Pacific Railroad, a few miles to the south of where that railroad crosses the Kings River. A detached portion of about 2,000 acres of the 76 Company's 30,000 acres lay on the railroad at that place. A portion of this 2,000 acre tract was used for a townsite and the remainder subdivided and sold as colony lots. The townsite was surveyed in March 1884, and named Traver, in honor of Charles Traver, one of the directors of the 76 Company.

On April 8 of that year an auction sale of lots was held in the partially constructed depot, which was the only building in town. The sales on that day and the day following amounted to $65,000.

In less than sixty days from the time the first lot was sold the town boasted of the following: two merchandise stores, one drug store, one agricultural implement store, two lumber yards, two hotels, two barber shops, two livery stables, three saloons, a post office, an express office and railroad depot, as well as the usual California Chinatown.

On April 8, 1885, when the town was one year old, they claimed a population of 400 and had an eight thousand dollar school house.

Activities in the colonies kept pace with those in town. Modest homes were built; orchards, vineyards and alfalfa fields were planted and a veritable paradise surrounded many of them in an incredibly short time. In many cases, all the improvements on the tracts represented the actual toil of the colonist and his family, which made the holdings double dear to their owners.

The town continued to prosper until October 30, 1887, when a fire broke out in L. Semorile's hotel on Front Street [Front Street's official name was Seventh Street (now Burke Drive). The hotel was on the southeast corner of Seventh and Bullard Streets.] Within a few hours a large portion of the business section was reduced to ashes. The fire originated in the kitchen when the Chinese cook let some grease boil over on the red hot range. The blaze quickly shot up the only stairway in the hotel. The occupants of the upper story were trapped and

Southern Pacific depot in Traver, circa 1924. According to McCubbin, the first building in Traver, and one of the last to be demolished.

compelled to shin down the porch posts in front.

Not long after the hotel fire, another fire was started in the 76 Company barn [located on the northwest corner of Eighth (now Zante Drive) and Bullard Streets]. It spread to nearby buildings and destroyed more valuable property. Eventually, these were followed by three other very destructive fires in the business section.

About the time of these later fires, the appearance of alkali in the colonies adjoining the town proved to be a serious problem for the settlers, and it was evident that some of the most productive lands still further out, were being encroached upon.

During the year 1888, the Porterville branch of the Southern Pacific Railroad was built out of Fresno. This line passed directly through the 76 Country, now known as the Alta District, which was the main feeder for Traver. The towns of Reedley and Dinuba were established on this branch line about twelve miles to the north and east of Traver, and both of these new towns drew heavily upon the population of Traver.

The colonists resorted to every known method in their efforts to protect their lands from the spread and corrosive effect of the alkali. At the same time the residents of the town were seeking in vain for a plan by which they could replenish their diminishing numbers. The alkali persisted, however, with deadly effect, until practically every tree, shrub and plant on many of the colony lots had been killed.

Finally submitting to the inevitable, and with marked composure, the colonists pocketed their loss and began to move to other locations. The exodus continued until everyone who had lived there during the prosperous days was gone. The migration from town kept pace with that of the colonies until there was not an individual who had lived there during the peak of its prosperity, nor any of their descendents left.

Today there is not a vestige of a building left in Traver that was there when fortune was smiling with favor on the town, except the old calaboose.

The colonist suffered worse than the businessman in town, for the greatest percentage of the investment was in his land, while for the businessman it was in stock that was moveable.

Although the burying of blasted hopes by the pioneers of Traver and the colonies was in some cases attended with bitter tears, seldom did a victim despair, nor were their lives soured by the great disappointment. Rarely did their sorrows find expression in the form of a dirge or tale of woe. The sad experience of one was only a duplicate of that of practically all the others, and it served as a tie that bound them together in a friendship that shall continue throughout their earthly existence.

With a population of about a thousand progressive and prosperous citizens, Traver had much to be proud of on the morning of October 30, 1887, the day of the first big fire. Incorporation as well as many lines of elaborate and substantial improvement were freely discussed.

Up to this time, if we except Tulare and Goshen to the southeast, no town in that part of the San Joaquin Valley, including Fresno, had any better railroad accommodations than did Traver. Tulare boasted of a little narrow gauge motor road connecting it with the county seat, but later this was torn up and moved away. Goshen had two branch lines in addition to the main line of the Central Pacific. One of these was the Central Pacific branch running through Hanford, and the other, which at that time was owned by private parties, connected the junction with Visalia. All the towns on the main line in the San Joaquin Valley had a passenger service that consisted of one overland and one local each way, every twenty-four hours, as well as the privilege of riding in the caboose on freight trains.

Traver's prospects of becoming a railroad center were very bright. The Tulare Valley and Giant Forest Railroad was actually under process of construction, with Traver as the proposed valley terminal. The office of this new railroad company was located in Traver. The present highway leading to Sequoia National Park was built over a portion of that old railroad bed.

Traver's three large warehouses, with a combined capacity of over 30,000 tons, were filled and re-filled each year. The 76 warehouse alone had 12,902 tons of grain stored in it at one time. The following figures will give a good idea of the business that was done. The station agent's books showed shipments of grain during the year of 1886 of 18,607 tons, and 17,203 tons for the first seven months of 1887, making a total of 35,810 tons. No other producing point in the United States had equaled that amount in shipments of grain during a similar period, yet there remained in storage about 15,000 tons.

There were three contributing factors that entered into these wonderful results. First, the vast acreage of exceedingly fertile land brought under cultiva-

Grain wagons from the Clark and Kennedy ranch on the way to Traver, circa 1887.

tion. Second, the favorable seasons, and lastly, the large volume of grain that was hauled to Traver by the growers in the Hanford and Visalia direction to save the short-haul freight rate from those two towns to the main line.

During the grain season it was a daily sight to see three long wagon trains, the front of each lined up at a separate warehouse, and the rear of the columns extending several blocks away. On one occasion one of these trains reached from the 76 warehouse to the corner of Hershey and Eleventh Streets, or 5,040 feet away, or practically a mile. [Hershey Street no longer exists, but was one block north and parallel to Jacobs Street. Eleventh is now Baker Drive. The 76 warehouse was located between the railroad tracks and what is now Burke Drive, three blocks south of Merritt Street.] At such times a team would take its place at the rear of the column and be two days working its way up to the front where the wagons could be unloaded. Those who could not afford to wait so long to unload, would unload alongside the railroad and, later, haul it to the warehouse or load it onto the rail cars from where it lay. Hundreds of tons were handled in this manner.

Since the advent of the motor truck, the long wagon trains with their beautiful animals have gone forever. No words can do justice to one of those wagon trains in motion. Nor can the imagination of one who never saw its counterpart produce more than a dim picture of that rare spectacle.

In memory I see one of those long wagon trains in Traver. The dust begrimed mule skinner sits patiently in his saddle, astride the near wheel horse at the rear of the long string of twelve animals that draw the three loaded wagons. His jerk line (the single line that controls the entire team) is in his right hand, his black snake whip in a loose coil is thrown around his neck. The wagons alongside the warehouse are emptied and moved away. The entire train of wagons prepare to advance the length of the warehouse, which is 500 feet. The crack of black snakes, the clank of fifth chains and the chuck of the wheels are heard, as well as the beautiful chimes of the sweet-toned hame bells that adorn the leaders. Over all is heard, sharp and clear, all up and down the long line, a volley of oaths poured forth by the teamsters. Many a good Christian name worn by those long-eared beasts of burden would be used as a nucleus around which vile epithets and profane language would be grouped with revolting effect upon anyone unused to such disgusting abuse.

As soon as a complement of wagons would be spotted alongside the warehouse, the train would again come to a halt, and the cloud of alkali dust that had partially obscured the procession would slowly float away in the almost motionless and super-heated atmosphere.

All day long and at comparatively regular intervals the train would continue to move forward and stop again, traveling the same distance each time. While it was slowly wearing away at the front, it was being replenished at the rear.

The storing and shipping of grain was only one of the many industries carried on in Traver. Kimble and Greene's machine shop was built especially for the manufacture of windmills, the patent on which had been secured by S. K. Greene, the inventor. Burke and Simpson manufactured cultivators on which Robert Simpson had secured a patent. George Lobb also manufactured windmills, and Wilson and Wilson had one of the best flouring mills in the San Joaquin Valley. It had a daily capacity of fifty-two barrels. It was located at the north end of town, on the canal, where it was run by water power during the irrigating season, and by steam the remainder of the year.

There were three newspapers published in Traver, but not all at the same time. They were the *Traver Tidings,* by Hayes and Starring; *The Traver Advocate,* edited consecutively by F. V. Dewey, F. A. Ziegler, and Harry Hurst; and the *Traver Tribune* by James McDonald. *The Traver Advocate* was moved to Dinuba, and its name changed to the *Alta Advocate,* but the two others died a natural death in Traver.

The businessmen believed in advertising and the local papers were liberally patronized. As a sample ad, the following is an exact copy:

> J. C. McCubbin, House, sign and carriage painting. Plain and decorative paper hanging. Shop on Eighth Street [now Zante Drive], between Bullard and Merritt.

There were seven secret societies represented by that many live local organizations.

Should we fail to call attention to the seamy side of life during the prosperous days of Traver, this sketch would be incomplete. A half score of saloons and gambling halls and their attendant places of evil were running unrestricted in that wide open town. With hundreds of laborers in the warehouses, at the ditch camps and on the ranches, most of whom collected their wages every Saturday night, the scenes that were witnessed in the town on Sundays beggar description.

Scores of drunken men would stagger up and down the streets trying to keep track of all the gambling games that were running. The drunkenness would increase as the day advanced. Crowds would assemble where an exciting game or other excitement was in progress, and not only fill the building but would extend clear out across the sidewalk and compel pedestrians to detour out in the street.

An occasional case of delirium tremens would be reported. Two sufferers from the "jim jams" were sent to the County Hospital in one week, and one of them died later while tramping back to Traver.

A miscellaneous lot of professionals, amateurs and "tin horns" made up the population of gamblers. One game was reported to have run continuously for two weeks, day and night, in which over 200 packs of cards were used. When one gambler would go broke or have to quit for any reason, another was ready to take his place. In one dice game it was claimed the stake was $200 a throw.

The two places "across the track" where men without self-respect and women without shame congregated, served as way stations on the road to ruin. The two places housed from fifteen to twenty women.

With so many saloons, it may be presumed there was no room for bootleggers. Such was not the case, for a woman did a profitable business in that line. As a sideline to her bootlegging, she kept a woman or two, who it was claimed were for immoral purposes. She would be arrested occasionally, but could never be convicted by a Traver jury.

The mining town of Bodie, in a neighboring county, that gave to the world the well-earned sobriquet, "The bad man from Bodie," was at that time well on the decline and as it held but little attraction for the toughs, they wandered over to Traver for their excitement.

September 1886 was especially replete with thrills, sufficiently wild and woolly to satisfy the most exacting. I'll quote from my diary of September 3, 1886. It reads as follows:

> About 11:00 o'clock last night as I was preparing to retire, I heard a pistol shot ring out on the night air. This morning at the Elite Restaurant I was informed that we had "another man for breakfast," and that a murder had been committed down in Burke's saloon. After breakfast, I went with others down to the saloon. The front door was closed and on entering at the rear we saw laid out near the billiard table the body of a handsome young man, still and cold in death. The bartender unbuttoned the undershirt of the corpse and exhibited a dark, ghastly bullet hole in the chest. We listened while he told how Worth Brown, while under the influence of liquor, had taken the life of Luther Brown, his own brother, about 11:00 o'clock last night. The description of the tragedy was given in saloon parlance and embellished with a liberal amount of profane language. This was the result of the shot I heard last night.

The woman who was the cause of the Brown fratricide is the same one [Maggie Rucker] who harbored Grat Dalton of the Dalton gang of bandits after he escaped from the jail at Visalia, where he was being held for the robbing of a train. The remains of Worth Brown now lie in the cemetery at San Quentin, where they fill a convict's grave.

The Traver murder was not the first time Worth Brown had figured in a shooting scene. Prior to the murder of his brother, he engaged in a gun battle with James Allison, a constable, while the officer was in the discharge of his duty. Brown shot Allison in the jaw and Allison shot Worth through the lungs. A pal of Brown's shot a hole through Allison's hat rim. Prior to the Brown fratricide, two Traverites had each killed his father-in-law. You will observe that each of these three murders was kept in the family.

Three weeks after the Brown tragedy, Carrol S. Hayes, associate editor of the *Traver Tidings* was murdered. He and another young man were spending the evening with two young ladies after they had been to church. All of the four young people were sitting in the parlor of one of the young ladies when a charge of buck shot was fired through the screen, and taking effect in the head and neck, killed Hayes instantly. A cousin of the young lady with whom Hayes was keeping company was arrested for the crime, but was never convicted.

During that same month while a brawl was going on in the "red light" district, a man was slashed across the abdomen, and an ugly knife wound reached near the internal organs. This wounded man's son, when grown, died with his boots on in Arizona, and a chunk of lead was found in his anatomy.

I will quote from another page in my diary, written three weeks after the Hayes' murder. It reads as follows:

> As I crossed the free bridge over Kings River this morning, four miles north of town, there was a trail of coal oil on the floor extending from one end of the bridge to the other. On reaching the west end of the bridge, I saw a fire smoldering in an old stump a few feet away. It had run out among some trash from the end of the bridge instead of attaching to that structure as was no doubt intended.

Suspicion for the attempt to burn the free bridge, rested upon the owners of the toll bridge a few miles below. Those men had enjoyed a monopoly of travel until this free bridge had been constructed a few months before the attempted arson.

Constable W. B. Blakemore had his troubles taking care of his prisoners before they built a calaboose for him. A box car was pressed into service, but if a man had been charged with a serious crime, he would be kept under guard until he could be taken to the County jail in Visalia.

John Ruggles, an ex-convict, and his brother Charlie, residents of Traver, robbed a stage in Shasta County, this state, killing the express messenger and securing $3,000 in gold. Charlie was so severely wounded in the jaw by the messenger that he required medical attention in a day or two. His manufactured story on how he got shot was not sufficiently plausible to prevent his arrest. That soon resulted in the arrest of his brother John. Two days after the second arrest, the passengers on the Oregon Express were presented with a gruesome sight as the train pulled into Redding just before sunup. The dead bodies of the two bandits were seen dangling from a telegraph pole. The remains of these bandits were brought back to Traver for burial.

An old drunk who had spent his last cent for booze and no saloon keeper would trust him for a drink, crawled under a store room one night and succeeded in loosening some twelve-inch boards from the floor, through which he spirited away some stale beer in tomato cans. A few days later the dead body of that poor old inebriate was found under an old combined harvester on a vacant lot among some tall alkali weeds with some of that vile stuff still by his side.

During a quarrel over a gambling game, a man who was always prepared for an emergency was quick enough and close enough to cover his loud mouthed aggressor with a dirk knife before the latter could draw his gun. The glitter from the long, shining blade, and the order to keep his hands out of his pockets, induced the man with a gun to cool down and seek a more quiet atmosphere in another gambling resort.

One of the characters of the town was in the habit of playfully flourishing a gun while under the influence of liquor. Though such a performance was not so exciting in Traver as it might have been in other towns, it caused quite a little inconvenience for the reason that this fellow had killed a man before coming to Traver. During one of his exhibitions his gun was accidentally discharged so close to the face of a member of Traver's underworld that the woman's face was badly powder burned.

When W. D. Tuxbury and C. F. J. Kitchener were on their way from Visalia with $2,500 in gold and silver for payday, an attempted holdup frightened their high-spirited team and caused it to run away. That runaway saved them their money and possibly their lives.

While a patron was in a drunken stupor in the rear of a saloon, late one night when business was dull, a pickpocket deftly drew the pocket of the drunken man up underneath the waistband of his overalls, and was just in the act of cutting off the portion containing the purse, when he was surprised by a command from the proprietor. On looking up the thief saw he was covered with a gun. The gun was kept leveled on the criminal until an officer could be summoned.

Some of the town wags finding an old boozer dead drunk, obtained a secret entrance to the warehouse of the local undertaker and placed the limp form of the intoxicated man very comfortably in one of the caskets. As the drunken fellow was naturally a little superstitious, his surprise on coming to was not very pleasant.

A young man who was a resident of Traver was converted at a revival meeting in a neighboring town. He proceeded at once to exhort others and direct them in the way of "true" Christianity. Soon afterwards it was learned that this young convert was a member of a gang of thieves that was operating in that part of the valley. As proof of this, he and another Traverite were sentenced to a seven year term in San Quentin.

Traver's Chinatown spread out over two city blocks, and travelers who had visited China claimed it was typical, both in dress and manner of living, of a community of those people in their native land. There were no Japanese in Traver. (According to the U.S. census, there were at that time less than 1,000 Japanese in the entire state, while there were 70,000 Chinese here.)

The places of business in Chinatown consisted of stores, hotels, laundries, gambling houses, etc. There were basements under many of their buildings with stairways leading, generally, through the front sidewalk. While gambling would be in progress on the main floor, opium smoking would be going on in the basement. Curious individuals of any nationality could enter or retire at will and watch either the gambling or the opium smoking, unnoticed by the Orientals. There was no law against either at that time.

Tin San was called the "mayor" of Chinatown. He was tall, a bright fellow, and spoke good English, which was the exception. He conducted a gambling house in connection with his labor contracting business. He would furnish men from one to a crew of any number on short notice. In those crews there was always one who could talk Pidgin English. All the others pretended to "no savvy."

Evenings would be made hideous in Chinatown when their orchestra would entertain their countrymen, which was almost every evening during summertime. It was always free to all. Their music might be described as a system of high-pitched, spasmodic, blurty shrieks or screams, accompanied with squeaks and strumming on their peculiar stringed instruments.

Depressions where opium dens have long since caved in are the only marks left to show were Traver's once populous Chinatown flourished.

After the town had passed the peak of its prosperity and the decline seemed to have reached the limit, it apparently remained stationary for a few years. Then there came a change, but the change was from bad to worse. Finally, the depot service was arbitrarily discontinued by the railroad company, and the place reduced to a flag station. The doors were locked, the windows boarded up and the old building was left as silent as the tombs. Later, the old building was torn down and moved away. On the opposite side of the railroad track from where the old depot stood, a white sign post was erected bearing only one single word, "Traver." That word means nothing to the multitude of travelers who are continually rushing along over U.S. Highway No. 99, only a few feet away, but what a wonderful flood of memory it brings to the mind of any early day Traverite.

At the present time, the fingers on one hand could represent nearly every building in Traver. These are all too few in number and too unpretentious in appearance to represent even the corpse of the once thriving town.

Viewing the place from an airplane, a vivid imagination might trace the rough outline of the gruesome skeleton, gigantic in proportion, formed by the white irregular shaped patches of alkali as it lays reaching its distorted limbs far out among dingy salt grass, as if portraying the bleaching bones of the once flourishing, though now comparatively dead and unburied city. Four other such gruesome and imaginary reminders of the past show where the once productive and thickly settled tracts of land known as Vina, Kitchener, Scaironi and Traver Colonies were located.

To the pioneer of Traver who chances to visit the old place now, a more uninviting scene could scarcely be imagined than the one presented to his view. Whole blocks that at one time exhibited solid business fronts are only a barren waste, white with alkali.

The awful dreariness is only intensified during the stillness of the night. Then the weird "cuck-oo-oo-oo" of the little Billie owl, perched on an alkali knoll, the faint response by another in the distance, the myriad-sounding "ki-yi-yi-yi-yi" of an occasionally wandering coyote or the defiant shriek of a locomotive as it rushes past the ghostly sign post and disappears in the darkness, are extremely depressing to the spirits. And to add a more ghostly atmosphere to the surroundings, the dry, bladder-shaped pods of the poisonous loco weeds, when disturbed by the night winds, respond with a gruesome death rattle.

Harry A. Burke, in whose saloon Worth Brown had murdered his own brother, was the last of the old timers to desert the town. Not only those in town, but all the early settlers in the colonies preceded him in their final departure. When the county voted dry, Harry sold his old saloon building and it was moved to another town. He then moved up near the depot and installed a small stock of groceries and notions in a little old weather beaten shack with rough board walls and rear, with battens over the joints. There he remained, tenaciously, until his was the only building on the entire street. He would sit out in front for hours waiting for a customer. No doubt as he sat alone on such occasions, while the gathering gloom of the fading twilight slowly closed in around him, he could have expressed himself in the language of others as follows:

All, all are gone,
And I alone am left
Of that gay throng.
Alone - bereft.
The merry voice,
Now silent as the tomb,
No more is heard -
All, all is gloom.
Now, only specters
Haunt the shrouded past,
And lingering here,
Weird shadows cast.
(Thornton Fisher)

I feel like one
Who treads alone
Some banquet hall deserted,
Whose lights are fled,
Whose garlands dead,
And all but he departed.
(Thomas Moore)

If the traveler will leave Traver where everything seems to present such a sad and solemn ruin, and take a fifteen minute drive to the northeast, he will enter the heart of the Alta District, a territory of some 200,000 acres, in which there is not a waste portion, which for quantity, quality and diversity of products, challenges the whole world. The intelligence, contentment, cooperation and thrift which characterize the people of this territory, are equalled by few communities in the country.

In April of each year, former Traverites and their friends gather in a reunion to celebrate the founding of the town and to commemorate similar occasions that were held in the old town in early days, when excursion trains brought thousands of visitors from all parts of the San Joaquin Valley to participate in the festivities.

[See Appendix C for a list of persons in business in Traver in 1887, and Appendix D for a list of those who made Traver their trading point. Not reproduced in this book due to their large size are two maps of Traver drawn by McCubbin. The first is entitled, "Main Business Section of Traver, Tulare County, California, 1886-1889," and measures 18 by 48 inches; the second map is entitled, "A Portion of Traver, Tulare County, California, as of 1886-89," and is 21 by 42 inches in size. Both maps, which are in the Reedley Historical Society McCubbin archive, identify the locations of businesses of the era. The first map deals strictly with the central business district around "Front" Street, and the latter covers the general area surrounding the central business district.]

Cross Creek - Grandview - Traver

Traver had a forerunner named Cross Creek and later Grandview. This place was about two and one-half miles southeast of the present town of Traver, and on the Southern Pacific Railroad. It was first named Cross Creek because it was located near one of the delta branches of the Kaweah River by that name. The exact location of Cross Creek was near the center of Section 27, Township 17 South, Range 23 East [on the Southern Pacific Railroad, about one-half mile of where Avenue 352 intersects with the railroad].

Replying to an inquiry I addressed to the United States Post Office Department they wrote as follows:

> According to the records of the Post Office Department in our custody, a post office was established at Cross Creek, Tulare County, on November 10, 1874, with Charles H. Robinson appointed as postmaster. Its name was changed to Grandview on December 4, 1876, and to Traver on April 14, 1884, on which date Charles J. F. Kitchener was appointed postmaster.

This latter appointment was made just six days after the first lot was sold in the new town of Traver.

When this writer first viewed Cross Creek or Grandview, in August 1886, there was nothing at the place except two warehouses, one of which was the Kitchener and Company warehouse, and two small white-washed buildings standing on the west side of the highway, one of which was used for a residence.

A few years later, one of the warehouses was sold and the purchaser moved it to Dinuba and located it on the Southern Pacific Railroad siding.

The two small buildings mentioned were also taken away about that time. The railroad company finally removed the siding. Now, for about fifty years, Cross Creek or Grandview has been only a memory.

The later maps used by the railroad company showed only the name "Cross" as their designation of the place.

Traver Warehouse and Business Association

The above named organization was the outgrowth of the former Kitchener and Company that for years conducted a business in Cross Creek, and transferred their operations to Traver when that town was established on April 8, 1884.

On February 5, 1954, I addressed a communication to the Secretary of State at Sacramento, California. Their reply read in part as follows: "The records of this office indicate Traver Warehouse and Business Association filed articles of incorporation March 5, 1887, but forfeited its charter December 14, 1905."

The incorporators and first directors as they appear in articles of incorporation are W. D. Nelson, J. M. Clark, A. W. Clark, L. B. Ruggles, and D. Burris, all of Traver, and C. W. Clarke (note the final "e") of Sacramento. C. W. Clarke was no relation whatever to J. M. and A. W. Clark.

The election of officers showed the following: Lyman B. Ruggles, President; Peter Jurgens, Secretary; Wm. D. Tuxbury, Treasurer; and Wm. D. Nelson, Business Manager. Jurgens and Tuxbury were both stockholders.

Having been personally acquainted with all these incorporators as well as the other stockholders, I'll add a few items concerning them.

Lyman B. Ruggles was a farmer in Mussel Slough, and had formerly served in the California Legislature as assemblyman from Yolo County.

Peter Jurgens had been bookkeeper for Kitchener.

Wm. D. Tuxbury had been the silent partner in the Kitchener and Company organization. He and James Sibley were associated as the owners of the original townsite of Dinuba.

Wm. D. Nelson had been with the Kitchener and Company after they established their business in Traver, and was a stockholder in this new company.

James M. and Amaziah Clark were brothers and farmers in Mussel Slough. Amaziah later on married Miss Marion Kennedy, daughter of Robert Kennedy and wife, who settled in 1873 out on the plains to the southwest of where the town of Dinuba was afterwards established. He was taken in as a partner with his father-in-law in his 3,000 acre farming activities on his own ranch.

David Burris was a large land owner in Mussel Slough and owned bank stock in a Santa Rosa, California, bank.

C. W. Clarke owned a 9,000 acre tract of land north of Traver, that extended about seven miles alongside and adjoining Kings River. He also owned several thousand acres of land just to the west of the town of Cross Creek besides other large tracts of land elsewhere. He owned the controlling interest in the Sacramento Bank.

C. F. J. Kitchener was a large owner in the newly organized company. He was one of the founders and a large owner of stock in the 76 Land and Water Company and served as its first president. Kitchener developed tuberculosis soon after the Traver Warehouse and Business Association was incorporated, and moved to Los Angeles where he died.

Speculating in wheat at an inopportune time, and the rapid and fatal decline of Traver, were perhaps the main reasons why the Traver Warehouse and Business Association failed to succeed and brought about the forfeiture of its charter on December 14, 1905.

Traver Flouring Mill

When the town of Traver, Tulare County, California, was established on April 8, 1884, Samucl Frey and Thomas W. Carr purchased a half city block near the northwest corner of the new townsite. Their property faced the railroad on the west and lay alongside the newly constructed Traver branch of the 76 canal system, now the Alta canal system. [The mill was at the north end of Seventh Street (now Burke Drive), on the east side of the road.]

Frey and Carr were practical millers. Frey had mastered the trade in his native Switzerland. A few days after making their purchase, these two men began the construction of an up-to-date flouring mill, with the capacity of fifty barrels per day.

At the time Frey and Carr launched their Traver enterprise, they owned and operated a flouring mill in Selma, Fresno County, twelve miles to the northwest of Traver. This Selma mill had been built by Samuel Frey and his brother William. It was on the canal, and before there was a town there. It was this mill that determined the location of the present city of Selma.

The construction work of both the Selma and Traver flouring mills was under the supervision of W. D. Reed, a practical millwright.

During the irrigating season, the motive power of both these mills was furnished by a water wheel in the canal. The remainder of the year they were run by steam engines.

On account of the land in the Traver district having a very slight fall, it was necessary to back the water up quite a distance in order to get a sufficient head at the fore bay. The immense volume of water thus formed proved a menace to the high banks of the canal, which were built of light soil. On more than one occasion the residents of Traver found their town flooded from a break in the canal bank.

In 1886, R. M. and O. P. Wilson purchased the Traver flouring mill and operated it under the firm name of Wilson and Wilson. Although their surnames were the same they were really no relation to each other. The Wilson and Wilson partnership lasted but little over a year when R. M. purchased his partner's interest and continued to operate the business alone.

In 1892 the Traver mill was taken to pieces and moved to a place about fourteen miles to the northeast, and reassembled on the Kennedy Slough, which was a natural channel used as one of the main laterals of the 76 canal.

The new location [on the north side of Manning Avenue near Zumwalt] was about two miles east of the town of Reedley. It was a favorable location for water power, for the reason that the banks of the Kennedy Slough were high, and the fall of the water was quite heavy in that locality. A good head was obtained without backing the water up very far.

With the exception of moving some of the heavier pieces of machinery, Wilson and one assistant did all the work of taking down, moving and reassembling the entire mill.

When R. M. Wilson purchased O. P. Wilson's interest in the Traver flouring mill it was a burr mill using the old-fashioned mill stones. But after he moved it to its new location, he changed it to the more efficient roller system. The old wooden water wheel used at Traver was replaced by a steel turbine that developed one hundred horsepower. When there was no water available a one hundred horsepower Atlas engine was used.

T. L. Reed, founder of the town of Reedley, two miles west of the mill, took the first load of wheat to be ground by the mill in its new location.

In its location near Reedley, the Wilson mill was a busy place for a few years. It was operated day and night, turning out thousands of barrels of flour, besides crushing vast quantities of barley.

Vineyards and orchards began to replace the vast grain fields and activities at the mill began to slow down. Very little wheat was ground after 1911. Traveling barley crushers were calling at the headquarters of the big ranches making it unnecessary for the farmers to take their barley to the mill.

Having no indebtedness and doing most of the work himself, Wilson managed to keep his place open for business until late in 1914, though he must have known long before then that the doom of his mill was sealed.

The final run was completed as the shades of nightfall were gathering at the close of a winter day, made unusually gloomy by the presence of a thick, chilly fog that had obscured the sun for several days. Wilson was alone at the time. He walked slowly up to the head gate and closed it down for the last time. As the old water wheel gradually weakened into silence, the old gentleman could have easily imagined there was a shudder in its frame and a gurgle in its throat as it slowly came to a dead stop. It had made its last revolution. The mill had ground its last grist, and now they were both silenced forever. Thus ended what was perhaps the final activities of the last independent flouring mill in California.

Intellectually, R. M. Wilson was above the average and kept himself well-posted especially on music and musicians. He owned the best phonograph he could buy and his collection of records was considered exceptionally good. He was slightly cross-eyed. His views concerning economic questions were considered quite radical.

At the death of Wilson, which occurred about 1919, his twenty-acre tract of land on which the mill stood passed into the hands of his daughter, Mrs. Lenora L. Wright, of Reedley. Either from sentiment or an inherited characteristic, Mrs. Wright refused to sell the old buildings. Neither would she permit the old mill to be wrecked. The framework being well constructed and of a high grade of material throughout, it remained sturdy and strong. Although, the outer unpainted shell, as well as the porch, showed plainly the ravages of time. The old building gradually became more unsightly as the years came and went, especially the porch, as the roof was left hanging where it had fallen in.

Mrs. Wright, being one of the victims of the general financial depression, lost her land about the year 1933. One of the first acts of the new owners was to wreck the forty-nine year old mill and salvage what they could of the material. Clearing away of the old, sad and solemn ruin afforded a wholesome relief to the landscape.

The old building had stood idle for nearly twenty years and was a mere ghost of its former self. Its size and badly dilapidated condition made it a conspicuous object and served as an inviting target for travelers with a hobby for collecting unusual snapshots.

Interest in the picture would have been greatly enhanced had the collectors known the full history of the mill and its former connection with the old ghost town of Traver.

Hotel Del Zante

The large brick building, originally known as Hotel Del Zante, and which for many years formed a conspicuous skyline in the ghost city of Traver, was destroyed by a fire that started about two o'clock on the morning of January 31, 1929. This building was not constructed during the prosperous days of Traver, as was generally supposed. Neither was its predecessor, which was an exact duplicate and which stood on the same foundation.

The original building was constructed by a local stock company during the winter of 1888-89 in a rather forlorn hope that it would aid in booming their city, which was already on the decline. That company was operating under the corporate name of Traver Improvement Company.

When the building was completed it was leased to one of the stockholders, who fitted the hotel up in first class style and established an up-to-date saloon in the corner of the building.

Before the new building had been occupied a year, a fire broke out near the roof, which destroyed the building and practically all of its contents. Suspicion rested upon the lessee of the building. This party owned all the furniture and fixtures of both hotel and saloon, all of which was well covered with insurance. These, together with his capital stock in the building, constituted practically all of his possessions in the rapidly dying town. The hotel fire also destroyed other nearby property and was a severe blow to the town as a whole.

Highly indignant over the loss of their fine new hotel, and with a spirit of loyalty to their town, the board of directors planned at once to rebuild. They augmented their insurance money, which was $5,000, with an assessment of $10,000 on the capital stock, and in 1890 rebuilt the hotel using the same plans and specifications that were used when erecting the original building.

Had the insurance money been distributed among the stockholders instead of using it to rebuild, no doubt the ruin of the town would have been more rapid and complete, but such a procedure would have relieved a prolonged agony and saved the hotel company several thousand dollars. The rebuilt hotel was finally sold for about fifteen percent of its original cost.

Long before the passing of the old landmark, alkali which had been carried up from the ground by capillary force, had eaten almost through the outer tier of brick in places near the ground.

For many years prior to the last fire, a very unsightly object was the old tank tower. Sections of its rust-eaten wall-covering would become detached one-by-one, and fall to the ground. Other sections still hanging by one side, would creak and rattle at every gust of wind. All of this, however, was in keeping with the general appearance of the old hotel building.

[The hotel was located on the northeast corner of Eighth (now Zante Drive) and Merritt Streets.]

The Seligman Company

Emil Seligman, a nephew of S. Sweet of Visalia, came from Germany when a lad and went to work for his uncle. After learning the English language and the routine of the general merchandise business, he was put in charge of their Hanford branch store.

Immediately after Traver was established, the S. Sweet Company established a yard in the new town and took Emil Seligman from their Hanford store and put him in charge of the new lumber yard [located between the railroad tracks and what is now Burke Drive, two blocks north of Merritt Street]. This Traver yard gave the S. Sweet Company another outlet for their lumber mill above Camp

Badger in the Sierra Nevada mountains.

Samuel Frey, a native of Switzerland, a grist miller by trade, was living with his family near the new lumber yard. An acquaintance was but natural between Seligman and the Freys. A romance developed between Emil and Frey's daughter that resulted in their marriage in the spring of 1887.

Previous to this, Sweet and Company had sold their Traver lumber yard to the San Joaquin Lumber Company and E. Barris was put in charge by the new owners.

The Levis, Sweet and Company was then organized. They built a store building on the north side of Block 112, facing Bullard Street, and stocked it with general merchandise. Emil Seligman was in charge of this new store. [There is a discrepancy between McCubbin's Traver map and this article. The map, which is probably correct, shows the store on the north side of Block *113,* facing *Merritt* Street. To be more exact, the map locates the store on the south side of Merritt, adjacent and east of the alley between Seventh and Eighth Streets (now Burke and Zante Drives)].

Although it has been reorganized several times, the Seligman Company of Dinuba, is the outgrowth of the Levis, Sweet and Company that started in business in Traver in 1887. It is the oldest mercantile establishment in the entire Alta District.

J. S. (John Simeon) Jones and Eppinger and Company

In the eighteen hundred and eighties, Eppinger and Company were extensive dealers in grain. They owned large warehouses in different parts of California. Their warehouse in Germantown, Colusa County (now in Glenn County), was 700 feet long and the longest warehouse in the state except those on tidewater.

Early in the year 1885, Eppinger and Company entered into a partnership with the 76 Land and Water Company. Under a special contract, Eppinger and Company was to have entire charge of the Traver warehouse under leasehold.

When the Traver warehouse was ready for service, J. S. Jones was transferred from their Germantown warehouse to their Traver warehouse. Jones served as their agent at Traver until early in 1889 when the 76 Land and Water Company purchased the Eppinger Company interest in the warehouse. [The warehouse was located between what is now Burke Drive and the railroad tracks, three blocks south of Merritt Street.]

Soon after the 76 Land and Water Company had come into entire ownership of the Traver warehouse, they sold 250 feet of the building to T. L. Reed who moved it to the new town of Reedley. About this same time, the other half was sold and it was moved to Alta, a switch on the Porterville branch of the Southern Pacific

Railroad a few miles to the southeast of the new town of Monson.

After Eppinger and Company had sold their half interest in the Traver warehouse, they leased the big brick G. W. McNear warehouse in Reedley, and continued their grain business without interruption in the 76 Country. J. S. Jones, the local agent of Eppinger and Company, negotiated all these local deals.

Jones was still in charge of the Eppinger Company local interests when their sensational collapse occurred, about the year 1903. When this collapse came, I had my desk in Jones' office in Reedley, closing up the business of the Reedley Lumber Company of which I was the local agent. That company had recently sold their yard and stock.

When the Eppinger and Company crash came, Jones was in Fresno, and the sudden news reached him there. He telephoned me to get Black, his warehouse bookkeeper, on the telephone. I combed the town until I located Black. He came to the office and closeted himself in their private booth where he and Jones had their private conversation. All of the Eppinger and Company business in the state immediately passed into the hands of a receiver.

J. S. Jones had valuable real estate in and around Reedley. Following the Eppinger and Company crash he moved to Fresno where he and other financiers organized the Union National Bank. The same group also organized the San Joaquin Abstract Company.

While in charge of the Eppinger and Company grain business in Traver, Jones received a telegram from O. J. Woodward, President of the First National Bank of Fresno, offering him the position of Cashier of their bank, which at that time was the largest and most influential banking institution in the San Joaquin Valley. Jones dropped into the 76 Company office and showed us the telegram. After due consideration, he wired back and declined the offer. His position with the Eppinger Company afforded him plenty of leisure to look after his land interests which the offered position would not give him.

The Traver Calaboose

Prior to December 1886, Traver constables had been compelled to use a railroad box car in which to confine their prisoners. The Tulare County board of supervisors had never made any appropriation for a calaboose in Traver.

Early in the month of December 1886, William E. Russell, the newly elected constable, took up a collection among the businessmen, and secured the money necessary to construct a local jail.

Russell purchased the material from Emil Seligman, who was in charge of the S. Sweet lumber yard. Seligman was a nephew of S. Sweet. Cisero Spears, the local drayman, delivered the lumber to the spot selected for the calaboose [according to McCubbin's notes, the jail was in the old Traver Park]. Harry F.

Winnes and Emery Barris did the construction work and the building was ready for occupancy that year.

The material used was two by six clear Oregon pine with redwood mudsills. When completed it had solid six-inch walls, floor, roof and door. There was no ceiling. The two by six pieces were securely nailed together with large cut spikes. The wire nails now in use, made their first appearance a few years later.

That old calaboose is now the only building left [written in 1953] that stood in the town during the peak of its prosperity.

Traver Churches

During the spectacular rise and fall of Traver, the town had four religious bodies, fully organized. Each one employing a regular minister at least a part of the time. These churches included the Cumberland Presbyterian, Christian, Methodist Episcopal and the Methodist Episcopal South. Each one had a place of worship of their own, except the South Methodist. The more fortunate ones were very liberal and when their buildings were not in use by their own people, they gladly opened their doors to their less fortunate sister church.

This sketch is intended to outline some of the activities of those religious bodies, up to and including the year 1889.

To get an idea of the location of these churches, we will use the school house as a starting point. Twelfth [now Canal] and Merritt Streets crossed each other at the southwest corner of the school yard. The Cumberland Presbyterian church was located one block west of that corner and on the southeast corner of the intersection of Eleventh [now Baker Drive] and Merritt streets. The Christian church was one block to the south of the Cumberland Presbyterian church and on the northeast corner of the intersection of Eleventh and Bullard Streets. The Methodist Episcopal church was two blocks to the north of the Cumberland Presbyterian church and on the northeast corner of the intersection of Hershey and Eleventh Streets [Hershey Street no longer exists, but was one block north and parallel to Jacobs Street].

Cumberland Presbyterian Church

The Cumberland Presbyterian folks were the first to have a house of worship of their own. Among the founders and pioneer members of this church were Mr. and Mrs. Osias Bingham, Mr. and Mrs. Robberson Jefferson King, Mr. and Mrs. Benjamin Gass and Mrs. Hattie Hackney, wife of Dr. J. E. Hackney.

I have been unable to learn when their building was first occupied, but the main auditorium was in use when I arrived in Traver on August 20, 1886. There was also a nice little Union Sunday School flourishing under the superintendence of Warren C. Bennett, a clerk in L. A. Rockwell's drug store. Bennett was affiliated with the Congregational church, in some other place.

The optimistic pioneers who outlined the original plans for the Cumberland Presbyterian Church building provided for a two-story structure, the lower one for auxiliary groups of the church, and the upper for the main auditorium. The builders reversed the regular rules of architecture and prepared the upper story for occupancy, leaving the lower one with nothing but the naked skeleton of the framework, in which condition it remained for years. Perched above that open frame work, the superstructure was occasionally referred to as "a castle in the air." That term could have been applied also to the ambitious plans of the founders of the organization. This building that had been planned on such a magnificent scale, stood many years as a monument to only *one* of the many forlorn hopes of the pioneers of Traver.

Although the town boasted of a public hall, many civic groups, fraternal organizations and traveling entertainers availed themselves of the use of the lofty auditorium of the Cumberland Presbyterian Church. My journal shows that on February 21, 1887, one H. H. Williams, who styled himself "Professor" gave an entertainment in that church. His program consisted of ventriloquism, sleight of hand and a temperance lecture.

Referring again to my journal, it states that on the evening of March 2, 1887, I attended church in that building and the congregation totaled six people.

Christian Church

The second building erected in Traver for religious worship was the Christian Church. Some of the principal ones who promoted that organization were Mr. and Mrs. Elias Tout, Mr. and Mrs. M. Milsap, Mr. and Mrs. L. S. Sproat, Mr. and Mrs. T. B. McCanne, Mr. and Mrs. J. W. Archer and Mr. and Mrs. J. A. Boyd. The Christian Church was dedicated on Sunday, April 3, 1887. The services on that occasion were conducted by Elder H. Frank Tandy. Additional subscriptions to the building fund secured on that day amounted to $500.

The interior of the Christian church was lined with cloth and papered with suitable decorations, a very popular method of interior finishing at that time. I did that particular part of the work on this building. I well remember that while putting the paper on the nineteen-foot ceiling, a trestle made by some careless carpenter gave way. My scaffold fell with such force it broke through the floor. A few bruises were the only injuries, and after rebuilding the scaffold, the work continued without further delay.

Methodist Episcopal Church

Subscription lists to the building fund of the Methodist Episcopal Church were circulated during the summer of 1887, but the church was not dedicated until May 27, 1888. Lyman B. Ruggles, one of the principal promoters of this church contacted me when soliciting subscriptions, and I donated a one hundred pound keg of white lead, which was sufficient to give the building two coats of paint both inside and out. The keg of lead was a part of the stock left over when I closed my paint shop in May 1887.

E. S. Weddle had charge of the construction work of the Methodist Episcopal Church. It was surrounded by a decorated cupola.

The first regular pastor of this church was Reverend G. W. Wood, who came directly from Connecticut to take charge. He arrived before the building was completed, and was tendered a reception by the members of his congregation and also by those of the other churches. The reception was held in the Cumberland Presbyterian Church. Mr. L. B. Ruggles, who was always at home in that capacity, served as Master of Ceremonies. Miss Eva Nelson presided at the organ.

The program of the evening included the following: Prayer by Reverend A. W. Baldridge, pastor of the Cumberland Presbyterian Church. Four numbers rendered by a quartet consisting of Mesdames L. M. Scott and John Mathews and Messers. L. A. Rockwell and S. M. Scott. A solo by Mrs. S. M. Scott. A reading by Miss Eva Nelson. Introduction of the new pastor and his response.

A luncheon that had been provided by the ladies of the church was passed out which was greatly enjoyed. This was followed by a social hour that closed a very enjoyable evening.

Ministers

Below is a list of some seventeen ministers who addressed Traver congregations prior to 1890, either as regular pastor, evangelist or guest speaker. The list is not complete, however.

Cumberland Presbyterian Ministers:

- Reverend Alexander Warren Baldridge, regular pastor.
- Reverend Warren Compton, regular pastor.
- Reverend J. O. McKlerkan, evangelist.
- Reverend "Father" Yager, guest speaker.

Christian Church Ministers:

- Reverend H. Frank Tandy, guest speaker who dedicated the church.
- Reverend W. E. Hawkins, regular pastor.
- Reverend Henry Shadle, regular pastor.
- Reverend Joshua "Pap" Lewis, residing in the Wilson District, guest speaker.
- Reverend James M. Gilstrap, resident and guest speaker.
- Reverend William T. Shelton, guest speaker.

Methodist Episcopal Ministers:

- Reverend G. W. Wood, regular pastor.
- Reverend Park, regular pastor.

Methodist Episcopal Church South Ministers:

- Reverend D. T. DeBelville, regular pastor.
- Reverend Archibald S. Hunsaker, regular pastor.
- Reverend Frank Burris, guest speaker. This minister was a brother of David Burris.

Other visiting ministers were T. J. Bauder, United Brethren minister from Selma, a guest speaker; and Reverend Reams, church affiliation not known, a guest speaker.

Reverend Hunsaker, Reverend Gilstrap and another minister whose name I cannot recall were dentists. Gilstrap was the only one who claimed to be a licensed professional dentist. The other two each kept a pair of forceps which they used when occasion required, without anesthetic, of course.

Reverend J. M. Gilstrap was progressive and had an up-to-date dental office in the Horace Haden building on Eighth [now Zante Drive] Street. He was a pioneer in the practice of painless dentistry, and employed this method in his Traver office. He claimed to use a special formula, entirely his own. He afterwards traveled throughout the state exhibiting his skill on the street. He was one of the very first dentists to adopt that method.

On one occasion, while I was watching him on the street in Merced, he extracted a tooth for a Chinaman. The Chinaman felt in his mouth and excitedly shouted with bloody mouth, "What for? You pull'em wrong tooth!" The doctor took hold of his patient and forcibly lead him off the platform and said, "You don't get me to pull two teeth for you for nothing. You come my office, I pull'em other tooth, one dollar."

The faithful members of early day Traver churches failed to realize their cherished hopes in the old town, but their efforts were not lost. Many of those same people assisted in establishing churches in other towns of the Alta District, where they continued their faithful services. May the loyalty to their religious convictions never be forgotten.

Traver Lodge No. 294, F. &. A. M.:

(Some Items Concerning Its Early History)

In the year 1888, a small group of men who were members of the Masonic fraternity and who were residing in Traver and the 76 Country decided that the time had arrived in the progress of their town that it should take its place among other thriving communities by having a Masonic Lodge. As a result of this local interest, a formal meeting was held in Traver during February of that year at which time and place committees were appointed to take up the preliminary work necessary for the securing of a dispensation. From then on regular meetings were held, and the work vigorously prosecuted until the 4th day of June following, when Grand Master Hiram Newton Baker issued the coveted dispensation for the formation of Traver Lodge.

The place selected to house the new lodge was the second story of a frame building that belonged to Brother J. N. Bowhay. It stood on the east side of Eighth

Street [now Zante Drive] about midway between Bullard and Merritt. That old building was destroyed by fire and was replaced with a brick structure, and the Lodge continued in its original location until it was moved to Kingsburg.

The original lodge quarters had formerly been used as office and press room for the old *Traver Tidings.* This paper was published by Carrol S. Hayes and Harry F. Starring. Hayes, who was the senior editor and leading spirit of the paper, was murdered in September 1886, and the publication began at once to decline, but hung on until Fred Dewey started the *Traver Advocate* in July 1887. The *Tidings* soon "petered out" and Starring left for parts unknown.

When Traver Lodge was organized its jurisdiction included the territory now occupied by four lodges and covered all of its present territory except a small strip that was taken over from Selma Lodge when Traver Lodge was moved to Kingsburg, practically all of the territory now covered by Dinuba Lodge, and the principal portion now occupied by the Reedley and Orosi jurisdictions.

Stated meetings of the new lodge were fixed on the Saturday on or before the Full Moon. The list of names appearing on the Dispensation included the following:

Lorenzo Anson Rockwell, Master
John Simeon Jones, Senior Warden
William Dennis Nelson, Junior Warden
Robert Lee Freeman, Treasurer
Sumner Fremont Earl, Secretary
Jasper Newton Bowhay, Senior Deacon
James Newton Agee, Junior Deacon
Anson John Rockwell, Marshall
Louis Hirshfeld, Senior Stewart
Robberson Jefferson King, Junior Stewart
Henry Houston Burum, Tyler
Ozias Bingham, Past Master
John Golden, Master Mason
James Polk Neil, Master Mason

The first formal meeting under dispensation was held on the 23rd of June 1888, and the first stated meeting on the second Saturday of the following month.

Among other matters that came before the first stated meeting of Traver Lodge was an application from this writer to become a member by initiation, and at the next stated meeting he was duly elected.

During that period, Inspectors were not so strict in their requirements of proficiency prior to installation of officers as they should have been, perhaps, and as a consequence of this apparent laxity on their part, the new lodge found itself in a rather embarrassing position with a candidate ready and willing to be initiated and the officers unable to confer the degree. The decision of the lodge to have their own members do all the work connected with their first candidate necessarily caused some delay. The delay occasioned in the Entered Apprentice degree was repeated, and for like reasons, in each of the succeeding degrees.

Early in the evening on which the first degree was finally conferred, I was told that they were not fully prepared and that I would have to wait another week. I repaired to my room and retired. After I was sound asleep, I was awakened by a rap on my window and accompanied with the words, "Johnnie, Johnnie." On responding to the call, which was from Brother Earl, the secretary, I was informed that the lodge was ready for me. Whereupon I arose, dressed and repaired to the lodge with the messenger where I was regularly initiated an Entered Apprentice Mason.

On the evening of the 17th of November following, all things being in readiness, I was raised to, "The sublime degree of Master Mason," and it was the first time in the history of Traver Lodge that a set of officers ever exemplified the work of the third degree. On the same evening, and immediately following me, Brother Allen E. McClanahan, a Fellow Craft of Selma Lodge, was introduced and also raised to "The sublime degree of Master Mason."

It had been the custom of local lodges, prior to that occasion, for the candidate, upon being made a Master Mason, to provide a banquet for all in attendance. A masonic brother by the name of Wright, though not a member of the Traver Lodge, was running a restaurant across the street to the west of where the Del Zante Hotel was afterwards built, and this brother prepared a magnificent supper for the occasion, which was thoroughly enjoyed by the forty brethren who partook of it. The expense of the "feed," which was $20 was divided equally between Brother McClanahan and myself.

I might say now, that the Master was not in full sympathy with the idea of a candidate furnishing a banquet for the crowd that witnessed his raising, but as neither Brother McClanahan nor myself wished to be considered "pikers," nor establish a precedent, we acquiesced, and the result was as above stated. This custom was continued far into the early history of the lodge, and was one of the factors that helped to establish the wonderful reputation the lodge enjoyed for its manner of entertaining visiting brethren.

Traver Lodge had a schedule of prices for conferring degrees which was $20 for one degree or $50 for the three. As I look back at it now, a rather amusing incident grew out of the raising of Brother McClanahan. The Master instructed the secretary to send a bill to Selma Lodge for $20 for the "services of conferring the third degree" upon their candidate. This the secretary did, and in due time a very courteous reply was received from Selma Lodge to the effect that though their Lodge had been fully prepared and willing to confer the degree themselves, but as a favor to both Brother McClanahan and Traver Lodge they had gladly complied with the request of the candidate and granted to Traver Lodge the privilege of conferring the degree. It was afterwards learned that when the bill was read in the Selma Lodge it afforded quite a little amusement, and that they decided that Traver Lodge was "a little green at the degree business."

The records of Grand Lodge [in San Francisco] were burned during the fire that followed the earthquake in 1906, but were partially rewritten from such material as it was possible to collect from available sources. Naturally, under such circumstances errors unavoidably crept in. One of these errors in particular is noted in the record of the early membership of Traver Lodge. In a communication from Grand Secretary John Whicher, he gives a list of nineteen Master Masons as being on the roll of Traver Lodge, August 1, 1888. Among these are the names of Brother Emery Barris, John E. Toler, Alexander W. Baldridge and myself. As a matter of fact, I was not raised until November 17th following, and Brothers Barris and Toler followed me. Brother Baldridge was not affiliated with the Lodge until 1889. The list of names referred to would apply to conditions as they existed in Traver Lodge one year later, and it is possible that a slip of one year is the result of a clerical error.

A portion of the Grand Secretary's communication referred to, reads as follows:

> The dispensation for the formation of Traver Lodge was issued June 4, 1888, by Hiram Newton Baker, then Grand Master. At the annual communication of Grand Lodge that year, and on the 11th of the month (October), the committee on charters reported as follows: "The records of Traver Lodge U.D. at Traver, in Tulare County, are in proper form and fairly kept, but a portion of them is without marginal references. Its first meeting was held June 23, 1888. Since then eight degrees have been conferred, and it now has fifteen members upon its roll. The records show that the Lodge is free from debt, but as it does not petition for a charter, your committee recommends that it be continued under dispensation until October 1, 1889." This was adopted.

At the annual communication October 10, 1889, charter was granted. Morris M. Estee was then Grand Master.

Membership as of October 10, 1889, date of charter:

Lorenzo Anson Rockwell
Robberson Jefferson King
John Simeon Jones
John Solomon Young
William Dennis Nelson
Ozias Bingham
Robert Lee Freeman
Emery Barris
John Cameron McCubbin
Henry Houston Burum
Jasper Newton Bowhay
David Theadore Cook
James Newton Agee
Christopher Dudley
Anson John Rockwell
Sumner Fremont Earl
Louis Hirschfeld
John Golden

Joseph "E" Hackney
Allen Ensley McClanahan
Albert Miller Mugler
James Polk Neil
William Rice Neil
John Byron Terrill
John Elwin Toler
Withdrawn: Alexander Warren Baldridge
(Signer) John Whicher,
Grand Secretary

Dr. E. M. Gebhart

Erasmus Manford Gebhart was born in Ottumwa, Iowa, April 1, 1855, and passed away in Los Angeles, California, January 19, 1945, at the age of eighty-nine years, nine months and eighteen days. He was of German and French extraction. His father was Noah LaRose Gebhart and his mother's maiden name was Martha Cotterman.

On March 4, 1878, Dr. Gebhart graduated from Miami Medical College in Cincinnati, Ohio. That institution is now known as the Cincinnati Medical College. After the completion of his intern work, the Doctor established an office in Kansas City, Kansas, where he practiced a number of years before coming to the Pacific Coast.

On coming to the Coast, the Doctor took plenty of time to look the country over before selecting what he considered a suitable location. Meantime, he visited various places from Seattle to Southern California. He finally went to Fresno and was in the office with Dr. [Chester] Rowell for some time while getting his bearings.

Traver, Tulare County, was then a new and rapidly growing town with a bright future and the place appealed to the Doctor. He opened an office there in June 1885, and was the first resident physician in what is now the Alta District. After practicing in Traver about six years, the Doctor moved his office to Dinuba, a new town about twelve miles to the northeast of Traver. He was the first resident physician of that place.

There was no drug store in Dinuba, and the Doctor established one and installed a full line of drugs and all accessories. He soon sold his store to E. A. Cutter, who in later years established the Cutter Laboratories in San Francisco where he specialized in the manufacture of vaccines.

It was while practicing in Dinuba that the Doctor met and married Miss Anne Farrington Bennett of Fresno. Miss Bennett was a native of Manchester, England. She passed away in this city [Los Angeles] on October 24, 1942. One child was born to the Gebharts, a daughter, who is now Mrs. Archer Norcross, and with whom the Doctor has been making his home for a number of years.

The Doctor continued his practice in Dinuba until about 1902, when he moved to Reedley, Fresno County. It was while in Reedley that the Doctor was appointed Health Officer of Fresno County, in which capacity he served two terms. At the close of the second term the Doctor retired from active practice, although he kept up his membership in the American Medical Association as long as he lived.

Peter Gebhart, the American immigrant, arrived in Philadelphia on September 25, 1741. His son, John Nicholas, great grandfather of the Doctor, served in the Revolutionary War from the beginning until July 18, 1782. He was under the command of Captain David Prauss, Company 4, 2nd Battalion of Lancaster County, Pennsylvania.

Noah LaRose Gebhart, father of the Doctor, crossed the Plains to California in 1850 and returned to his home in Ottumwa via the Isthmus of Panama in 1854. Coming again to California via the Isthmus route in 1855, he was in various places but finally located in Aurora, where he acquired mining and other interests. He died there about 1861.

Aurora was the county seat of Mono County, California, when Nevada was admitted as a state in 1861. A careful survey was then made of the state line between California and Nevada, and it showed that the townsite of Aurora was really located in the state of Nevada. This surprising discovery made it necessary to transport all county property that was moveable across the state line to Bodie, California, the newly established county seat of Mono.

At the time of his death, Dr. Gebhart had been a member of the Masonic order over sixty-five years, a distinction very rarely attained by any member of the order. He was also in good standing in the Independent Order of Odd Fellows.

The Doctor's son-in-law, Archer Norcross, received the degree of Masonry in St. John's Lodge, Boston, Massachusetts, where he still holds his membership. That lodge has the distinction of being the first Masonic lodge ever established in the American colonies. Its charter was granted by the Grand Lodge of England in 1733. Mr. Norcross holds a very important position as District Manager of the American Bitumuls and Asphalt Company. His territory covers several states in the southwest, as well as a portion of Old Mexico.

Dr. Gebhart was in full possession of his mental faculties until within a few days of his death, when he suffered a severe stroke that rendered him unconscious, and in which condition he remained until the end came.

His was a Masonic funeral conducted in the Little Church of the Flowers in Forest Lawn Memorial Park, Glendale.

The near relatives surviving are Mrs. Archer Norcross, the daughter mentioned above, and Miss Ardath Anne Norcross, a granddaughter, both of Los Angeles.

William E. Ross

William E. Ross

William E. "Billy" Ross was a native of Indiana, and served as a volunteer with the Indiana Cavalry during the Civil War.

After his father's death, his mother married a Mr. Hill. Five children were born to this second marriage. Their names were: George, Charles, John, Sarah and Emily.

During the early seventies, W. E. Ross and all the Hill family moved to Fresno County, California, and purchased land in Hills Valley on which they made their home most of the time until 1886 when they moved to Traver, Tulare County. Mrs. Hill had a brother, Mr. Barton, who had come to Fresno County in the later sixties and purchased a tract of land in the 76 Bottom on the Kings River.

In 1874, J. W. Mitchell purchased the Smith's Ferry and Hotel, and all the real estate along with them. He then formed a partnership with William E. Ross in the management of the hotel and ferry. Ross took charge and placed his mother, Mrs. Lorena Hill, in the hotel as landlady. J. W. Mitchell was the father of W. D. Mitchell, who was one of the supervisors of Fresno County for several terms.

The new Southern Pacific Railroad that had recently been built down the San Joaquin Valley was encroaching more and more on the Smith's Ferry and Hotel business, and so at the end of 1874 both were discontinued forever. W. E. Ross had the distinction of being the last man to operate a ferry on the Kings River.

In 1886, as stated above, W. E. Ross and all the Hills, except Charles, sold all their Hills Valley interests and moved to Traver and purchased a colony lot near the town. W. E. Ross formed a partnership with Homer Hall, and they conducted a real estate business in Traver under the name of Ross and Hall.

While living at Traver, W. E. Ross was married to a lady in the east.

During the late nineties, W. E. Ross sold out all his Traver interests and moved to Sawtelle [California] where he purchased a home at 16652 Colby Avenue. He also purchased other real estate that eventually became quite valuable.

W. E. Ross and wife had two children, a son and a daughter.

W. E. Ross died at his home in Sawtelle on August 21, 1927. Although Ross had never been an inmate of the Old Soldier's Home, both he and his wife are buried in the National Cemetery at that place.

Mary A. Clarke, nee Graves

History shows that in 1846 a belated emigrant train bound for California, and under the leadership of Captain George Donner, was trapped by early winter snows at an altitude of 6,000 feet, just before the caravan reached the summit of the Sierra Nevada mountains. There were some eighty persons in the party, nearly half of whom perished from cold and hunger during that terrible winter, which has been described as one of the most severe ever recorded in that locality.

Miss Mary A. Graves was a member of the Donner Party and one of its real heroines. She, with her father and sister, Sarah, and Sarah's husband, Jay Fosdick, helped to make up the little group known as the Forlorn Hope, who started out from Donner Camp over the deep snow in a supreme effort to cross the summit and enlist aid for those who were perishing. Leaving camp on December 16, with scant rations for only six days, it was twenty-five days before they reached a small Indian village and contacted their first human beings.

Of the fifteen persons composing the Forlorn Hope, eight perished on the way over the mountains, and among those were W. F. Graves, father of Mary and Sarah, and Jay Fosdick, Sarah's husband. Later, Elizabeth and W. F. Graves, Jr., mother and brother of Mary and Sarah perished while attempting to make the trip out with the Second Relief Party.

C. F. McGlashen, in his history of the Donner Party, states that the hearts of Mary and Sarah Graves "failed not during trials which crushed strong men." This same author in describing Mary at the time of the Donner Party tragedy, says,

> Mary Graves was then about nineteen and a very beautiful girl, of tall and slender build, and exceptionally graceful carriage. Her features, in their regularity, were of classic Grecian mold. Her eyes were dark, bright and expressive. A fine mouth and perfect set of teeth added to a luxurious growth of dark, rebellious wavy hair completed an almost perfect picture of lovely girlhood.

From the same author we also learn that in May 1847, Mary Graves married

Edward Pile, and that in 1848, Pile was murdered by a Spaniard. The murderer was executed for the crime and was the first man ever hanged in California under the laws of the United States.

Mrs. Pile remained a widow until 1851 or 1852. She then married J. T. Clarke. In 1879, Mrs. Clarke was making her home with her son, Robert F. Clarke, at White River, Tulare County.

From McGlashen's list, given in 1879, of the offspring of Mr. and Mrs. Clarke, I quote as follows:

> Robert F., born in 1852, is married and living in White River, Tulare County. Mattie, born in 1854, and now the wife of P. Bequette, Jr., Visalia. James Thomas, born in 1857. An infant who died soon after birth. Belle, born in 1860, died in 1871. Alexander, born 1865. Daniel, born 1872.

When Traver, now a ghost town, was enjoying its boom, Mrs. Clarke moved with her son, Robert F. and family, over to the new town. That place being in the same county as White River.

During the summer of 1887 I was boarding with a private family in Traver by the name of Spears, on the east side of Eighth Street [now Zante Drive] between Jacobs and Hershey [just north of Jacobs] Streets, and next door to the Robert F. Clarke family. I would frequently see Mrs. Mary Clarke over at her son's place, but was never personally acquainted with her. She was then about sixty years of age, and apparently ambitious and quiet in her manner. Despite the awful suffering and sorrow she had experienced as a member of the Donner Party, one could still plainly see by a careful study of her intelligent face, that she had fully measured up to every item in McGlashen's complimentary description of her as a young lady.

Daniel Rhodes

Member of the First Group That Went to the Rescue of the Donner Party

When William Eddy, a member of the Forlorn Hope, reached Johnson's ranch in the Sacramento Valley, bringing the first news of the Donner Party who were perishing from cold and hunger beyond the summit of the Sierra Nevada mountains, he was so near the jaws of death it had been necessary for the Indian that had joined him to practically drag him the last few miles.

It was John Rhodes who volunteered to carry the news on to Fort Sutter, thirty-five miles away. Rhodes was compelled to go on foot, and at times, wade through icy waters three feet deep. Sacramento Valley, in that locality, was a veritable quagmire, making it utterly impossible for any beast of burden to travel over it.

On the receipt of the news of the awful plight of the Donner Party, Captain Sutter organized a relief party at once and dispatched a group of men with supplies to go to their aid. John Rhodes and his brother, Daniel, volunteered as members of that party, which was known as the First Relief Party. Using pack animals, until the snow became so deep it was impossible for them to travel further, they cached a quantity of their own supplies and sent the pack animals back. From there, ten men on snowshoes and with packs on their backs, started on over the deep snow. Three of these men soon became discouraged claiming it was absolutely impossible for any human being to cross the summit. Those three men returned to the valley. The other seven, including the two Rhodes brothers, said they would endeavor to reach those who were perishing, even if they died in the attempt.

Just at nightfall on the nineteenth of February 1847, those seven brave men reached the camp of death. The next day, with some of the smaller children on their backs, and a number of the older people who were still able to travel, the Relief Party started back for the Sacramento Valley, but several of those who had started with them perished before reaching the settlement.

Later, John and Daniel Rhodes were pioneer settlers of Tulare County. Daniel's ranch contained 1,000 acres, much of which was unusually fertile soil.

I was well acquainted with "Uncle Dan" Rhodes, as he was familiarly known, and was hospitably entertained over night in his home in May 1889. The next morning he took me out and showed me his artesian well that was discharging two separate streams of water, each containing a different mineral. He explained how he had bored down about 500 feet, using a large casing, and had struck a flow that was not entirely satisfactory. Dropping another casing inside, he went on down about 250 feet further to where he encountered another good flow of water that was satisfactory. The two flows could be separated, and while the good water was carried off in an irrigation ditch, the other stream could be run off in a wasteway.

Louie Roes' Traver Residence

A saloonkeeper by the name of Louie Roes built a residence on the southwest corner of Block No. 69, Traver, in the early summer of 1887. It was by far the finest dwelling ever built during the history of that town. [The Roes residence stood on the northern corner of Tenth (now Bowhay Drive) and Kitchener Streets. These streets have since been shortened and no longer intersect.]

Joe Long, the painter, always had an unpaid bill for booze at Louie's saloon. Louie figured that now was his chance to get his pay out of Joe by having him paper and paint his new house. When he engaged Joe to do the work he said, "Now, Joe, if you will not get drunk until you have finished this job, I'll buy you a new suit of clothes." Joe solemnly promised to stay sober until the job was completed.

Joe managed to stay sober until he got the painting done and started on the papering. The weather was hot and Joe thought he would go down and get "just one drink." But one drink called for more, and Joe took several drinks. He came back on his job, but he was too full, and the second strip of paper overlapped the first one by about three inches at the bottom. So, Joe left his paste brush in the paste, where it stayed, and went to some saloon, but not Louie's, and went on one of his regular sprees.

I had closed out my paint shop and had accepted a regular job as main yard man in the San Joaquin Lumber Company's yard. Louie came to me and after telling me his troubles with Joe, asked me if I would come and paper the new house for him. I told him I had quit the painting business because it was effecting my stomach, and had a steady job in the lumber yard, and could not do the work for him. Louie then went in the office and took up the matter with E. Barris who was agent for the lumber company. Barris had purchased lots adjoining Louie's new house and was interested in having the house nicely papered. Barris came out to me and said that if I would go and do the papering for Louie at the regular papering wages, which was one dollar more than I was getting in the lumber yard, we would split the dollar and get another man in my place until I got back. That suited me for it was in the shade and I liked to hang paper.

I talked the matter over with Louie and told him that he should have something better than he had planned for his parlor, and that I had some of the material left over that I used in decorative paper hanging. It was gilt picture moulding and a half-round gilt moulding and some material we called velvet flocking. It was a deep red colored velvet-looking paper. This I used about four inches wide between the picture mould and the half-round bead below. Joe never did a real decorative job in his life, so my suggestion just suited Louie, and I went over and finished the job with which he was highly pleased, but he didn't give me any new suit of clothes.

I never paid Louie nor any other man a nickel for booze.

Years later this same house was moved to Reedley by cutting it in two, vertically, and reassembling it at the end of the journey. I papered the same house in its new location. [This became the W. H. Carpenter house, which still stands at 1396 S. Reed.]

Bee Gumm

Bee Gumm and his "White Elephant"

An exblacksmith was running a house of ill fame in Traver in 1886 on the southeast corner of Block 158. It was on the first street back of Chinatown. [The house would have been one block south of the present Golden State/Highway 99, on Merritt Street, an area now a part of Freeway 99.]

Two Italians came down from Merced, looked the situation over, and decided there was justification for another one in the fast growing town. They made the first payment on the lots in the northeast corner on the same block in which the exblacksmith was running his house. They had plans and specifications drawn for their building and submitted them to the contractors of the town.

On the three bids submitted, Bee Gumm was the successful bidder. We are calling him B. Gumm because that was not his name. [Bee Gumm, according to McCubbin's correspondence, was his friend, Homer Hall.] After making a small payment in advance to Gumm, the men returned to Merced.

Gumm had Cisero Spears, the drayman, haul the lumber he had purchased from the S. Sweet Company lumber yard to the lot and put his men to work.

While the house was in process of construction neither of the Italians came to inspect the work. Gumm had written them inviting them to come and see the house. Getting no reply to his communication, Gumm made a trip to Merced and learned that the Italians had gone, leaving several unpaid bills behind. Gumm waited a reasonable time, then filed a lien on the building and attached the lots on which it stood.

As Gumm was a moral man he was greatly embarrassed at being compelled to take such an action against that class of building. He purchased lots on the west side of Block 113 [on Burke, between Merritt and Bullard Streets] in the main part of town and moved the building to there.

Bee Gumm had his Chinatown lots only a few months when a Spaniard came along and purchased them, and had a house built thereon to be used for immoral purposes. He soon had it tenanted with senoritas.

Bee Gumm Orders a Room Papered

About a year after B. Gumm had moved his house to the main part of town and sold, he wanted a room papered that he expected to occupy with his new bride.

I was working for a man who was running a paint shop in the town. One morning the boss told me that Bee Gumm was going to Visalia to get married and wanted a room papered and ready for occupancy when he got back with his bride. He told me he would show me the place. We took our tools and material, and he took me to the house and showed me a room, and then went away.

I tore the old paper and lining all off and piled it up in the back yard and proceeded to tack on new lining. After I had worked about a half hour the boss came back in a hurry and said, "Hold on, Johnny, we are in the wrong house." Gumm had previously owned this house, but had sold it to the capitalist of Traver. The painter that I was working for was great on the booze, and perhaps was half drunk when Gumm gave him the order and thought Gumm still owned the house. Gumm gave the order without going to the place and showing the painter the exact room he wanted papered.

The boss took me to the next block north and showed me the right place. I had it all nicely papered when the newly married couple arrived.

A Traver Tidings Local Item

Jim Doody, one of the five "Front" Street [now Burke Drive] saloonkeepers, had an elevated tank for his water supply, something unusual for Traver. All toilets were outside and open. Doody's, like many others, had a two-by-four cross bar on which to stand or sit.

On this particular occasion to which I will refer, in the spring of 1887, one of the old drunks toppled over and fell in. Being unable to extricate himself, he called loudly for help, which was immediately forthcoming.

The drunk was fished out and lain on the salt grass, where he was drenched with water from the hose, and when as clean as he could be made, was left on the grass to dry off.

In the next issue of the *Traver Tidings,* Harry F. Starring, the editor, had among his local items the following quote: "One of our popular saloon men had a friend interred last week." That occurred just a few weeks before Starring tramped out of Traver one night for parts unknown.

Chapter 4

Reedley

Looking south down the Kings River from the east side of the old wagon bridge at the present Manning Avenue crossing, Fall 1887. L. to R., T. L. Reed, J. H. Harris; Mules, Madam and Matt. Photograph by C. C. Curtis.

Beginnings in Reedley

{*McCubbin wrote over twenty short sketches on the early history of Reedley. Since his articles were largely intended to stand on their own, many of the pieces contain similar background material, and repeat information or stories in articles on related subjects. In order to avoid unnecessary and potentially confusing repetition, McCubbin's Reedley sketches have been edited and compiled into the following thirteen articles.*}

In 1884, the area that came to be Reedley was largely owned by the 76 Land and Water Company. When their canal system was well along toward covering the district, they began recruiting men who would come in and farm their lands. Some of the company's stockholders knew a man named Thomas Law Reed as a tenant on their Yolo County properties and managed to induce him to come down and farm portions of the 76 Company lands.

Reed and his family arrived in the area on November 19, 1884, and took up residence in the old Smith's Ferry Hotel building which was then owned by the 76 Company. They lived in that old building somewhere between twelve to eighteen months, until their own dwelling was ready for occupancy on their own land. Their land was the west half of Section 22, Township 15 South, Range 23 East [this section is bounded by Manning, Reed, and South Avenues; and the Kings River].

The 76 Company lands were nearly all sold on time contracts. While I was in the office (which was all except the harvesting season) I filled out all those contracts. The most important one that I ever filled out was dated July 12, 1888, by which T. L. Reed purchased from the 76 Company 1,259.3 acres. The purchase price was $51,341.25. It averaged about $40 per acre. Upon delivery of that contract, Reed gave his personal check in favor of the company for $10,000. That was the largest check I ever handled. Soon afterward Reed gave the company another personal check for $15,000.

The land described in that big contract adjoined the original townsite of Reedley on three sides — the east, west and north. It was one quarter of a mile on the east and north sides of town, and extended clear to the river on the west side. This purchase increased Reed's local land holdings, including his townsite, to approximately 2,500 acres. He also owned other detached bodies of land in the 76 Country.

Reed's own lands, as well as those he was farming under lease, were nearly all in a virgin state when he took charge of them. His plows turned the first furrow that was ever turned in either of those large areas.

The Railroad

By March 1888, the Southern Pacific was running their construction trains across the Kings River on a temporary bridge, about 300 feet downstream from the present Southern Pacific bridge [this bridge no longer exists, but was just fifty feet south of the remaining Santa Fe bridge]. These construction trains were delivering material to the crews that were laying track through the 76 Country to the southeast of their river crossing. As soon as the permanent railroad bridge was completed the temporary bridge was removed entirely, except where they cut the pilings off near the water level.

About the time Reed made the large land purchase mentioned earlier, he deeded a one-half interest in 360 acres of this 2,000 acre tract to the Pacific Improvement Company, a subsidiary of the Southern Pacific Railroad Company. The railroad required a half interest in all townsites in which they located as a consideration for so doing. Reedley was no exception. The townsite was three-quarters of a mile square [bounded by North, East, Dinuba and Reed Avenues]. The southwest corner [Reed and Dinuba Avenues] was located at the center of the south line of Section 27, Township 15 South, Range 23 East. The townsite of Reedley was surveyed by L. D. Norton in May 1888, but the map was not filed in the County Recorder's Office until November 20.

Finishing the Southern Pacific railroad bridge across the Kings River, 1888.

First Developments in the New Town

First Residence and Post Office

The first home built in Reedley was the F. S. Knauer residence. It was located on the northwest corner of "F" and Eleventh Streets, facing on "F" Street. The Wahtoke Post Office was moved into this home from the F. M. Merritt home two miles to the north, and Mrs. Flora Knauer handled the mail as the assistant of Mrs. F. M. Merritt. This arrangement continued until the name of the office was officially changed from Wahtoke to Reedley. At this time Mrs. Knauer received her regular appointment as the Reedley postmaster. She held the position continuously for over thirty-one years, until her resignation on March 31, 1920. In 1923 the building was moved across the railroad tracks to the southeast corner of "J" and Thirteenth Streets.

Knauer obtained his lumber for his building from the San Joaquin Lumber Company in Traver. T. L. Reed's grain teams, usually returning empty, hauled it up and unloaded it in the grain stubble where the house was to be built. This was in 1888.

First Railroad Depot

As soon as the Porterville Branch of the Southern Pacific Railroad was completed through Reedley and was ready for business, a caboose was set out on a siding and used as a depot. Early in July 1888, T. L. Reed's teams began hauling

Flora and Frank Knauer, circa 1908.
Photograph by George Besaw.

his grain crop to the new townsite and piling it on the ground alongside the switch, there being no depot platform facilities ready to receive it. John Pearl was the teamster who hauled the first load of grain. The grain came from land John R. Reed, T. L. Reed's brother, rented near Smith Mountain.

T. B. McCanne, a colonist near Traver who had formerly served as a railroad agent in a Missouri town, was employed as the first Southern Pacific agent in the new town of Reedley. When the new depot was completed, a man by the name of Humphrey was employed as the first permanent agent. [The depot was on the north side of the Southern Pacific tracks, and on the south side of Eleventh Street.]

First Warehouse

Late in 1888, T. L. Reed purchased, from the 76 Company, 250 feet of their 500-foot long "76 Warehouse" in Traver, and moved it to Reedley, and had it ready for his 1889 grain crop. It was the first warehouse in the new town. Joel G. Wright was in charge of the weighing and Ed. Miles was in charge of the house interior. This warehouse had originally been owned jointly by the 76 Company and Eppinger and Company. [The warehouse was located on the north side of Eighth Street, between the railroad tracks.]

"F" Street looking northwest. Old Knauer home and post office on left, Catholic Church on right, circa 1912.

First train arriving in Reedley at the Southern Pacific Railroad depot, 1888.

Reedley's first warehouse is shown just right of center in this photograph taken from the southwest corner of "G" and Ninth Streets, looking west, circa 1912. Note parachutist.

First Eating Places

In 1888 a portable cook house, which had been built on a regular ranch wagon, was hauled in from one of T. L. Reed's ranch camps and parked on the new town site near the intersection of the present Frankwood and North Avenues. This structure had a kitchen in one end and the remainder was supplied with tables and benches. Access was gained through the opposite end from the kitchen by means of a short flight of detachable stairs. This style of cook house was common then on the big ranches and for the threshing crews.

A Chinaman cooked and served meals in this cook house until John Fairweather built his residence on his newly acquired colony lot. That residence stood on the northwest corner of the intersection described in the above paragraph. The Fairweather daughters did the cooking and the meals were served family style.

In 1889, T. L. Reed built a hotel on the southwest corner of Block 37 [northeast corner of "G" and Eleventh Streets], where the Simpson hotel is now located. H. E. Barnum was placed in charge of the hotel, and Mary Fairweather served as the waitress.

For many years in the early history of Reedley all meals cost 25 cents.

First General Merchandise Store

In the autumn of 1888 when this writer was employed as Assistant Superintendent of the 76 Land and Water Company, Emil Hirschfeld came into the Traver office and made arrangements with me to draw up a contract for the construction of a store building in the new town of Reedley. The building was to be located on the northwest corner of Block 51 [southeast corner of Eleventh and "H" Streets] of the new town. The building was on the south side of Eleventh Street, facing the railroad reservation and depot. Later, when the carpentry work was nearing

John Fairweather. Established one of Reedley's first eating places. Fairweather arrived in Reedley in 1889 and was appointed Justice of the Peace in 1892. In 1896 he and his son purchased the Reedley Exponent. *Fairweather was elected to the California State Assembly in 1898.*

completion, I was also engaged to draw up a contract for painting the building.

On the completion of the building, which was about December 15, 1888, it was stocked with general merchandise and operated under the firm name of E. Hirschfeld and Company. The silent partners were Zelinsky and Gutfeld. Gutfeld was a brother of Charles Gutfeld, a clerk in the Louis Hirschfeld store in Traver.

The company continued in business until the depression of the early 1890s, when they closed out the business and retired from Reedley. After standing idle for a few years, the building was rented to a Fresno firm [McCubbin thinks this may have been the Nobel Brothers] that operated it as a raisin packing house.

[In letters to Neva Hunsberger, McCubbin writes that "Gosliner's general merchandise store followed the closing of the Emil Hirschfeld Company store. It was located on the northeast corner of Block 52 {the southeast corner of Tenth and "G" Streets}, in a two-story brick building. The upper story was the Masonic Hall. Before the Gosliner building was constructed, Harry F. Winnes had a small stock of men's coarse working clothes, notions, tobacco, cigars, etc. There was perhaps another {general merchandise} store, but I can't recall whose it was."]

Pioneer Telephone Lines

The 76 Land and Water Company built their private telephone line in 1885. It extended from Traver, via Wahtoke Dam, to their headgate. It was a one-wire line, yet it worked fairly well.

When E. Hirschfeld and Company opened their general merchandise store in Reedley about December 15, 1888, they made arrangements with the 76 Company to run a line from the store and connect it with the company's line. In March 1889, I took two men out from Traver and we set the poles and strung the wire. This branch line came into town from the east, and came down the south side of Eleventh Street to the Hirschfeld store, where I installed Reedley's first telephone.

About the time this branch was built into Reedley, we built another line connecting the California Fruit and Wine-Land Company's headquarters with our line. That connection was about a mile north of where the Reedley store line was connected with our line. This second line was also a one-wire line. The California Fruit and Wine-Land Company was on the natural mound that stands a mile or two north of the north end of Smith Mountain.

In late 1888 or early 1889 the Sunset Telephone and Telegraph Company built a line from Visalia to Traver. Miss Lizzie Egenhoff was the "Hello Girl" in Traver. Her office was in the Mariposa hotel, which was operated by her father. When this Visalia to Traver line was built there was no telephone line south from Fresno. Sometime during 1890 the Sunset Telephone Company ran their line down from Fresno to Selma.

Some Other Reedley Firsts

The first church building in Reedley was the United Brethren Church on the southwest corner of Block 31 [northeast corner of Tenth and "F" Streets]. The Baptist Church was the second church building in town.

The first hotel in Reedley belonged to T. L. Reed, and H. E. Barnum was the proprietor. It was built on the northeast corner of "G" and Eleventh Streets where the Simpson Hotel now stands. The present building is the third hotel to stand on that corner, the two former ones having been destroyed by fire.

The first livery stable was owned by T. L. Reed [and rented to Reese Bourland and Joe Miller]. James W. Shipe was the proprietor [in later years]. It stood on the northeast corner of Block 29 [southwest corner of Eleventh and "E" Streets]. The old Will. McCreary livery and feed stable had been established earlier, but was not in the town proper but on his colony lot [at the corner of North and Frankwood Avenues] just to the north. It was in the southwest corner of his lot that faced the road that runs out to the Great Western School. When the Shipe stable was built it took McCreary's business away and brought it "up town."

Reedley's Chinatown started in 1889 with the establishment of a Chinese hand laundry.

In 1889, L. A. Rockwell of Traver put in a stock of drugs. W. W. Green was in charge of the store. Later, Green purchased the stock from Rockwell and ran the business until about 1903. In the early 1900s [1908?], W. W. Green sold his store to C. H. Green and moved to San Jose. The Greens were no relation.

Joe. B. Moomaw had a jewelry store and was the watchmaker. His shop was on the west side of "G" Street, about midway between Tenth and Eleventh Streets. In 1889, Moomaw and Joel G. Wright, whose wives were sisters, each purchased five-acre lots adjoining each other and also adjoining the new town on the north. This is where they had their homes.

The First National Bank was the first one in Reedley. It was promoted by Jesse

TOP: Reedley's first church, the United Brethren, circa 1908. Photograph by George Besaw. MIDDLE: The Reedley Hotel, the town's first, circa 1893. L. to R., starting with fifth person, Camillia Simpson, Ora Simpson, Mrs. Bob "Ma" Simpson, Bob Simpson (proprietor), other persons unidentified. Note the sign identifying the Justice Court office of John Fairweather. BOTTOM: First livery stable in the city of Reedley, owned by T. L. Reed. Photograph circa 1888.

Early Reedley street scene showing "G" Street, looking northwest. Photograph taken from the balcony of the Arlington (or Grand) Hotel at Twelfth and "G" Streets, circa 1892.

"G" Street, looking southeast from Ninth Street, circa 1905.

Jansen, and first located in the northeast corner of what was formerly the Gosliner store building.

In 1898, the San Francisco and San Joaquin Valley Railroad was built from

Stockton to Bakersfield via Reedley. The road was eventually turned over to the Santa Fe Railway Company.

In either 1902 or 1903 the Reedley Chamber of Commerce was organized. T. L. Reed was elected president and I was chosen secretary. They had their meetings in the real estate office of T. L. Reed and A. E. McClanahan. The office was where the Bloyd real estate and law office is now located.

Jesse Jansen erected his building, called the Jansen Opera House in 1902 [1903?]. It was the first [opera house or theater] in town. [Still standing at 1720 Tenth Street.]

Thomas Law Reed

I first met T. L. Reed in Traver about September 1, 1886. We were introduced by A. E. McClanahan. I only had casual meetings with him from that time until March 1888 when I began work in the Traver office of the 76 Land and Water Company.

Reed's vast farming operations in the 76 Country included several thousand acres of the 76 Company lands. In addition to this he had extensive private business relations in Yolo County with some of the company's board members.

Thomas Law Reed, circa 1885.

T. L. Reed family, circa 1892. L. to R., top, Jessie, Horace, Nina, Edmond; bottom, Dollie, Amantha, T. L., Imogene.

This was the reason for his frequent calls at the office. During the harvesting season it was my duty to keep in close touch with all the 76 Company lessees. Since T. L. Reed was one of the largest lessees, I naturally became familiar with all his farming activities.

T. L. Reed as born at Chester, Ohio, on November 13, 1847. In 1863, at the age of sixteen, Reed enlisted in the Union Army at Chester. He was wounded at the battle of Shilo, yet served until the close of the Civil War in 1865.

On November 5, 1868, Reed married Miss Amantha Ann Smith at Chester. Shortly after their marriage, the Reeds moved to Kent County, Michigan, where T. L. took charge of a cheese factory at Campbell, Michigan.

In the summer of 1876 Reed traveled to Yolo County, California, arriving in Woodland on May 1. He spent that summer working for Byron Jackson. [According to T. L. Reed's daughter, Imogene Reed Maxwell, her father had come to California to look for his father, George Reed. The elder Reed had come to California by ship in 1849, via the Isthmus of Panama, during the Gold Rush. He had written back that he had struck it rich in the Mother Lode, but then the family lost contact with him. He was never located, nor heard from again.] By the end of the summer, Reed had decided to settle in California. He returned to Michigan for his wife and three children, who had remained behind. The family landed in Woodland on November 16, 1876. The following year (1877) Reed rented the Allan ranch of 400 acres and farmed it to wheat. Eight years later the Reeds moved to the 76 Country.

T. L. Reed home and ranch on what is now the site of Kings River Community College, circa 1891. Photograph by C.C. Curtis.

The Reed Ranch

The old T. L. Reed homestead was located one-fourth of a mile north of Reedley (fractional west half of Section 22, Township 15 South, Range 23 East [the site of Kings River Community College]). In the summer of 1887, Reed purchased from the Traver branch yard of the San Joaquin Lumber Company enough coast redwood pickets and posts to fence his entire home ranch of a half section. After setting the posts, a man with a machine wove the pickets and wire together alongside the post and attached it to them as he went. When completed it was the best fenced ranch in central California. When his tank tower was first completed, Reed had me come in to see how substantially it was constructed.

In March 1888, when I purchased the forty acres where the famous gum tree now grows, there were but four families that owned and occupied homes on the twenty-one mile stretch from Cross Creek on the south, to the Kings River on the north where the Reed ranch was located. Adjoining the T. L. Reed home ranch on the north was the James H. Harden ranch and home. Across the road from the Hardens, and slightly to the north was the Pat. Segrue ranch and home. The McCubbin homestead cabin was six miles from the T. L. Reed home. There was nothing more in the nature of a dwelling north to the Kings River, or the Morrow Slough — one of the delta branches of the Kings River.

There was no public road on this line from Cross Creek north to the Fresno-Tulare County line. From there on north was a public road leading through the present city of Reedley and past the four homes mentioned. Leading down from the plains to the river bottom, the road detoured to the east and ran diagonally down to the flat below. From there it returned to the main line.

Other Accomplishments

T. L. Reed was one of the main promoters of the Alta Irrigation District and served as a member of the first board of directors of that organization. T. L. Reed was no doubt the first man to advocate the construction of a dam on the Kings River where the present Pine Flat Dam is located. He continued to boost for that project as long as he lived. But he never lived to see his dream a reality.

It was Reed who first promoted the building of the present Sand Creek Road. It was also through his influence that the first bridge on what is now Manning Avenue was built. In one of our conversations back in the 1880s he said to me, "If I were supervisor I would overhaul every bridge in my district and make them wide enough for two teams to pass each other simultaneously in perfect safety."

T. L. Reed advanced the best theory of the final disposition of the body of William Wooton, who mysteriously disappeared in the early 1890s [1894]. The location of that body is just as deep a mystery now as it was when he disappeared. For details see my story about William Ruth.

Reed had an unusual talent for judging horse flesh. His was the best and finest buggy team that ever drove the streets of Traver.

When any of his pioneer neighbors needed seed, feed, or provisions, they would go to T. L. Reed, who never refused them. He never made a book account of such loans, but trusted to their honesty and never dunned them. Some of those men would take advantage of his generosity and never pay him, though the honest ones would. He would never take a cent of interest.

There was nothing in the way of arrogance or egotism in the nature of Reed. He would stop to chat, but for a minute only, with the most humble man in a group.

A short time before Reed passed away in 1911, his daughter Imogene said to me, "Papa wants to see you." I replied, "I'll go right up and see him." She said, "No. This is one of his bad days. I'll let you know when he gets better." But he never rallied. I'll never know what it was he wanted to see me about after our long years of friendly relationship. He never told his family what it was and he has taken that information with him on into the eternal silence.

Harvest morning on T. L. Reed's ranch, August 15, 1892. Photograph by J.S. Wintemute.

The Reed Family: Vital Statistics

Thomas Law Reed was born in Chester, Ohio, November 13, 1847. Married to Miss Amantha Ann Smith in Chester, on November 5, 1863. Reed died at Reedley, Fresno County, California, September 11, 1911, at the age of 64 years, 2 months and 2 days.

Amantha Ann Smith was born in Chester, December 11, 1848, and died at Reedley on June 17, 1916, at the age of 67 years, 6 months and 6 days.

Their children were:

Daniel B. born in 1869 and died when three-and-one-half years old.
Horace M. born in 1872 in Kent County, Michigan. [Died in 1954.]
Nina E. born in 1874 in Kent County. [Died in 1954.]
Edmond R. born in 1875 in Kent County. Died in October 1941.
Jessie V. born in 1881 in Yolo County, California.
Sarah born in 1883 in Yolo County. Died when one week old.
Imogene Edith born in 1888 in Fresno County, California.
Dollie born in 1890 in Fresno County.

T. L. Reed had two brothers living in the 76 Country. Sam. Reed farmed lands near the north end of Smith Mountain that he had rented from Simon, Jacobs Company. John R. Reed farmed lands near Smith Mountain and further south than that farmed by Sam. Reed. John rented lands from Mrs. Pennsylvania Crow, nee Haas, who had been widowed when her husband [Walker J. Crow] was killed during the Mussel Slough Tragedy.

ABOVE: Amantha Reed and daughters. L. to R., Nina, Imogene, Mrs. Reed, Dollie, Jessie. Circa 1900. RIGHT: T.L. Reed and sons. L. to R., Edmond, Horace, Mr. Reed. Circa 1900.

J. R. Reed family and ranch, east of Smith Mountain and south of the present Manning Avenue. L. to R., J. R. Reed, Mrs. Reed, Addie, Bernice, Rayson on mule, and Chinese cook.

Smith's Ferry School, circa 1888. Seated at the center is teacher Frank Knauer.

Smith's Ferry School District

During that period when the T. L. Reeds were still living in the old Smith's Ferry hotel building, they resided in the Riverbend School District [the school was located on what is now the southwest corner of Lac Jac and Adams Avenues]. But since there was no way of crossing the Kings River, the three Reed children, Horace, Nina, and Edmond, were unable to attend school until the following year, 1885, when the bridge was built at the present Manning Avenue. By this time the Reed's had moved into their new home.

Since other families with children were also settling in the locality, a group headed by T. L. Reed organized the Smith's Ferry School District. Reed donated land for a school in the northwest corner of Section 23, Township 15 South, Range 23 East, and a school was built there [the southeast corner of Frankwood and South Avenues]. At that time, Reed owned all of Sections 22 and 23 laying on the east side of the Kings River [this would be all of the land between Manning and South Avenues to Buttonwillow Avenue]. Reed was made clerk of the board. Among other patrons of the school were Samuel C. Helm, Patrick Segrue, James

Reedley Grammar School, circa 1892.

H. Harden, E. W. Holmes, F. M. Merritt, and Silas Gregg.

Miss Edith Hatch, of Selma, was the first teacher and served during the 1886-87 term. Miss Hatch later married Al Simpson, a local farmer. Lola Wallace was the teacher for the 1887-88 term. She later married John Carpenter. Following Miss Wallace was Frank S. Knauer, the first male teacher for the school. Mr. Knauer taught during the 1888-89 term. Professor Simon followed Mr. Knauer, teaching the term of 1889-90.

Plans were discussed for moving the schoolhouse into the new town of Reedley, but there were some objections. Nevertheless, in February 1890, the trustees ordered the schoolhouse moved into town. The house mover had elevated the building and placed skids underneath, ready to start the move early the next morning. During the night [February 14, 1890] the building mysteriously caught fire and destroyed the schoolhouse and all the housemover's equipment.

Professor Simon, who was the teacher at the time, moved his classes into the newly constructed United Brethren Church on the southwest corner of Block 31 in Reedley, where he completed the term. The following school term, 1890-1891, was taught by Lola Wallace Carpenter, with classes continuing to meet in the church building.

Bonds were promptly voted for a new schoolhouse, and in due time a good brick schoolhouse was constructed on Blocks 79 and 86, the site of the present Washington School. The first sessions were held in the new building on September 14, 1891, with Clara Boyer as principal, and Carrie Weaver the teacher of the lower grades.

[Records of the Fresno County Schools office indicate that the name of the district was officially changed from Smith's Ferry to the Reedley School District on February 8, 1898. It is unclear, however, whether the new school itself retained the Smith's Ferry name during the six and a half years between its opening and the district's name change, or was known from the beginning as the Reedley Grammar School.]

The Reed Colony

About the time Reedley was established, T. L. Reed came into the 76 Land and Water Company office in Traver and requested that I draw a map for his proposed colony at Reedley. This was the first colony to be placed on the market in the vicinity of Reedley. The map would be used by the surveyor in making the subdivision of the colony property. All of this kind of work I did on my own time.

Reed's original plan was to include all his property that adjoined the townsite on the east, west and north sides of the townsite — about 500 acres. It extended one quarter of a mile deep on the east and north sides, and extended to the river on the west. All of the land on the north and east sides was to be cut into five- and ten-acre lots, and that on the west was to be cut into large lots extending from the townsite westward to the river.

After we talked the matter over, Reed decided to cut all of the land facing the townsite on both the east and north sides into five-acre lots that would extend back half way across the quarter of a mile. That portion to the back of these lots would be cut into ten-acre tracts. All of the lots on the west side were to be much larger and extend clear back westward to the river.

Among the first buyers of lots on the north side of town were: A. T. Simpson, J. G. Wright, J. B. Moomaw, a Mr. [Charles?] Gummow, E. F. Austin, John Fairweather, William McCreary, and J. L. Gilbert. Simpson also purchased the three-cornered lot between the new railroad and what is now Manning Avenue. Among the first purchasers of colony lots on the east side of town were: Harry F. Winnes, Rev. [O. L.] Franbes, and A. L. Ayers. Among the first purchasers of the larger lots on the west side of town were: Samuel Reed, brother of T. L. Reed; Rev. T. J. Bauder, minister of the new United Brethren Church in Reedley; and Daniel L. MeKeel.

Harry F. Winnes Buys the Hirschfeld Building

Harry F. Winnes was a carpenter and contractor in Traver from 1885 until he moved to the new town of Reedley in 1889. When Winnes moved to Reedley, he first opened a little store in which he carried a stock of tobacco, stationery,

Harry F. Winnes, in Traver, 1887

"G" Street, looking southeast from Eleventh Street, circa 1908. Note the retirement of H. F. Winnes General Merchandise store at right. Photograph by George Besaw.

After the Reedley Hotel fire in 1910, looking south. Prior to the construction of the Winnes (now Burgess) Hotel on opposite corner. Photograph by George Besaw.

candies, canned goods, etc. In 1894 his business had grown until he was conducting a general merchandise business on the northwest corner of "G" and Eleventh Streets.

In 1895 Winnes married Miss Anna Payne. Miss Payne had come to California from Missouri with her parents in 1892.

In 1897 Winnes took in S. F. Earl as a partner in his general merchandise business. After two years, Winnes bought his partner's interest in the business, and the Earl residence. Late in 1899 Winnes purchased the lots on the southwest corner of Eleventh and "G" Streets. That street-crossing was then and is yet the logical business center of Reedley.

[In a letter to Neva Hunsberger on January 17, 1956, McCubbin wrote that Winnes and Earl "made an unsuccessful attempt to burn a kiln of brick near the center of Block 61 in Reedley. Their plan was to construct a brick building where the Hotel Winnes now stands." Block 61 is that area between the Santa Fe and Southern Pacific railroad tracks, between Fifteenth and Sixteenth Streets. The Hotel Winnes is now known as the Burgess Hotel.]

Early in 1900 Winnes bought the Hirschfeld Company property. He then owned the two corners, properties with only an alley between them. He then moved the [Hirschfeld] building across the alley to the east, turned it around and faced it in the opposite direction. Its new location was on the southwest corner of "G" and Eleventh Streets, where the Hotel Winnes now stands. Winnes moved his stock of merchandise from the building across Eleventh Street into his own building.

Winnes then erected a new building on the lot facing the depot. A part of this new building he used for his furniture and undertaking business and the other

Public gathering at the intersection of "G" and Eleventh Streets, and showing a full view of the Winnes Hotel, circa 1917.

portion was used for a skating rink.

In 1913 Winnes sold the old Hirschfeld building and the purchaser moved it to Chinatown, where it was cut up into several units and rented to Chinese. Winnes then built a good two-story brick building on his Eleventh and "G" Street property. The ground floor was used for his general merchandise store and the upper portion was furnished and operated as a rooming house under the name Hotel Winnes.

Winnes continued his regular business until his health failed in 1918. When he retired he had been in business in Reedley continuously since he opened his modest little store the first year Reedley was in existence. His business had grown with the town until it was one of the leading mercantile institutions in the entire Alta District. His business had survived that of every competitor he ever had. Winnes, who had been born in 1864 in Decator, Indiana, and raised in Muncie, passed away on March 4, 1919, at 54 years of age.

Mrs. Anna Winnes, the widow, married Mr. A. Helm-Kennedy, a teacher in the Reedley schools. Mrs. Helm-Kennedy divided the upper story of the large brick building and rented out the units separately. In 1922 they remodeled the building, added a lobby, and turned the upper portion of the structure into a regular hotel. [In an earlier version of this article, McCubbin wrote that Winnes had opened a grocery store in Taft in 1914, and had operated it in conjunction with his business in Reedley. Later, according to this account, Winnes had a one-story brick building constructed across the alley from the hotel building, closed the Taft store, and brought his stock back to Reedley and placed it in this new building. Whether this information was left out of McCubbin's most recently dated version through inadvertence, for the sake of brevity, or because he determined that the information was inaccurate, is unknown.]

Harry F. Winnes, circa 1910

Pioneer Lumber Yards in the 76 Country

When the first sale of lots was made in Traver on April 8, 1884, S. Sweet and Company of Visalia purchased Block 136 for the purpose of establishing a lumber yard. There was no lumber yard in the entire 76 Country at that time.

Emil Seligman, who was in the S. Sweet General Merchandise store in Hanford, was brought over to take charge of this Traver lumber business. Seligman remained in charge of this Traver yard until it was sold to the San Joaquin Lumber Company in January 1887. Yancey was the General Manager of the chain of yards belonging to this company. E. Barris of Traver was employed as the local agent. A few years later Barris bought the yard and stock. But Traver was already on its fatal decline, and after a few years Barris moved his entire stock to Dinuba where he continued the business.

I had been familiar with the lumber business practically all my life. My father had been in the hard wood lumber business in Illinois since I was a small boy. I was in charge of the Traver yard from June 1887 until March 1888 at which time S. F. Earl, Secretary of the 76 Company came to me and offered me a position in the 76 Company. I accepted this offer and resigned my position with the lumber company.

When making my home in Selma during the nineties, John A. Bishop, local manager of a branch lumber yard belonging to one of the big Fresno lumber companies, and I would occasionally talk shop.

Believing it was an opportune time to establish another big lumber business in

Fresno, a group of capitalists organized the Fresno Lumber Company and employed John A. Bishop as their business manager.

This new company purchased lots at the corner of "I" (now Broadway) and Ventura Avenues and installed a complete stock of lumber. They also established close connections with some of the other lumber companies in the valley, as well as establishing some new chain yards.

On October 25, 1890, the Puget Sound Lumber Company purchased Block 68 [bounded by Tenth, "I", and Eleventh Streets and the Southern Pacific railroad tracks] in Reedley, and put in a complete stock of lumber. Soon afterwards the depression of the early nineties halted building operations, and the Reedley yard was unable to make expenses. The entire stock was moved to another point where it could be disposed of. The lumber office, shed and yard in Reedley lay idle for several years.

About 1900, E. Barris, who had a lumber yard in Dinuba, rented the old Puget Sound lumber plant in Reedley and put in a small and inferior stock of lumber and placed D. L. MeKeel, a local man, in charge. It was apparently a "dog in the manger" move to discourage other lumber men from doing anything in Reedley.

It was about a year later that I met Bishop on the street in Fresno and he invited me to come down to his office. I accepted the invitation and that afternoon I visited his office. He arose from his desk and took me out in the yard and showed me what they had in stock. We then sat down in the shade and he asked me what they had in the way of a lumber yard in Reedley. I described it to him and told him it could not be called a lumber yard in the full sense of the term.

According to appointment, Bishop came down to Reedley in a few days. We got a livery rig and I drove all around the lumber yard where he could get a good idea of the so-called stock of lumber. We then drove all over the immediate territory of Reedley and then down to Dinuba. When Bishop was ready to return to Fresno, he said he could not say for sure what his board would do, but he believed they would put in a good stock of lumber in Reedley.

In the meantime he requested that I go around and take orders for enough lumber to fill a car, and he would ship it to me. This I did, and secured sufficient orders to make three cars. These he shipped to me, and I delivered them.

While this was going on I received a communication from W. R. Spalding, a big lumberman in Visalia, and who had a lumber yard in Dinuba, desiring to employ me as local manager of a lumber yard they desired to establish in Reedley. I telephoned to Bishop and told him I would like to see him in his office that evening.

I met him according to appointment and showed him Spalding's letter. He was somewhat surprised and said that he and Spalding were friendly competitors. He put in a call for Spalding on the telephone and got a prompt reply. While I was on one of the office phones, Bishop was talking to Spalding on the other one. Spalding said he thought perhaps I was acting for some other lumber concern that might not be a congenial competitor, but had not thought of interfering with the Fresno Lumber Company's interests.

Before and during this activity title to the Puget Sound property in Reedley passed to G. M. Dopkins, then to W. R. Spalding, then to John A. Bishop. This conveyance to Bishop was dated March 25, 1905. Bishop, of course, was the General Manager of the Fresno Lumber Company at this time. The result was that a full and complete stock of lumber was put in the old Puget Sound lumber yard, and I was employed as the local agent.

I had no idea when I was manipulating the lumber business for the Fresno Lumber Company that I would have anything to do with it after it was completed. I was interested only in getting a good reliable firm established in the town. Bishop had expected to have his brother come up from Arizona and take charge of the yard. But his brother found he was unable to make the change. Then Bishop said to me it was up to me to take charge, which I did.

The other big lumber companies in Fresno were never pleased with the idea of the Fresno Lumber Company entering the field and acting independently and doing business on a twenty per cent gross profit when they were combined and charging all the traffic could bear, which sometimes reached nearly one hundred per cent profit.

Consequently, the other firms launched a lumber war to force the Fresno Lumber Company to enter the combination. This war lasted nearly two months, but the combination found their foe was too strong for them, and they finally withdrew, shipped their outside, newly established competitive yards' stock to their other yards. The Fresno Lumber Company then went on as they had before the war.

The big lumber combination sent a man to Reedley with nothing but a scratch pad, a pencil and a big stock of egotism. I continued my prices and business as usual, which was aimed at a twenty per cent gross profit. Had it not been for two local merchants who threw all ethical methods to the winds and each gave the agent an order without even giving me a chance to bid on them, the agent would never have gotten a dollar's worth of business.

My yard was the only one in our chain that showed a net profit during the war.

After I had this new Reedley yard thoroughly established, M. Sides of Selma, one of the big stockholders in the Fresno Lumber Company, bought and took over the Reedley yard, but it continued to operate as a member of the regular chain of yards, so far as purchasing was concerned.

This sale and transfer was made from the Fresno Lumber Company to Sides, and the real estate passed through the name of John A.Bishop. This occurred on January 28, 1904.

Shoemake and Curtis

During the early eighties David T. Curtis and Albert B. Shoemake, who were residents and large land owners of Stanislaus County, California, purchased a tract of land containing 2,880 acres that lay across the Fresno-Tulare County line, east of the Kings River.

The north end of this body of land adjoined what was later the townsite of Reedley. The legal description of the land was as follows: The east half of Section 34 and the entire Section 35, all in Township 15 South, Range 23 East [bounded by Dinuba, Buttonwillow, Floral and Reed Avenues], in Fresno County, and containing 960 acres; and all of Sections 2, 3 and 10 in Township 16 South, Range 23 East [these sections are contiguous and bounded as follows: Sections 2 by Avenue 432, Road 64, Avenue 424, and Road 56; Section 3 by Avenue 432, Road 56, Avenue 424 and Road 48; and Section 10 by Avenue 424, Road 56, Avenue 416 and Road 48], in Tulare County and containing 1,920 acres, or a total of 2,880.

The land was all rented out for dry farming until 1889 when the Level Orchard Land Colony was established. The colony included all of Sections 3 and 10, Township 16 South, Range 23 East, in Tulare County. It was subdivided into thirty-two lots of forty acres each, making a total of 1,280 acres. The map was filed in the office of the Recorder of Tulare County, January 20, 1889.

In 1890, D. T. Curtis took charge of all the unsold portion of the original tract and continued in charge of the farming activities thereafter. Although his home was in Stanislaus County, Curtis spent most of his time at the ranch. The headquarters was always in the extreme southeast corner of Section 34 [northwest corner of Frankwood and Floral Avenues] on the Fresno County side of the Tulare-Fresno County line. When it was first established, it was near the old Stockton-Los Angeles stage road that was still in use by the traveling public. That road passed about 200 yards to the southwest. Its course was southeast.

The map of the Curtis and Shoemake Tract (a colony subdivision) was filed in the office of the Recorder of Fresno County, November 24, 1893. The land included in this colony was described as east half of Section 34, and all of Section 35, Township 15 South, Range 23 East, and contained 960 acres.

During the middle nineties Shoemake and Curtis dissolved their partnership. By special arrangement, Curtis took over all the Tulare County portion of the land, as well as the southeast quarter of Section 34 in Fresno County. In addition to this property, Curtis owned 640 acres in Stokes Valley and another 640 acres located about ten miles south of Reedley. On this latter section, about the year 1918, a vicious mule actually kicked Curtis' brains out.

On Thanksgiving Day 1899, I purchased from A. B. Shoemake Lot 29 of the Curtis and Shoemake Tract. It was located in the extreme southwest corner of Section 35 [northwest corner of Frankwood and Floral Avenues], in Fresno County, and on the north side of the Fresno-Tulare County line. When the deed was executed it was signed, "A. B. 'X' (his mark) Shoemake," which indicated he was unable to sign his name. He was a shrewd businessman and succeeded in acquiring about $100,000 worth of property despite his lack of education.

Reedley Cooperative Packing Company

About January 1, 1904, the Reedley Cooperative Packing Company was incorporated. The directors were T. L. Reed, T. M. Lane, W. H. Graham, A. E. McClanahan, and myself, J. C. McCubbin. T. M. Lane was elected president and I was chosen secretary. The First National Bank of Fresno was treasurer.

Shares for the company were fixed at $100 each. After securing 100 paid up shares ($10,000) the company built a granite packing house on the northwest corner of Block 49 by the Santa Fe tracks [still standing at 1760 Thirteenth Street, and now owned by Peloian Fruit Distributors].

The company secured their stone from the south end of Smith's Mountain. The Santa Fe had not yet worked up enough business to justify a daily freight train both ways. Instead they had one train that started at Calwa and went via Reedley, Visalia, Corcoran, Hanford, and back to Calwa. All the stone used in that granite packing house was hauled by the railroad over 100 miles, clear around the "loop," and delivered within six miles from where it started. The packing house was in the process of construction in the spring of 1904, with Paul ______, a stonemason of Dinuba, in charge. This stonemason was a newphew of "Tobacco" Wilson.

That packing house should stand for thousands of years!

Reedley's Great Raisin Vineyards

{*This article appeared in the December 1914 edition of* The Earth, *a publication of the Santa Fe Railway. The article carried the following preface, "Mr. McCubbin is secretary of the Reedley Chamber of Commerce. It is a district long famous for peaches, pears, and grapes, and now citrus fruits are coming. The statistics of production given by Mr. McCubbin are of 1913. Production in 1914 was very much greater, and the market better; but full reports are not yet in."*}

It would interest the general public very little, should we repeat simply the well established fact that Fresno County, California, is the greatest raisin district in the world, but definite information concerning the locality which contributes most toward this distinction no doubt would be worthy of attention.

After giving the yield of one vineyard in order to prove the fertility of the soil,

Reedley's "monster" raisin packing house, circa 1908. Photograph by George Besaw.

all further reference in this article will deal with the product generally.

Among the records of the California Raisin Grower's Association, which included every raisin vineyard in the state, we find that a twelve-acre vineyard, one-half mile south of Reedley, Fresno County, owned by A. B. Clark, of Fresno, and farmed by Carson Reid, of Reedley, shows the greatest yield of any vineyard in the state. The crop grown on this vineyard in one year was 59,875 pounds, or practically, two and one-half tons per acre.

At the present there are six packing houses and one cannery in Reedley, in which all varieties of fruits are prepared for market. However, for the purpose of this article, special reference will be made to only one of these establishments.

"When wheat was king," busy scenes were witnessed in three large warehouses here, but since grain no longer is grown over great areas, large storage for the storage of that commodity is not required. Owing to this the California Associated Raisin Company was enabled to purchase one of these houses. This was converted into a raisin packing house, and it is the largest for this use in the world. [Still standing on Tenth Street, between the Southern Pacific and Santa Fe railroad tracks.]

Monster Packing House

It is 60 by 348 feet, inside measure, and 16 feet high in the clear. An eight-foot porch extends the entire length of one side; the main roof extending out beyond. The material used in the house is of a most durable character and in keeping with substantial construction; the walls being of brick and the roof of corrugated iron. There are no posts in the house; the roof is supported by trusses. The floor of the house proper contains 20,880 square feet and the porch 2,800 more, making a total of 23,680 square feet.

None of the space is taken up for office room; that department together with the wagon scales is under a separate roof near the end of the main house. Instead of a ground lease, which is the only title usually held by packing firms, the California Associated Raisin Company holds a deed to this magnificent property. In its acquisition of this house, the company certainly is to be congratulated, especially on account of its favorable location. Situated as it is, between the Santa Fe and Southern Pacific railways, it has service of two transcontinental lines.

J. P. Kane, the local manager, says that there were more raisins in this house at the close of business, December 31, 1913, than ever were collected under one roof before. A statement from his books taken at that time shows as follows: Pounds raisins in house, 5,017,629; pounds raisins shipped out, 4,465,252; pounds raisins handled by house during 1913, 9,482,881, or 4,741 tons.

More Room Required

Although this is the largest raisin packing house in the world, it was found to be inadequate for handling the business, and the company was compelled to lease additional space in two other packing houses. A statement of the business transacted at these two places is as follows: Pounds in leased storage, 2,681,678; pounds shipped out, 1,964,553; total handled in leased storage, 1913, 4,646,231; total handled in company's own house 1913, 9,482,881. Grand total, season 1913, 14,129,112 pounds, or more than 7,000 tons.

In order to arrive at a proper estimate of the entire Reedley raisin crop, it would be necessary to add the number of pounds handled by other companies, but unfortunately it would be very difficult to ascertain the exact amount of these goods, and the task was not undertaken.

To understand the full significance of the above figures, the reader should take into consideration that the raisin crop of 1913 was only 70 per cent of normal.

The stemmer used is one of three machines manufactured expressly for the California Associated Raisin Company. They are exactly alike and are the largest raisin stemmers ever built.

That the greatest strength and efficiency might be attained in the operation of this gigantic machine (weighing 26,500 pounds), it was necessary to assemble the parts at the manufactory, where powerful machinery specially adapted for the purpose, may be employed.

Exclusive of the elevator which conveys the stem waste from the packing house, and the elevated walks for the use of the operators, the stemmer measures 36 feet in length, 7 feet 11 inches in width, and 12 feet 10 inches in height. An 18-horsepower gas-engine supplies the motive power and, running full capacity, will stem seven tons of raisins per hour, requiring services of twenty-three men.

During the busy part of the past season it was run an average of twelve hours daily. When there was a rush, the time was extended to fifteen hours, when it turned out over 200,000 pounds of raisins daily.

How the Work is Done

Four men, working in couplets, truck the loaded sweat boxes to the stemmer, where two feeders with wet sponges over their noses, to protect them from dust, dump the contents of the boxes into a hopper leading directly to the cylinder.

This cylinder is a large drum made of heavy galvanized steel wire, woven with a one-eighth inch mesh and revolves inside of a system of concaves of the same material and construction as the cylinder. The centrifugal force, aided by the action of the air, detaches the stems, after which, the raisins with their trash are hurled against the face of a vertical elevator provided with a set of transverse troughs, which lifts them to the top of the stemmer, where they are deposited in a shaker which hangs on a slight incline and vibrates with a vigorous lateral motion. This shaker spreads them evenly over its surface. Underneath the shaker is a huge fan revolving at the rate of 800 revolutions per minute. In dropping from the shaker to a conveyor below, the raisins are exposed to a blast of air from the fan above referred to, which removes all the trash and forces it upward at a moderate angle for a short distance, from where it passes by gravity beyond the conveyor and drops through another, though weaker, blast of air, where many good berries are rescued which had been blown over with the trash by the first fan. An elevator takes the refuse at this point and dumps it beyond the wall of the house.

Returning to the raisins, we find that the conveyor on which they drop, acts with a gentle pitching motion and carries them along over its surface. This conveyor is thickly perforated with round holes of four different sizes. The first, or smaller set allows the "one crowns" to drop through, and the holes increase in size as the raisins move forward over them, until the "four crowns" drop through at the farther end.

There are four chutes running through the stemmer from one side to the other, which are built on an incline and provided with a system of ball-bearing rollers in lieu of a floor. The empty boxes are fed into these chutes on one side and glide along until they emerge on the opposite side under continuous streams of raisins running from spouts connected with each of the four bins above. The thin sides of the boxes crowding each other prevent any raisins from dropping between. An attendant stops a box until filled, when it is allowed to pass on to the weigher who draws it on the scales, which are on a level with the top of the rollers. Here he adds to or takes from its contents, until the indicator shows fifty pounds net, then another attendant shoves it under the press and applies the power. After this it is ready for the lid; when this is nailed on it is lifted for the first time, placed on a truck and wheeled away.

Great Raisin Center

Viewed from the volume of products for the past twenty-five years, since the time when the Reedley district really emerged from the desert, it is demonstrated that Reedley is the center of one of the most magnificent agricultural districts in the world.

The great warehouses still standing, together with the records of the quantity of grain shipped out, are proof that this locality was unsurpassed for grain, and during the brief period of fifteen years since the industry was established, results have demonstrated what can be accomplished in the production of raisins.

Citrus trees only three years old passed through the unprecedented cold weather of the winter of 1912-1913 without the least protection and produced a good crop of exceptionally fine fruit the following season.

To fully appreciate the large size and fine flavor of the many varieties of deciduous fruits, it would be necessary to visit the orchards when the crops are ripe. The vast area of full-bearing citrus and deciduous orchards, together with the ever-increasing areas coming into bearing yearly, promises soon to entitle this district to claim production records for fruits equal to that which it now holds as in the production of raisins.

Smith's Ferry Historical Landmarks Destroyed

The old Smith's Ferry site with its historical setting constituted one of the most valuable heritages of any spot in the San Joaquin Valley. Reedley would still be in possession of that priceless heritage had it not been for the actions of a small group that carried on a campaign of destruction until the last one of those interesting landmarks was obliterated.

The land where the old Smith's Ferry site was located passed into the possession of the 76 Land and Water Company and formed a part of their twenty thousand acres.

On April 22, 1889, W. G. P. Thomas died at his home near Traver. He was the father of Mrs. Samuel C. Helm, who with her family, was living two miles north of the old Smith's Ferry site. Without the knowledge or consent of the 76 Company or any of its officers, the Thomas body was buried near the James Smith grave.

I was serving as Assistant Superintendent of the 76 Company at the time, and I lettered a conspicuous, strongly lettered notice to the effect that any future trespassing on that property would be promptly prosecuted, and posted the notice on the tree at the foot of the Smith grave. That notice prompted the organization of the Reedley Cemetery Association.

Troubles in the Cemetery Association

The association seemed to work fairly well for a number of years, until a new and arbitrary secretary was elected. No progress was being made with the passing of the years. Among other things, lots were being sold at about half their value and to anybody with no restrictions as to the class of people being interred in the heart of the cemetery. In one case, a lot was sold to a man who buried his dog in it.

At one of the annual meetings I succeeded in having a committee appointed whose duty it was to prepare a new code of Bylaws, and also make needed suggestions for the guidance of the board of directors. I corresponded with several other cemeteries to get information on their methods of management. I also secured from the Secretary of State a copy of the law governing such organizations. All the material I had gathered was turned over to the committee.

After waiting nearly two years with no action by the committee, I got the material I had given them and framed a code of Bylaws, getting legal advice on its preparation. I then prepared a list of recommendations to be given the board of directors. Among those suggestions was one regarding the preservation of the old Smith's Ferry landmarks.

After examining what I had prepared, the committee signed them, and they were presented at the annual meeting. No mention was made, however, of the part I had taken in their preparation. Verbally, I added to the recommendation regarding the importance of the old landmarks, and gave a short sketch of the activities during the early days around the ferry site. After a stormy discussion, the report was adopted without a single change.

The new Bylaws prevented the illegal board members from being reelected. There were, however, enough of the embittered ones returned to the board to obstruct any move toward the preservation of the old landmarks. The board, together with the angry secretary, launched a campaign of destruction that continued until the last landmark was obliterated.

After this meeting, the Fresno County Historical Society appointed a committee to confer with the Cemetery Association board regarding the old landmarks at the ferry site. As one of the members of the historical society committee, I telephoned down from Fresno to the president of the cemetery board on the day of the board's regular meeting, stating what had been done, and that our committee would be down immediately after lunch to confer with them. The cemetery board hurried through with their work and went home before our committee could reach Reedley.

First Act of Destruction

The first act of destruction was when the sexton backed his truck down the old road and dug away the old steep bank at the ferry landing where room had been made for the stages and other vehicles to land or board the ferry boat. His excuse was to get dirt to spread out on his yard. That soil taken below the surface as everyone knows was worthless for such a purpose.

The old road that ran from the ferry landing diagonally through the Reedley city property, up the hill to the front of the old hotel, was still well defined. I took up the matter of its preservation with the Mayor and suggested that a row of trees or shrubs could be planted along each side of the road. But he was not interested. The city then located their septic tank directly across the old road bed.

China Trees of Heaven Destroyed

In 1862, James Smith planted a row of China Trees of Heaven in front of his hotel. When the survey was made for paving the Fresno County highway that now passes in front of the cemetery, those old trees were found to be exactly in line of the proposed highway.

I went to Chris Jensen, the County Surveyor, and gave him a brief history of the trees and asked if it were possible to have the trees preserved. He was very cooperative, and assured me that he would resurvey that portion of the highway and make a detour around the trees. This he did, and I felt the trees, being on county property, would now be safe. But, I was over optimistic.

J. H. (Herbert) Carpenter, whose dwelling was on the east side of the road opposite the trees, boasted that he was going to destroy those trees because sprouts would come up on his place. When Oscar P. Noren learned of Carpenter's threats, he went to him and pleaded for the preservation of the trees. Ignoring Noren's pleas, Carpenter did go out onto Fresno County property and wantonly grubbed up and destroyed those interesting landmarks.

Monument is Moved

Mrs. Clayborne Wright, who had formerly been Mrs. James Smith, came from Monterey County in 1874 and had a brick wall constructed around her late husband's grave and monument. The wall was not exactly east and west, the east end bearing slightly to the south. The cemetery board had it torn down and moved, together with the monument, about eight feet to the north, where it remained for a number of years, when it was taken entirely away. The monument was returned to the Smith grave, but was not placed at the head of it.

Deed is Corrected

About 1912, I examined the deed that the 76 Company had given to the Cemetery Association and found that by mistake they had described land six miles to the east of the cemetery. As I had formerly served in the 76 office, I took up the matter with the officers of that company and they executed an instrument that cured the defect in the deed. This I had recorded at my own expense and said nothing about any of those corrections to the cemetery board.

Miscellaneous Items on Reedley's History

The Dalton Brothers' Uncle

In September 1886, I was painting on the new Lyman Ensley two-story building located about two miles to the southwest of the Smith's Ferry site, on the old stage road. The painters and carpenters kept their bedrolls in the barn where they slept. Early one morning I climbed to the platform on the tank tower to get a better view over the plains. To the northwest, the T. L. Reed home was about four miles distant and was the first house in that direction. The Henry Roes dwelling was the only one I remember seeing between the Smith's Ferry site and Smith Mountain to the east. Looking to the south, the Dewitt Dopkins dwelling was the only one between where I stood and the Robert Kennedy home five mile

Wheat threshing on the J. R. Reed ranch, circa 1892. Photograph by C. C. Curtis.

away. Down the river and through the 9,000 acre Clarke ranch, there was no family residence for twelve miles from Smith's Ferry. Scattered over that broad expanse were several ranch camps where foremen or renters and their families lived.

One evening a Mr. Oldham, from one mile east of Kingsburg, stayed over the night at Ensley's and slept in the barn with the rest of us. Oldham was a lame man having been wounded in the leg while serving in the Confederate Army during the Civil War. Oldham was an uncle of the Dalton brothers, the Oklahoma bandits. The Daltons would visit their uncle, but no one knew at the time that they were bandits.

Charlie Flewelling, a butcher in Reedley, told me that when he was living in Kingsburg he once went to a dance there with the Dalton brothers. Before they went in to the dance the Daltons left their guns hidden under the porch and said to him, "We want these where we can get at them easily, for we may need them in a hurry."

Early Doctoring

Dr. [B. F.] Day was the only doctor and really a poor excuse for a doctor. His office was on the rear of the Knauer post office and residence lot and his office faced on Eleventh Street, next to the alley. When H. E. Barnum accidentally shot himself in the shoulder, Dr. Day sewed up the wound. When Barnum was getting very low with the wound a subscription was raised in Traver to secure the services of Dr. [Chester] Rowell in Fresno. The doctor came down and amputated the arm. He removed a piece of the jumper from the wound that Dr. Day had sewn up into it.

After recovering from the gunshot wound, H. E. Barnum was elected Constable, and later on to the office of Auditor of Fresno County. He held the office as long as he was able to attend to the duties.

Local Library

In 1909 a committee was appointed by an informal group to prepare a

Old Kings River wagon bridge at the present Manning Avenue, looking east, circa 1908. Photograph by George Besaw.

constitution and bylaws for a local library. That committee consisted of Mrs. Gallager, wife of the local United Brethren minister; Miss Alice M. O'Connor, teacher in the grammar school; and myself. We met at Gallagers but the work was turned over to me and I prepared the bylaws, which were adopted as I had presented them.

The library was regularly organized, and local parties donated a miscellaneous lot of books. My contribution consisted of about 250 books, and a flat-topped walnut desk. The books were kept in the S. D. England ice cream parlor until the County Library established a branch in Reedley, when all the local material was turned over to Fresno County.

Lac Jac

Lachman and Jacobi, a firm doing business in Petaluma, California, built the Lacjac winery where the new San Francisco and San Joaquin Valley Railroad (now Santa Fe Railway) crossed the Porterville Branch of the Southern Pacific. The first syllable of each partner's name was used to make the name of their new winery.

Chapter 5

Around the District

Wahtoke

Unusual record set by using word on eighteen occasions

The practice of applying a succession of different names to one particular place, during different periods, is a common one. In fact, some of the principal cities of this state, among them San Francisco and Sacramento, have been known in the past by other names than the ones in use at the present time.

A radical departure from this custom is to be found in Fresno County, California, where the method has been reversed and one name has served on no less than eighteen different occasions, and fourteen of the eighteen were within a radius of three and a half miles. We refer to the name "Wahtoke." "Wahtoque" is an Indian name meaning "pine nut."

Indian Nation

There was an Indian nation known as the "Wattokes," composed of four tribes, viz: the Wattokes, Ituches, Chokemnies, and Wechummies. Their territory was along the tributaries of the upper Kings River, and included the country east of Centerville and north of Reedley.

During the Indian war of 1850 and 1851 the Wattoke nation cooperated with all the other Indians from the Tuolumne region on the north to the Kaweah on the south.

There are numerous pictographs, done in various colors, and some wonderful carvings, still visible on the rocks throughout the territory originally occupied by the Wattokes. If any present day Indians have any knowledge of their meaning or have any tradition as to when or by whom the writings or carvings were made, the information has never been communicated to the white people.

All local place names that have been adopted in the past, as well as those still in use, and whose spelling is similar to that of the Indian nation referred to, could no doubt be traced back to those people. Among the names used at different periods, five different methods of spelling are to be found.

[Some of the above information is in need of clarification and correction, the result of exhaustive research conducted by ethnographers in the years since McCubbin wrote this article in 1924. Frank Latta was perhaps the foremost authority on the Yokuts Indians — the Indian "nation" of some sixty tribes that populated the floor of the San Joaquin Valley and portions of the foothills. Latta's book, *Handbook of Yokuts Indians* (1977), is the source for most of these notes.

Each tribe of the Yokuts was independent and held its own territory. However, there was considerable similarity in their customs and tribal practices. The dialect each tribe spoke was distinct, yet similar enough to other Yokuts dialects to allow partial intelligibility throughout the valley. The Indians used the word Yokuts as we use "everybody," or "people."

Wahtoke was the chief of the Choinumne Yokuts at the time whites arrived in

THE FRESNO MORNING REPUBLICAN, SUNDAY, MAY 11, 1924.

Shows Use Of Name Wahtoke

This map has been drawn by Mr. McCubbin to accompany his study of "Wahtoke" as a Fresno county place name. It locates, in a territory north of Reedley and around Mt. Campbell, the various uses of the name since it was first applied to Wahtoke creek in the early fifties. For purposes of comparison, to show sizes and distances, the central Mt. Campbell property, belonging to J. C. Forkner of Fresno, is one mile east and west by three fourths mile north and south.

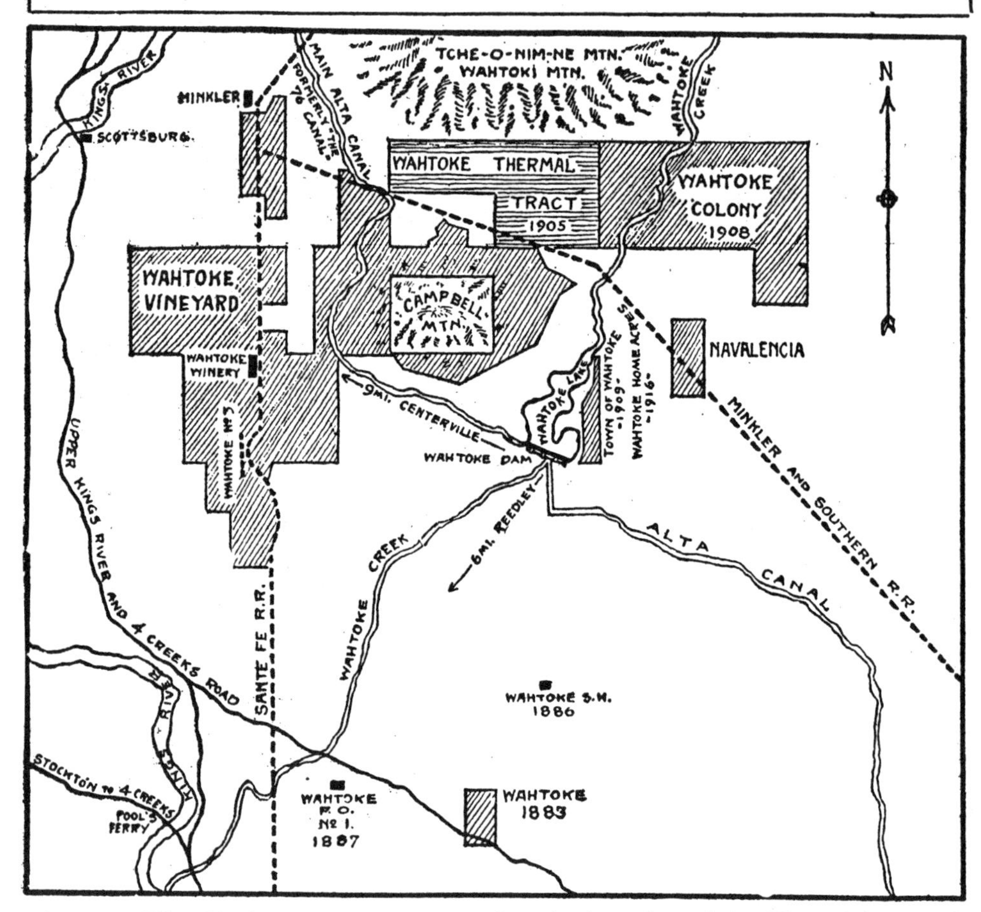

the area. The Choinumne were centered at the junction of the Kings River and Mill Creek, but ranged south of there along the river.

Other tribes in the immediate vicinity of the Wahtoke district included the following. The Itecha were located on the south bank of the Kings River, around Sanger. The Wechikit were on the north bank of the Kings River near Sanger, but ranged as far as Centerville and Reedley. Oscar Noren, a local historian who took a special interest in the Indians of the area, located over twenty Indian habitation sites, including two villages, in the Reedley vicinity. The village of Musanau was in the Sanger river bottom, and Wewio was along Wahtoke Creek.

The Wechummies, mentioned by McCubbin, are presumably the Wukchumne. The Wukchumne were not, however, a Kings River tribe. They lived on the Kaweah River in the vicinity of the present Kaweah Lake.

Latta took particular care in trying to determine the original pronunciation of Indian names and words. As a result, he altered some formerly accepted

Wahtoke head gate, circa 1908. Photograph believed to be by George Besaw.

spellings. The reader will note the similarity of Latta's names with those mentioned by McCubbin.]

Wahtoki Mountain

The mountain standing between Clarks Valley and the river bottom to the west, and now known as Tche-o-nim-ne [Choinumne], was at one time called Wahtoki mountain. [Presumably this is Jesse Morrow Mountain.]

Wahtoke Creek

The written record made as early as 1854 shows that the name Wahtoke was already applied to the stream that drains Clarks Valley. Joseph A. Tivy, a surveyor, who was under contract with the State of California to subdivide certain townships, including the territory through which this creek runs, mentions Wahtoke Creek repeatedly in his field notes.

Wahtoga Lodge

On December 2, 1880, a lodge of the A. O. U. W. [Ancient Order of United Workmen] was instituted in Centerville, with fourteen charter members. It was named Wahtoga Lodge, and O. M. Thompson assisted by Messrs. Pedler, Jensen, Litten and Doyle, acting as grand officers, installed the following officers: P. M. W., Dr. Wadsworth; M. W., Max Frankenau; O. F., M. W. Hobler; O., H. G. Kidd; Recorder, L. Weil; Financier, George Kerann; R., A. A. Henry; G., R. M. Wood; I. W., E. Stack; and O. W., J. G. Chism. This spelling, Wahtoga, may go back to a name familiar in the American Revolutionary period. It was chosen at Centerville, perhaps because of the local name Wahtoke.

Wahtoke Dam

When the 76 Land and Water Company made their survey for what is now the main Alta Canal, it was found necessary to cross Wahtoke Creek. Instead of fluming the creek, as is often done in such cases, a restraining dam was constructed across the chasm, which formed a lake, known as Wahtoke Lake.

Wahtoke Lake

The reservoir formed by Wahtoke Dam was called Wahtoke Lake. It was originally about a quarter of a mile wide just above the dam, and nearly a mile long. It furnished boating and fishing, but has since filled up with silt. It was nearly twenty-five feet deep on the upper side of the dam. The water from the canal would enter the lake on one side and continue on its course by entering the mouth of the canal on the opposite side of the lake. A spillway was provided to take care of any excess water that might enter the lake from Wahtoke Creek. The spillway let the water flow back into the channel below the lake.

Wahtoke (Town No. 1)

In the year 1883 the 76 Land and Water Company surveyed and platted a townsite in the northeast quarter of the northeast quarter of Section 13, Township 15 South, Range 23 East [southwest corner of Adams and Englehart Avenues], and named the place Wahtoke. It was three miles south and one-half mile west of Wahtoke Dam. In a short time a general merchandise store, a blacksmith shop, and a hotel were established at the place. A Mr. Jacobson was proprietor of the store, John S. Cole ran the blacksmith shop, and Dan. Bowman provided hotel accommodations. This place was near the upper detour of the old Stockton-Los

Mount Campbell with Wahtoke Lake in the foreground, circa 1908. Photograph by George Besaw.

Angeles Stage Road that was still in use by the general public.

All three of the establishments at Wahtoke did a thriving business until Traver, seventeen miles to the southwest, began to enjoy the first thrills of its wonderful boom. The business at Wahtoke began to slump and soon afterwards the store and blacksmith shop were moved bodily to the new railroad town. Bowman discontinued his hotel business and moved his family to Wahtoke Dam where he took charge of the boarding house for the 76 Company.

On April 16, 1924, under the heading of "Forty Years Ago Today," there appeared in the *Fresno Morning Republican* the following item:

> The 76 Land and Water Company has ordered a telephone line constructed from Traver, to the head of their canal, a distance of 30 miles. In all probability, a telephone will be built from Fresno to the head of the Fresno Irrigation Company's canal during the summer, and connection will be made with the 76 Company line, of about fifty miles in length and making connections with Centerville and the new town of Wahtoke.

The old town site of Wahtoke has been in vineyard for years and very few people now living know there ever was such a place.

Wahtoke (Town No. 2)

Twenty-five years after the 76 Land and Water Company's town of Wahtoke had been abandoned, W. N. Rohrer filed a map covering a tract of land near the Wahtoke Dam as a townsite and called it, "Town of Wahtoke." The map was filed in the office of the County Recorder of Fresno County on May 3, 1909, and was described as, "That portion of Section 30, Township 14 South, Range 24 East, lying east of Wahtoke Creek." [This would be northwest of Central and Alta Avenues.] It contained thirty-five blocks and a private park of 12.41 acres. The grove in the park was provided with the accommodations usually found in pleasure parks, and Wahtoke Lake, adjoining, was furnished with boats for the use of the public.

Wahtoke Home Acres

After selling a few lots in Wahtoke Town No. 2 and waiting seven years without a single structure making its appearance, except a few temporary ones in the pleasure park, the land was resubdivided by the owners, of which there were then fifteen. The map was filed in the office of the Recorder of Fresno County on December 6, 1916. The name was changed from "Town of Wahtoke" to "Wahtoke Home Acres." Two blocks and the pleasure park were reserved from this second filing.

Wahtoke (Town No. 3)

The place now known as Wahtoke (May 1924) is located near the northwest corner of the northeast quarter of Section 34, Township 14 South, Range 23 East, and on the Wahtoke branch of the Santa Fe railroad [the southeast corner of Central and Reed Avenues]. It is about five miles north of Reedley. On September 12, last [1923], a fire destroyed everything at the place except one packing house. The first house at this point was built in 1906 by H. V. Rudy.

With the exception of the five cheaply constructed packing houses, which stood in a row alongside the railroad prior to the fire, there was not a building of any description at the place. These houses occupied the land by a temporary leasehold only, and their business was limited strictly to the packing and shipping of fresh fruit and grapes.

The group of houses mentioned nestled near the base of the bluff, and with the exception of a small portion of the roof of one of the buildings, the place was entirely obstructed from view when a person was standing a quarter of a mile back from the edge of the bluff.

The business done in comparison with the modesty of the place was simply marvelous. It didn't even have a depot, everything being billed out through the office at Reedley. The station agent's books at the latter place show that during the season of 1922 there were 596 cars shipped out from Wahtoke. Had empty cars been available this number would have been increased to fully 800 cars. If the 596 cars could have been grouped, they would have been equal to ten long freight trains.

The revenue paid to the railroad company on these shipments was approximately $475,000. To this amount should be added several thousand dollars paid on about forty cars of incoming freight, such as shook used for packing and lumber for "staying" fruit boxes and crates while being loaded for shipment. As the fresh fruit season lasts only about five months the revenue in freights averaged about $100,000 per month.

Wahtoke Post Office (No. 1)

On January 27, 1887, Wahtoke post office was established and Mrs. Rosie Merritt was appointed postmaster. The Merritt ranch home, a small pioneer cabin built of rough lumber and covered with split shakes, was used for the post office. The old house is still standing on its original location on the north side of the road near the southeast corner of the southwest quarter of Section 11, Township 15 South, Range 23 East [north of Adams Avenue, a quarter to a half mile east of Frankwood Avenue], or about two miles north and one-half mile east of Reedley. Since the time when it was used for a post office, there has been a small addition to the building and the roof has been renewed. Yet it looks quite familiar to the old timers. The land now belongs to M. D. Minasian.

The mail was first carried out from Traver twice a week over a star route. A road cart was used for the purpose and F. M. Merritt, husband of the postmaster, was the mail carrier, but he soon turned the work over to Miss Clara Glass, Mrs. Merritt's sister.

The records of the old Wahtoke post office show the following:

Cancellations for 1887	$1.38
Cancellations for Sept. 1887	1.44
Cancellations for Oct. 1887	2.59
Total	$5.41
Sale of postage stamps for July 1888	$ .68
Sale of postage stamps for Aug. 1888	1.00
Sale of postage stamps for Sept. 1988	1.15
Total	$2.83

On October 31, 1888, the name and site of the Wahtoke post office was changed to Reedley and Mrs. Flora S. Knauer was appointed to succeed Mrs Rosie Merritt. Mrs. Knauer held the position until her resignation, which was accepted March 31, 1920. At the time of her resignation she had served her patrons continuously for over thirty-one years.

The Knauer residence [in Reedley] into which the Wahtoke post office was moved in 1888, remained on its original location in the southwest corner of Block 37 [northwest corner of "F" and Eleventh Streets] until February 1923, when the building was moved across the railroad to the southeast corner of "J" and Thirteenth Streets and located on the northwest corner of Block 80. R. A. Rasmussen and George E. Rice, officers of the Reedley National Bank, had very recently purchased the Knauer house and lots.

This old Knauer house was the first residence erected in Reedley, and was then conspicuous as it stood out alone among the wheat stubble.

Wahtoke Post Office (No. 2)

Nearly seventeen years after the original Wahtoke post office had its name and location changed to Reedley, it was re-established under its former name. This took place on July 27, 1905, when it was located in a little country store that stood about a half mile to the northeast of Wahtoke Dam, and C. L. Croyle was appointed postmaster. In 1910 Croyle was succeeded by C. B. Kern, who held the position until the office was discontinued on September 25, 1916.

The reason for discontinuing the re-established Wahtoke post office was quite similar to the one given for changing the name and location of the original one. A railroad had been built but a short distance away and a new town established. In the case of the re-established office it was the Minkler Southern railroad, and the new town was Navelencia, while on the former occasion the railroad was the Porterville branch of the Southern Pacific and the new town was Reedley.

Strange to say, neither one of the three places known as Wahtoke ever had a post office, nor was either one of the post offices called Wahtoke ever in a town.

Wahtoke School District

Wahtoke School District was established on May 7, 1886, and a school house was built that summer on the northeast corner of the northwest quarter of Section 7, Township 15 South, Range 24 East [the southwest corner of Lincoln and Pedersen Avenues]. It was two miles south of Wahtoke Dam. On account of some delay in the construction work of the building, Miss Nellie Baird of Selma, who was the first teacher, had to open her school and teach the first day in the home of W. R. Neil. Mr. Neil was the clerk of the school board. His report for the first term of the school showed the following:

Number of pupils enrolled (all white)	25
Average daily attendance	12
Amount of state money received	$156.00
Amount of county money received	344.00
Total money received	$500.00

From the territory forming the original Wahtoke district there have since been established, either whole or in part, the following six districts: Mount Campbell, Navelencia, Citrus Cove, Mount Olive, Fink and Frankwood. After contributing to all these districts there is still a healthy school left.

Four of these newer districts have since united in two separate groups, and with the addition of one outside district, formed union schools. The Navelencia Union School District, which was established July 1, 1918, included within its territory the Navelencia, Citrus Cove and Clarks Valley districts; and the Great Western Union School District is composed of the Mount Campbell and Fink Districts. This was formed July 23, 1920.

A comparison of the report from the Wahtoke School District, made for the first term, with the last one submitted for practically the same territory grouped: is as follows:

	1886-87	1922-23
Teachers:	1	11
Average daily attendance:	12	232
Total expenditures:	$500.00	$34,302.25
School property		
Estimated value:	$500.00	
Actual value:		$80,500.00

This territory is also a part of the Reedley Union High School District, and furnishes its proportion of its students for that institution, and in addition to its property in the country, it has its interest in the $450,000 high school property in town.

Wahtoke Vineyard

The first move toward establishing the Wahtoke vineyard was made in the fall of 1901. At that time the Great Western Vineyard Company purchased their first tract of land for that purpose. It was in the Kings River bottom five miles north of Reedley, and consisted of 1,480 acres. During the spring of 1902, 1,340 acres of grapes were planted. This planting was all done in twenty days, or at the rate of 67 acres per day. In 1903 and later they made additional purchases of raw land aggregating 760 acres, 590 acres of which they planted to grapes, which increased their acreage in vines to 1,930. To these they added by purchasing adjoining vineyards as follows: the Janowitz, 320 acres; and a portion of the old Carmelita, containing 336 acres. This brought their total acreage of vines up to 2,586. All were wine grapes and of several different varieties. In addition to the vineyard, there were 310 acres planted to alfalfa and grain, which were also a part of the unit. To the above should be added 900 acres of pasture lands which were a part of the tract, making a total of 3,796 acres.

There were five camps located at convenient points in the vineyard, from each of which a group of workmen farmed a separate portion. Although the buildings for the hands were constructed years before the law was passed requiring employers to provide certain specified housing and sanitary conditions for their employees, the Great Western Vineyard Company had their buildings fitted up far better along those lines than the law now requires.

The Wahtoke vineyard was not the largest (there being one exception), yet on account of the fertility of the soil and efficient management its product far exceeded that of any other vineyard in the world. For the season of 1913 its crop reached the enormous amount of 11,000 tons of fresh grapes.

The headquarters of the vineyard was located at the edge of the mesa near the south end at an elevation of about twenty-five feet above the main tract, from which a magnificent view of the vineyard was to be had. Not only from the headquarters, but from two other sides a magnificent panoramic view was spread out before the eye. Looking eastward from the summit of a natural mound on the western boundary, across the vineyard to Mount Campbell on the eastern side, or from the side of Mount Campbell itself, is a very inspiring experience.

Everything around the grounds at the camps, including the implements and work stock, always presented the same neat clean appearance that was to be found throughout the entire vineyard.

Sanitary measures were carefully looked after and the men were not only provided with tub and shower bathing facilities, as well as other conveniences, but were required to make regular use of these accommodations.

Running the entire length of the vineyard from north to south are two avenues, each one lined on either side with rows of fig trees. These avenues as well as every row of vines, are perfectly straight.

[McCubbin's correspondence provides some details about the "old Carmelita" acreage mentioned in the first paragraph. He writes, "Stockholders in the 76 Land and Water Company promoted the Carmelita Colony. Moses Samuel being the principal one. Sometime during the summer of either 1890 or 1891, I drew the map of Carmelita colony, and from this map the survey was made. Preparations were begun immediately for planting the main portion of this colony out to fruit,

Wahtoke Winery, circa 1908. Photograph by George Besaw.

grapes and hops during the following winter. The hop growing venture was soon abandoned, just why, I don't remember."]

Wahtoke Winery

In 1905 the California Wine Association built the Wahtoke Winery selecting a central point in the vast Wahtoke vineyard for its location. In 1907 the plant was enlarged by increasing the size of the first buildings and adding others, and when completed it was the largest sweet wine producing plant in the world.

The group consisted of the following: two storage buildings, each 120 by 220 feet, combined capacity of two million gallons; one fermenting cellar 200 by 260 feet; three crushers, combined capacity of 400 tons grapes per day; one power plant, distillery, grape juice and brandy room combined; one machine shop; one tank tower; one steam pump; one electric pump and one gas pump; one supply warehouse; one office building; one kitchen and dining room combined; and one sleeping quarters for men.

In 1913 the Wahtoke Winery had its largest run. In addition to its own crop of 11,000 tons, there were 5,000 tons from other vineyards, running the one season's crush up to 16,000 tons.

On July 2, 1919, these immense holdings, including both vineyard and winery, were sold to a group of financiers: W. B. Nichols, J. H. Lindley and J. J. Farrar.

John Rankine, now of Oakland, California, was the superintendent and had entire charge of both of these vast enterprises from the time of their origin until they were sold in 1919. Rankine was Scotch.

Wahtoke Branch Railroad

When the Santa Fe Railroad Company built their branch line out north from

Reedley they called it the Wahtoke branch. It ran through the Wahtoke vineyard, and the Wahtoke Winery buildings were on both sides of the track. It continued on up the river to where the town of Piedra was established.

Wahtoke Thermal Tract

A tract of land containing 1,043 acres, located in Dunnegan Gap [along Kings Canyon Road, between Campbell Mountain and Jesse Morrow Mountain], two miles north of Wahtoke Dam, was subdivided into colony lots and the map was filed for record by W. N. Rohrer, December 12, 1905. It was named Wahtoke Thermal Tract.

Wahtoke Colony

On March 2, 1908, a map was filed in the office of the Recorder of Fresno County by the 76 Land and Water Company and San Francisco Savings Union and named Wahtoke Colony. The subdivision adjoins the Wahtoke Thermal tract on the east, and contains 1,640 acres.

If there is any blame to be attached for this overworking of the name Wahtoke, Uncle Sam should come in for his share of the censure, for it appears that he was not satisfied with appropriating it once, but used it as a "warmed over" article for his post offices.

William Ruth

William Ruth was born in Queens County, Ireland, in 1840, and died at the National Soldiers Home, Sawtelle, California, February 18, 1921. He had been in the Old Soldiers Home about a month prior to his death.

When William was ten years old he moved with his parents to New York where he grew to manhood.

At the beginning of the Civil War, William Ruth enlisted in Company B, 14, New York Volunteers, and served his adopted country continuously until the close of the war. A portion of his service was spent in the Navy.

Upon his discharge from the army, William Ruth came to Fresno County, California, and accepted employment with Simon, Jacobs and Company on their large cattle range, with their headquarters near the north end of Smith Mountain.

After about eighteen months in the employ of the above firm, Ruth resigned his position and engaged in the cattle business for himself. He continued in that same business until his health failed about the year 1914.

In 1867 Ruth filed on a homestead located about six or eight miles northwest of Visalia, near what was then the upper end of the timber on Cross Creek. Having been in the United States service four years, he had to remain on the land only about a year until he could perfect title to the land.

In 1873, Ruth purchased 160 acres of land from the railroad company. This land was located east of the Kennedy Slough about four miles northeast of where the town of Reedley, Fresno County, was later established. He paid the railroad company $2.50 per acre for the land. Ruth made his home on this land for over forty years. [In handwritten notes made at a later date, McCubbin refers to this land as a half-section (320 acres), rather than the 160 acres mentioned here.]

Ruth also owned a tract of land in Squaw Valley, Fresno County. His cattle ranged far and wide, with other cattle, over vast territories in the foothills.

After some of Ruth's cattle had been mysteriously disappearing at intervals from his Squaw Valley herd, the San Joaquin Valley Cattlemen's Association alerted all their members. O. S. Brewer, a member of the association who lived about two miles north of Traver, chanced to be awake about two o'clock one morning when he saw some cattle being driven by his home. Being suspicious, he telephoned the officers in the direction which the cattle were being driven. An officer had no difficulty in meeting the two men and caught them with Ruth's cattle. They were driving to their hide-out in Mussel Slough where they had been slaughtering and disposing of the meat from former looted stock. As a result, Jack Works and Avery Marlar were tried, convicted and served terms in San Quentin Prison for the theft.

During the boom that occurred in the late 1880s, Ruth offered his half-section for sale, but at an exorbitant price. Consequently, there were no offers. He held it at the high price even after land prices dropped all over the 76 Country.

O. L. Abbott, a man Ruth had known about five years, came to Ruth with a proposition from his son, Milt, who would purchase the land under certain conditions. O. L. Abbott had been a "jack leg" lawyer [shyster] back in Missouri years before and managed to secure a license to practice in California.

By the plan Abbott proposed, Milt would purchase the land from Ruth at the very high figure provided Ruth would accept a very small down payment with a long term payment on the remainder. Ruth having no education failed to see the joker in the deal until it was too late. The joker was in a clause in the mortgage by which in case the interest was unpaid when due it should be added to and become a part of the principal and bear a like rate of interest. But, it had no clause giving the mortgagee the option of foreclosure in case of default of the interest payments. By this scheme you will see that the purchaser got possession of the land, and could avoid paying either interest, taxes or rent.

Milt might have made one payment of interest, but I am not sure. With Milt in undisputed possession, getting the entire crop, letting both interest and taxes lapse, Ruth had to step in and pay the taxes to protect himself.

Under these conditions it appeared highly beneficial to the Abbotts if by chance Ruth should mysteriously disappear and allow the notes to run the statute of limitations.

At the end of the second year, Ruth finally got very insistent that Abbott make some payments. Abbott eventually came up with a plan to release his claim on the ranch, which Ruth agreed to. O. L. Abbott, his son Milt, and another man, came to Ruth, and the four of them were to go to Fresno where all the papers were to be executed. The Abbotts had a plausible reason for going by a certain place in Clarks Valley. Milt and the third man went ahead in one rig while O. L. Abbott and Ruth came along behind in Ruth's two-horse buggy.

Before they got to Clarks Valley, Ruth became suspicious and wanted an explanation just why this side trip had to be made. O. L. Abbott was rather evasive, which led to a heated argument and eventually to a tussle during which the quick and agile Ruth dumped Abbott out on the road, and quickly turned his team around and headed for home. He was soon out of sight of the three men.

Ruth claimed it cost him over $1,000 to repossess his land. This land was purchased by Amaziah Clark about 1903 or 1905. It was later deeded to James Clark, a nephew of Amaziah. I think Ruth moved onto his Squaw Valley land following the sale of his land to Milton Abbott.

The mysterious disappearance of William Wooton, which occurred in the early nineties [about February 1894] and whose body was never found, is well remembered by those who were living in Fresno County at the time. O. L. Abbott also figured in this case.

Wooton was a native of England, and an old bachelor, living alone on his foothill ranch in a cove a few miles north of where Orange Cove is now located. Wooton had no relatives in America, nor had he been in communication with his relatives for years. After Wooton's disappearance, a deed was produced, which was supposed to be a forgery, conveying Wooton's land to two men named Knausch and Graves, supposed to be myths, and also a deed conveying this same land from Knausch and Graves to "Professor" W. A. Sanders' son. The fact that Wooton's body could never be found, prevented "Professor" Sanders from being convicted for murder. He did, however, serve a term in San Quentin for forgery in connection with the case.

When Sanders was on trial in the Wooton case, O. L. Abbott claimed that he had known Knausch and Graves (the mythical characters) at one time when they had "grub staked" a prospector. Abbott was the only one ever found who claimed to have known such persons.

The Abbotts had possession of the Ruth half-section when Wooton disappeared, and T. L. Reed had the best theory as to the disappearance of Wooton that I ever heard. T. L. told me that he believed Sanders took Wooton's body out on that half-section, buried it, soaked down the dirt in the grave and Milt Abbott plowed over the grave as he was plowing over the ground there at the time for either summer fallowing or seeding. If that were done, it would have been difficult to locate the spot.

When I was Assistant Superintendent of the 76 Land and Water Company under Joseph Peacock, I came in contact with O. L. Abbott on many an unpleasant occasion. He could stir up trouble for people but never could get them out of it.

Kennedy, Ryce and Ross

Robert Kennedy, Henry Ross and their father-in-law Andrew Crawford Ryce, helped to make San Joaquin Valley history beginning in the early 1870s.

In 1863 Robert Kennedy, Henry Ross and John Treadwell took passage on a sailing vessel from Liverpool, England, bound for Australia. While on their long voyage the ship's crew mutinied. After getting the mutiny quelled and the mutineers placed in irons, the male passengers, including the three young men mentioned, worked the vessel into port at Sydney.

During their four years in Australia, the three young men were partners in the building and contracting business. In 1867, they transferred their operations to San Francisco, California. In 1870, when they each decided to engage in other lines of business, they dissolved the partnership, but the ties of their staunch friendship remained strong throughout their lives.

About 1865, Andrew C. and Margaret Wilson Ryce moved with their family from Edinburgh, Scotland, to Australia. The names of their six children were: Margaret, Elizabeth, Marion, Jessie, James and Jeannie. About 1868, the Ryce family moved to San Francisco.

While in Scotland, Andrew C. Ryce was employed as an accountant, in which activity he continued until he moved from San Francisco to Fresno County in the early 1870s. His last employment in San Francisco was with a commission house.

When Kennedy, Ross and Treadwell dissolved their partnership in 1870, Treadwell went north to Alaska, and engaged in the mining business in the Juneau locality. He was very successful, and to enlarge his business, purchased the three Duncan and Harris mines, thus forming the great Treadwell group. From 1885 to 1915, the Treadwell group was ranked as one of the largest gold mines. By running day and night, their stamp mills crushed over 250,000 tons of ore per year. It was not a high-grade ore, but during that thirty year period the group netted their owners over $20,000,000. The city of Treadwell, Alaska, was named after John Treadwell.

In 1869 Robert Kennedy and Henry Ross made an inspection tour, traveling practically all over the San Joaquin Valley. They were mounted on horse back, minus saddles. Their object was to find a suitable place to engage in the sheep business.

While they were living in Australia, Henry Ross was acquainted with the Ryce family. Kennedy knew a portion of the family, and that by sight only. After they moved to San Francisco, Henry Ross married Miss Margaret Ryce. Robert Kennedy became acquainted with the Ryce family in San Francisco, and in 1870 married Miss Marion Ryce.

Soon after they were married, Mr. and Mrs. Robert Kennedy together with James Ryce, Mrs. Kennedy's brother, went by boat to Stockton, and from there drove their wagon and team of horses to Millerton on the San Joaquin River. Millerton, at that time, was the county seat of Fresno County.

Kennedy first located a few miles below Millerton where he began his sheep business, but the place proved to be too restricted. In 1872 he transferred his operations further south and purchased a large tract of land in Tulare County, and established his headquarters about three miles to the southwest of where the city of Dinuba is now located. Visalia, twenty miles away, was the nearest trading point.

All that portion of Tulare and Fresno Counties, lying to the south and east of the Kings River, and in which the Kennedy ranch was situated, was then known as "The 76 Country." So named on account of a brand worn by vast herds of cattle that roamed over that part of the San Joaquin Valley and beyond.

After the Central Pacific (now the Southern Pacific) Railroad was built through the San Joaquin Valley in the early 1870s, settlers began to come in. In the fall of 1882 the 76 Land and Water Company began construction work on their canal system (now the Alta Canal). With irrigation water available, land values made a substantial and permanent increase.

When it was demonstrated that dry farming was feasible, Robert Kennedy rented a portion of his ranch out for wheat growing. Prior to this he had added to his holdings until his ranch consisted of 3,000 acres in the home ranch and 2,000 acres of grazing land in the foothills about Sand Creek. Among the tenants that farmed the Kennedy Ranch were James and Amaziah W. Clark, ranchers from Mussel Slough.

In addition to his wool growing, Robert Kennedy specialized in raising a very high-grade of lambs for the market. They and their mothers were given the very best of care and kept in fine condition. When ready for market, these lambs commanded extra prices and the wholesale butchers competed for them.

In 1891, Mr. Kennedy sold a small portion of his home ranch to Amaziah W. Clark, one of his tenants. Afterwards they operated the ranch in partnership and grew grain and alfalfa, and raised cattle and sheep.

In the fall of 1892, Robert Kennedy purchased a fine residence at 2907 Mariposa Street, Fresno, and moved there with his family. He traveled back and forth between Fresno and the ranch helping to handle the vast ranch interests.

After moving to Fresno, Mr. Kennedy purchased the Sequoia Hotel, which at that time was the best hotel in the city. He also purchased other income property including bank stock.

The names of the Kennedy children were, in the order of their births: Marion, Margaret, Jessie, Elizabeth, Ethel and Helen. A son died in infancy.

In 1893, Miss Marion Kennedy married Amaziah W. Clark and moved back to her childhood home, in which her husband then owned an interest. She passed away in January 1899. In 1908 the large Kennedy ranch was sold to Kleinsasser who later subdivided it and sold it off in small tracts.

Miss Margaret Kennedy married E. A. Cutter, a druggist, in 1897. He was a native of Canada who came to Traver in 1889 and accepted a position in the L. A. Rockwell drug store. He later purchased a drug store in Dinuba, which he sold to Brady Doyle in 1893, and then went to San Jacinto, California, where he bought another drug store. That store was disposed of in 1896. He then went to Fresno and purchased another drug store.

Cutter eventually disposed of all his San Joaquin Valley interests and moved to Berkeley, California, where he established the Cutter Bacteriological Laboratories and specialized in the manufacture of vaccines and serums. Products turned out by this laboratory are sold all over the United States in large quantities. E. A. Cutter died in 1934, but the laboratories that he founded are still owned by the Cutter family.

Miss Jessie Kennedy married F. Dean Prescott of Fresno. He is the General Manager of the Valley Lumber Company. This organization operates yards in various towns in the San Joaquin Valley. This company was incorporated in 1899 and took over the Prescott and Pierce Lumber Company of Fresno. That was one of the oldest lumber companies in the San Joaquin Valley.

Miss Elizabeth Kennedy married Ward B. Minturn of Fresno. The railroad station at Minturn, Merced County, was named for Ward's father, who was a pioneer of that county. Mr. Minturn packs and ships large quantities of fresh fruit from many points in the San Joaquin Valley. Mr. Minturn assisted Mr. Robert Kennedy in the management of the Kennedy property, and after Mr. Kennedy's death in 1924, he had entire charge of the vast estate for the heirs: Mesdames Cutter, Prescott and Minturn.

Neither Ethel nor Helen Kennedy married. Ethel died in Fresno in 1909. During that same year Mr. and Mrs. Kennedy and their daughter Helen moved to Berkeley, California.

Robert Kennedy was born in Liverpool, England, March 23, 1839, and passed away in Berkeley, California, on November 1, 1924, at the age of 85 years, 7 months, and 9 days. Mrs. Kennedy passed away in Berkeley in 1938.

Let us return and take up the Andrew C. Ryce family.

Miss Margaret Ryce [daughter of Andrew] married Henry Ross. After a short time in San Francisco, they moved to Fresno County about the fall of 1872, and purchased a ranch about six miles northeast of where the town of Selma was afterwards established. This ranch was about ten miles to the north of the Robert Kennedy ranch and across the Kings River. Ross immediately engaged in the sheep business in which his brother-in-law, Kennedy, was already established.

Kennedy and Ross would graze their sheep on the plains during the winter, and in the spring drive them to the mountains where they would remain until the fall rains would start the feed on the plains. They would then drive them back to the valley.

By common consent, each sheepman had his separate grazing area, both on the plains and in the mountains. Headquarters for the Kennedy mountain range was in the beautiful and now famous Kings River Canyon. The Henry Ross mountain range centered at Dinkey Creek.

On one occasion when Henry Ross had his sheep in the mountains, and left them in charge of his herder, and was hurrying along over a brushy trail, he suddenly rounded a sharp turn and ran directly face to face with an old she-bear and her two cubs. What occurred I'll let Mr. Ross relate in his own words in a letter he wrote to his sister and her husband.

> Dear Brother and Sister,
> In answer to your last letter of December 11th this leaves us all well hoping that it may find you well. You wish to know how I came by my accident. I came on the bear by accident laying in the long grass with her cubs so she jumped on me at once and caught my face in her mouth at the first leap. I had nothing to fight her with at all so I thought the only chance was to make on that I was dead but it was hard to do when she was chewing me up so. I had a shepherd dog along with me and when she thought that I was dead she went along after him. Then I seized the opportunity and tried to get a safer place and I struggled to a small tree and got up it about five feet but I could not climb fast as my left arm was broken in two places. I had only one hand to hold on by so she came at me again and chewed my legs fearful and tore off all my clothes. Bleeding like an ox I gave up to die in earnest. Then the two cubs came up and they all went off together so then I got to my feet and got a look at myself. I concluded that I was the most pitiable sight that ever stood in this world 5 miles from my camp and not the least shadow of ever getting there so I lay there for three days and four nights in the cold and frost naked on my body as I was born and nothing to eat. At the end of that time I concluded that I might be able to crawl or walk a little now and then so I started and got to camp and got one of the men to fix me a little. I got tied on the saddle the next day and went 16 miles on the way to the doctor but then I got speechless so I staid and sent for the doctor. By that time I was pretty low but then things took a turn and I commenced to get better. (Then followed personal items)
>
> (Signed) Henry Ross.

There were five children in the Henry Ross family. Namely, Margaret, Alice, Henry Jr., George and Edwin.

Margaret married Rev. George Miller, who is now Bishop in the Methodist Episcopal Church.

Alice married George Rice, who was a nephew of her Uncle James Ryce's wife. Alice died in 1937.

Henry Ross, Jr. married Miss Blanch Roberts. He died in 1949.

George died several years ago.

Edwin was killed in an auto accident in 1942.

Mrs. Margaret Ross, widow of Henry Ross, Sr., married J. R. Baird who was also a pioneer of Fresno County.

Henry Ross was born in Inverness, Scotland, in 1842, and died in Fresno County, California.

Miss Elizabeth Ryce married Captain Thomas Patrick Henry Whitelaw. Captain Whitelaw operated a fleet of vessels and salvaged sunken craft along the Pacific Coast. He and his wife were both natives of Ayrshire, Scotland. Mrs. Whitelaw passed away in 1931 and her husband died in 1932.

James Ryce married Miss Jessie Rice. She changed but one letter of her name and the pronunciation remained the same. The names of their seven children were: Andrew, Jessie, Elizabeth, Flora, Jamie, Margaret and Edwin. After the death of his wife Jessie, James married a widow, and one son was born to them and they named him Clarence. James sold his ranch near Kingsburg and bought a small place north of Selma where he spent the remainder of his life.

Miss Jessie Ryce, daughter of Andrew C., married William L. Jones a blacksmith of Selma.

Miss Jeanie Ryce married David Freeland, also a native of Scotland. They had two children, a son and daughter. They died in Novato, Marin County, California, when their children were small.

The slough that heads in Clarks Valley and runs thence in a southerly direction for a distance of about ten or twelve miles is called Kennedy Slough, and is so named for Robert Kennedy. It flattens out near where the Kennedy residence stood and soon looses itself on the plains. The natural channel of the Kennedy Slough for several miles served as a part of the main lateral of the 76 canal and still is used for the same purpose.

Andrew C. Ryce and his son James each purchased a tract of land a few miles west of Kingsburg soon after Robert Kennedy and Henry Ross had settled on their ranches. Andrew and his wife spent the remainder of their lives on that place.

Pioneer Beekeeping in California by John H., Charles C. and Fred M. Hart

{*The following article was published in the April 1936 issue of* Bees and Honey.}

The original apiary, which was the beginning of a fifty-two year period of continuous commercial beekeeping in California conducted by members of the same family, was established by John H. Hart, near Gilroy, Santa Clara County, in 1856.

John Hudson Hart was born near Goshen, Connecticut, January 5, 1828, where he grew to manhood. Just as he reached his majority the great gold discovery excitement in California was spreading all over the world. The lure caught young Hart, and he joined a company that embarked early in 1849, on a sailing vessel bound for San Francisco, via Cape Horn.

John Hart taught school in his early days in California, but engaged in mining as his first venture in the West, as did practically all the forty-niners; but when his brother Charles C. arrived in 1857, John was already established in the bee business — an industry in which he continued for the remainder of his life.

Charles Conkling Hart was born near Goshen, Connecticut, March 6, 1826. He married Helen Payne, of Georgetown, New York, October 20, 1856. Early the following spring, this newly married couple started for California. Going via the

Isthmus of Panama, they arrived at their destination in May 1857, and settled near Gilroy, where, as stated above, John H. Hart, brother of Charles, was located.

According to previous arrangement, John took his brother in as a full partner in his bee business and also the dairy business, as John was engaged in both enterprises.

In 1859 the Hart brothers moved over the Coast Range Mountains into the San Joaquin Valley, going via Pacheco Pass, and established their home about one mile east of Visalia, the county seat of Tulare County, on a half-section of land they had previously purchased; 160 acres of this land was under fence, and it was the largest body of land then enclosed in the upper portion of the San Joaquin Valley.

In July of that same year, the Harts moved about 100 colonies of bees over the mountains from Gilroy and located them on their Tulare County land.

The Harts were not the first to bring bees into Tulare County; that distinction belongs to a man by the name of J. B. Stevens, who had moved ten colonies in about a month before the Harts landed with their 100 colonies.

The first sale of bees by the Harts, after their arrival in Tulare County, was made in the spring of 1860. It consisted of thirty-five colonies and the purchaser was Dr. Cobb, of Millerton, which was the county seat of Fresno County at that time. The purchase price was $100 per colony, delivered at Millerton.

In the summer of 1860 an advertisement was run in the *Visalia Delta* of which the following is a copy:

> Bee Advertisement
>
> For sale: On and after the first of September next, a choice lot of bees in good condition. Price, $50.00 per swarm. A farm or grain will be taken where it suits the purchaser better than to pay the money.
>
> J. H. and C. C. Hart

In 1866 Charles Hart took up a homestead near where the little village of Farmersville is now located, on which he conducted general ranching together with bee culture.

During the first few years the Harts were in the bee business, they sold all their surplus honey at one dollar per pound. It was marketed either as "chunk" honey or melted up and strained and sold in liquid form. For many years their honey was practically all sold from a peddle wagon, in which John, who did the peddling, covered a wide territory, as the country was very sparsely settled at that time.

About 1863 John H. Hart established an out-apiary near where the present town of Lemoore, Kings County, is located. Another out-apiary was later located on a tract of land John had purchased that is now on the road connecting Tulare and Lindsay.

Charles Hart eventually disposed of all his bees, after which he devoted all his time to farming and stock raising. He owned, individually, 320 acres of land and a half-interest with his brother in 320 acres more, besides a half-interest in 640 acres with his son, C. W. In addition to their own land, the father and son rented outside lands, and at one time they were farming about 3,000 acres.

Charles Hart was a staunch supporter of both school and church, he and his wife being members of the Baptist Church.

At the time of his death, which occurred near Visalia, when sixty-six years of age, the estate of Charles C. Hart was valued at $35,000.

In 1878 Charles Hart gave his son Fred fourteen colonies of bees. After Fred had built these up to a good sized apiary, he went into partnership with his uncle John. Their combined number at first was 300 colonies, which was increased the following year to 400.

During the seventies, John and Fred Hart moved all their bees into what is now Kings County, where they remained permanently. Their home apiary was located on a forty-acre tract that belonged to John, and is described as the northeast quarter of Section 4, Township 19 South, Range 22 East. One of their first out-apiaries was located near Burris Point, an old landmark on the Kings River.

Fred Hart was the first man to take honey from the combs with an extractor in Tulare County. The extractor was a two-frame machine, composed principally of wooden material and Fred had made it himself.

When Fred Hart married in 1889, he and his uncle John dissolved their partnership and ran their bees separately. They cooperated, however, in much of their work, as well as in the purchase of supplies and selling their honey.

John H. Hart was instrumental in organizing the Central California Beekeepers' Association, and served as its president from the time it was organized, which was about 1890, until their regular annual meeting held in Selma, Fresno County, on March 6, 1895. His name had been presented for reelection, but being sixty-seven years old at the time, he made a special request that he be allowed to retire and that a younger man be placed in the office. His wishes were complied with, and the result was that I was elected to succeed him.

John H. Hart was one of the pioneer school teachers of California, having taught here during the early sixties. He was an active member of the Grange from the time it was first organized in this state. His hobby was music, and his rich tenor voice was invariably heard in the choir of some church wherever he lived. His melodeon was among the first instruments of its kind to be shipped into California following the gold rush, and it was quite a curiosity at that time. The vocal numbers, which he sang to his own accompaniment, were always pleasing features on programs at local entertainments. He also assisted freely at similar functions given at any other place within reasonable distance of his home. He was very congenial as well as humorous, and he usually had a good supply of comic songs which would be rendered with telling effect when the occasion suited.

John H. Hart was never married. He was generally known as "Honey Hart" though it would have been quite appropriate to have called him "Sweet Hart." He died in Kings County in 1898, at seventy years of age.

At the death of John Hart, all his bees and equipment passed on to his nephew, Fred. This addition increased Fred's stock over 100 per cent.

It is not known how many colonies of bees the Harts had at the peak of their operations, but in 1905, when Fred decided to close out his bee business, he had 1,100 colonies distributed among six apiaries, scattered from the Kings River to Cross Creek. Able assistance rendered by Mrs. Hart and the children made it possible to do all the work connected with those 1,100 colonies with a small amount of outside help.

In 1905 Fred decided to sell all his bees and retire from that line of work. His first sale, which was made that year, was to A. F. Smith, Kings County Supervisor, and consisted of 200 colonies. Smaller lots were disposed of at intervals until 1908 when he made a final clean up by selling the remaining 750 colonies and all his equipment to Perry Griswold, a beekeeper of Kings County, and an old employee of Fred and his uncle John. Soon after Fred Hart had disposed of all his bees he moved to Exeter, Tulare County, where he remained permanently.

At the time of the Mussel Slough Tragedy on May 10, 1880, when eight men lost their lives in a battle over land troubles between settlers and the Southern Pacific Railroad Company, John and Fred Hart were working in one of their out-apiaries and were near enough to hear the shooting.

Frederick Miles Hart was born near Gilroy, Santa Clara County, California, October 28, 1857, and was married to Miss Kizbiah Sarah Smith in Visalia, February 17, 1889. Miss Smith was born and reared in Centerville, Iowa. The children born to them were: Elmer D., Leona M. and David P.

Fred Hart was a member of Hanford Lodge No. 275, I. O. O. F., and the Encampment. He and his wife were members of the Rebekahs. Fred was also a member of the Hanford Parlor No,. 37, N. S. G. W. He owned 640 acres of land in Kings and Tulare Counties, much of which was improved to fruit, grapevines and alfalfa. He passed away at Exeter, Tulare County, California, on January 3, 1933, at the age of 76 years, 2 months and 6 days.

The Hart Brothers were not only pioneers in California beekeeping, but they were "stayers" as well. Their original business was conducted uninterruptedly and on a commercial scale in the Hart family for over a half a century, overlapping three generations.

When Fred Hart made his final sale of bees in 1908 it closed the last chapter of what had been a very important and unusual apicultural enterprise — one that had long outlived practically all its California contemporaries of the first fifteen years of its activity.

It was the spirit of adventure, backed by indomitable courage, that prompted John H. Hart to leave his comfortable surroundings in Connecticut and brave the dangers of that long and tedious voyage around the Horn to California in 1849. It was faith in his ability to succeed that spurred him on a few years later to launch the pioneer enterprise of beekeeping in the Far West. Those worthy qualities were a natural heritage handed down through a long line of American ancestors, dating back two centuries to 1632 when Stephen Hart, a native of Braintree, Essex County, England, came to this country and settled in Massachusetts Bay Colony.

History records the fact that during the early Colonial period, Stephen Hart and his posterity were foremost in exploring and settling the wilds of New England. They were also active in both Church and State and from among them men were chosen to fill responsible positions of public trust in religious, civic and military capacities. Hartford, Connecticut, was named in honor of Stephen Hart.

Fred Hart, who represented the ninth generation of Harts in America, was no exception to his worthy ancestors. He had served the public satisfactorily in other capacities, and for that reason he was chosen to fill the office of Bee Inspector of Kings County, when that office was first established, and he always discharged his duty with credit to himself and honor to his county.

Early Day Beekeeping in Fresno County

The route traveled by the first honey bees to their destination in Fresno County, California, was from New York state via the Isthmus of Panama, San Francisco, Santa Clara County and Tulare County.

The *Alta California* of San Francisco, in its issue of July 1, 1852, published an item as follows:

> We were yesterday surprised and gratified to learn that a gentleman arriving on the *New Orleans* had brought with him from New York state, a hive of bees in good working condition. This is the first importation of the honey bee to these shores.

The man's name is not mentioned, which is a serious omission, for he undoubtedly brought the first hive of bees to California. This item being the last known mention of this colony, it is doubtful if they lived to swarm and increase.

In the of November 23, 1869, issue of *Pacific Rural Press,* S. L. Watkins, a beekeeper of Placerville, gives an account of a man by the name of Shelton who purchased twelve swarms of bees from a man in Aspinwall, on the Isthmus of Panama, who intended trying bees in California, but after reaching Aspinwall became disgusted with the experiment and returned to New York.

According to Watkins, Shelton landed his bees in San Francisco in March 1853. The following winter they dwindled to one colony. In the spring he moved this colony to San Jose, where they made an increase of three swarms. Soon after, Mr. Shelton was killed by the explosion of the ill-fated *Jenny Lind*. In December, two of the Shelton colonies were sold to settle up the estate, and were bought by Major James W. Patrick at $105 and $110 respectively.

About 1855, Clayborne and Enos Wright, brothers from Ohio, acquired about

McCubbin comb honey apiary, seven miles southwest of Selma, in 1892. McCubbin is on the right.

1,100 acres of land on the Kings River, below and adjoining what was later the Jack Sutherland holdings. The Sutherland holdings were a part of the original Laguna de Tache land grant. About 1856 the Wright brothers brought five colonies of bees from San Jose and located them on their land near the brick corral, which was about ten miles below Kingston. The brick corral was near the old Tulare-Fresno County line. These are supposed to be the first honey bees brought to the Kings River. "Uncle" Dan. Rhodes' daughter, who lives on her father's old homestead, could probably give some definite information regarding the location of the old brick corral. In that way, it could be determined whether the Wright bees were located in Tulare or Fresno County.

John H. Hart, who came to California from Goshen, Connecticut, via Cape Horn, in 1849, established an apiary in connection with his dairy business near Gilroy in 1856. His brother, Charles C. Hart, came with his bride, also from Goshen, Connecticut, via the Isthmus of Panama, and arrived in Gilroy in May 1857, and was taken in as a full partner by his brother in both enterprises.

In July 1859, the Hart Brothers moved 100 colonies of bees over the Coast Range mountains, via Pacheco Pass, and located them on their newly acquired 320 acre ranch, about one mile east of Visalia.

In the spring of 1860, the Hart Brothers sold thirty-five colonies of bees to Dr. Cobb of Millerton, Fresno County. The price paid was $100 per colony delivered. Cobb, of Cobb-Evans of Fresno, is a son of Dr. Cobb and could perhaps give some further information concerning his father's early venture in bees in the county.

During the sixties, Richard Smith, who was familiarly known as "Eating" Smith, on account of his insatiable appetite, had an apiary on the Kings River below Kingston. In Mrs. Ernestine Winchell's column [in the *Fresno Morning*

Republican], under the heading of "Fresno Memories," dated April 3, 1927, giving an account of the high water of 1867-68, she wrote as follows:

> At the mouth of the Kings River, Richard Smith loaded one ton of wild flower honey on a flat boat, having floor space about equal to an average living room, and assayed the journey to San Francisco, over the lake that spread from the Kings River to the San Joaquin, along the course of the submerged Fresno Slough, and on down the great river to the bay. There he sold his cargo and felt content with the expedition.

Mrs. Perry Phillips, of Kingston, told this writer that the last time she saw "Eating" Smith was sometime during the seventies when he came by their place peddling honey and distributing religious tracts.

David Secord, who passed away in a hospital in Paso Robles, California, September 23, 1934, was a veteran of the Civil War and was ninety years old at the time of his death. Secord was one of California's pioneer beekeepers. As early as 1875, he was engaged in the bee business in the foothills of Fresno County in the Coast Range mountains where he had an apiary continuously for a period of nearly sixty years. During the later years of his life he limited his apiary to only a few colonies. During the later eighties, Secord had John Bray as a partner, and they numbered their colonies by the hundreds.

In 1882, George Sargent, a beekeeper of Mussel Slough, brought a wagon load of bees to Fresno County and peddled them out from house to house a few hives in a place. Among Sargent's customers were George B. Otis and his brother, Philo, of Selma; D. S. Orr and his son-in-law, Charles Sweift of Wildflower; and Mr. Styles of Central Colony. With the exception of George B. Otis, all of Sargent's customers soon built their colonies up to commercial sized apiaries and kept them in up-to-date moveable frame hives.

Orion S. Davis, of Newburn, Iowa, answered an ad in *Gleanings in Bee Culture,* in 1880, and as a result, came to California that year and accepted a position with O. F. Coon, a beekeeper of Lemoore, and worked in Coon's apiaries about two years.

Cyrus M. Davis, a brother of O. S., came to California in 1882, and the two brothers began in the bee business on a small scale that year. The following year they moved their apiary consisting of about 35 colonies from Mussel Slough to their 80-acre tract, recently purchased, and which was located about two miles southwest of Selma.

On account of their optimism regarding a winter supply of nectar, the Davis Brothers left their bees only a limited amount of stores in the fall of 1863, and as a consequence their loss during the winter was very heavy. But, by 1886 they had built their apiary up to over 100 colonies and were securing good honey crops of both comb and extracted. They were progressive and always kept their apiary and equipment up-to-date.

O. S. Davis was badly handicapped on account of lameness, and he ran a peddle wagon and disposed of their honey crop during the winter, while C. M.

did most of the work on the ranch. Their territory covers a goodly portion of the central part of the San Joaquin Valley, where they wholesaled to stores and retailed from house to house.

At the close of the honey season of 1888, the Davis Brothers had about 200 colonies of bees, all in good ten-frame Langstroth hives. At that time they dissolved their partnership, and C. M. moved his portion of the bees to the Coast Range mountains where he had filed on a homestead in the Zapatha Chino canyon.

Early in 1889, O. S. Davis took **R. E. Zimmerman** [McCubbin's brother-in-law] in as a partner in the production end of both apiary and vineyard. At the end of the honey season of 1889, this writer took over the O. S. Davis interests in bees and equipment and he and Zimmerman ran the business jointly until the close of the 1890 season. They then dissolved the partnership, though both continued in the bee business.

Phineas Loucks engaged in the bee business in Fresno County about the early eighties, and in 1888 he had an apiary of about 100 colonies located near Centerville. He was enterprising and was possibly the first man to introduce a honey extractor and comb foundation mill into the county. The extractor was a four-frame nonreversible, and the mill was small and would accommodate only a six inch sheet of wax.

The sudden disappearance of Loucks in 1889 from his mountain cabin located above Markwood Meadows in the Sierra, is yet, after over a half century, an unsolved mystery, as no trace of him has ever been reported. As Mrs. Loucks passed away in this same cabin the year before, the seven small children were left without either parent.

The Loucks honey extractor was a Root "Novice," and was in the possession of several parties before I purchased it. After equipping it with a new gearing, I used it several years, then removed the gearing and converted it into a honey tank.

During the years 1900 and 1901 a very noted beekeeper in the person of John H. Martin, whose nom de plume was "Rambler," was in charge of this writer's apiaries. When E. R. Root, editor of *Gleaning in Bee Culture* was visiting Rambler at Reedley in 1901, he stated to this writer that Rambler's writings were the most popular of all the contributors to current apicultural literature.

The ten-frame Langstroth hive has been the one always used by practically all Fresno County commercial beekeepers.

Prior to 1894, approximately eighty percent of all honey produced for market in Fresno County had been stored in small sections 1½ x 4¼ x 4¼ inches, weighing a fraction over three-quarters of a pound. About that time the bee men began to extract more of their product, and by 1900 the proportion of comb honey had been reduced to about five per cent of the entire output, and it has since remained at that point or below.

It was about 1895 that the new five gallon honey cans and cases were adopted by Fresno County bee men. These new containers soon replaced the coal cans and cases that had previously been used exclusively.

In preparing the second hand oil cans for use, the original cap would be melted off and a new one soldered on in its place after which the cans would be thoroughly washed out with a solution of concentrated lye. The screw caps used at that time were much smaller than the ones used at the present time.

The production of comb honey in Fresno County reached the peak about 1892. During that year this writer owned an apiary of 206 colonies located about seven miles southwest of Selma. The bees remained in that same location throughout the entire year and stored what is believed to be the largest crop of comb honey ever produced in one apiary in the entire history of the San Joaquin Valley. The apiary was in an extra good location and the season was a long and ideal one in every respect. Alfalfa was the main source of nectar, and at that time the growers permitted their alfalfa to stand until it was well along into the blooming period, whereas they now mow the crop as it is coming into bloom.

On this particular occasion, the queens were all young and vigorous, having been reared the fall before from pure Italian stock. The colonies were given the best of care, and were fed over a ton of well-ripened honey in the brood frames just as the bees had stored it the year before.

From his collection of books and periodicals on bees and honey, this writer has donated over 800 items to the University of California. This is said to be the largest single donation of its kind made by any individual in the state. Eight separate bee periodicals have been launched in California. Early copies of seven of these, beginning with 1887, were included in the above donation. Also, a lithographer's sketch of the front cover page of another bee journal that "died a boomin'" was among them.

This writer has also donated a number of miscellaneous articles to the Apicultural Division at Washington D. C. They included the following: Six rare volumes on bee culture of which the Division had no duplicates; six sections of comb honey that had been stored in his apiaries near Selma; and a 1894 group picture containing photographic reproductions of 100 men and women who were

The "last homestead cabin in the Alta District" at McCubbin's "Eucalyptus Ranch" in Tulare County, and used as his honey house. The photograph was taken in 1900 by J. H. Martin and pictures R. H. Frey, a Traver beekeeper, along with his dog.

considered the most outstanding beekeepers in the United States and Canada prior to 1900. In this donation to Washington was also the queen rearing outfit used by Rambler while he had charge of this writer's apiaries. This queen rearing outfit is enclosed in a glass case made especially for its reception. The six sections of comb honey mentioned above are also in a special case.

O. W. Stearns, who made his home in Selma for nearly fifty years, passed away February 22, 1941, at the home of his daughter, Mrs. J. M. Powell, in Sebastopol, California, at eighty-five years of age. Beginning in 1898, Stearns was continuously engaged in the bee business in Fresno County for a period of about thirty-five years or longer. Viewing his activities from the standpoint of strenuous work, efficiency and net profits, he was undoubtedly the most successful beekeeper that ever operated in the county.

Stearns knew bees from A to Z and most always secured the maximum crops from his apiaries. His equipment was always simple but thoroughly efficient. In fact, economy and efficiency were always manifest throughout his entire operations. There was never any superfluity connected with either apiary, equipment or management. His plan was to keep a sufficient number of colonies to completely occupy his entire time during the main season. He would occasionally hire some help during a rush.

Stearns was modest in manner, stout and healthy. He used neither tobacco nor intoxicants in any form, and his powers of endurance were wonderful. These characteristics, coupled with agility and no lost motion, made every stroke count for practically one hundred per cent. Despite his unusual activity, Stearns was a believer in relaxation, and took regular vacations with his family, but never at a time that would interfere with any necessary work with the bees.

J. H. Martin "The Rambler"

{*The following article appeared in the September 1937 issue of* Bees and Honey. *The journal appears to have edited McCubbin's submission, since the typescript version of this article is different. According to McCubbin's notes, Dr. E. F. Phillips, who is mentioned in the article, requested that McCubbin write this sketch because no person had been in closer contact with "Rambler" during his time in California.*}

John Henderson Martin was born in Hartford, Washington County, New York, December 30, 1839, and died in Havana, Cuba, January 13, 1903, at sixty-three years of age.

Let the reader picture in his mind a man of unusual intelligence, a close observer with keen perception, and one who is also a humorist. This rare combination of characteristics would represent somewhat, those of J. H. Martin, who was better known to the beekeepers of the world by his nom de plume, "Rambler."

John H. Martin, "The Rambler"

In "Rambler's" make-up there were two elements in strong contrast with each other. One of these abounded in humor of a high class, while over the other, melancholy seemed to reign supreme, yet there was never anything in the nature of a grouch associated with that dejection.

During his low spirited periods, which were usually of short duration, "Rambler" would never write for publication, for it was his desire to give his readers a one hundred per cent article. Consequently, his "Rambles" always contained, not only valuable information, but also an interesting description of some laughable incident, presented in a most pleasing manner, with an original cartoon to "cap the climax."

Always deeply interested in everything that pertained to practical or scientific beekeeping, he would permit nothing to interfere with his duties along that line.

For the first few years his work with bees was confined to northern New York. This was followed by a ten year period in California and closed with over a year in Cuba.

During the time he was in this state, "Rambler" had charge of apiaries in seven different counties, and the work was well distributed over a territory that extended practically the entire length of the state. This brought him in direct contact with the three distinct features of our climate: the coast, the interior valleys and the mountain districts.

During his "Rambles" he visited hundreds of beekeepers in many parts of the United States and Cuba. This, together with his practical experience in so many different places, gave him an opportunity for observation, enjoyed, perhaps, by no other man of his day.

Many of our leading authorities on apiculture hold that the "Rambler's" writings were not only in a class by themselves, but that they were the best of their kind the beekeeping world has ever known. His serial story, entitled "Beekeeper Fred Anderson or the Mystery of Crystal Mountain," which was published in *Gleanings* in 1896-97 is alone sufficient to substantiate this claim.

Being familiar with many of the places mentioned in "Rambler's" serial it was doubly interesting to me, but it had a much deeper significance after he had explained who some of the characters represented and that many of the attending circumstances, though far removed from their original setting, reflected incidents in his own life and those of some of his late relatives.

"Rambler" was well educated and his specialty, next to beekeeping, was geography. He could give off hand the exact location of practically every place of any importance on the globe. There were but few teachers anywhere, perhaps, as well informed as he on this subject.

Being mechanically inclined, and really quite a genius, he manifested a desire when about sixteen years old to enter a machine shop as an apprentice. As he was the only child in the family, his parents were not entirely willing for him to leave home, so he abandoned the idea.

Had some enterprising individual been privileged to personally direct the talents of "Rambler," and promote them freely for the sole purpose of making money, it would be difficult to estimate what the possible results might have been. Such a proposition however, would have been spurned with utter contempt, for no money consideration or allurement of fame could have tempted him to depart from the modest life he spent among bees and beekeepers.

His view of the individual was a peculiar one. Such matters as material wealth or important positions of those with whom he came in contact never interested him in the least. He would enjoy an evening with the occupants of the most humble mountain cabin, far removed from civilization, with apparently the same degree of pleasure that he would visit with some important personage in a palatial city home, and would be equally at ease in both places. This peculiar characteristic, together with his unusual alertness, enabled him to acquire valuable information that would have escaped the ordinary person.

As intimated above, the desire for fame or to acquire wealth were entirely foreign to his nature. With sufficient funds to meet modest current requirements, he was perfectly satisfied. By this it must not be construed that he was negligent of his obligations or that he was a spendthrift, for he was quite the reverse. He carried sufficient life insurance to supply any possible deficiency that might have occurred at the end.

He was a very pleasant conversationalist, and being of a modest and retiring disposition, was a good listener and never monopolized the time.

He had definite views, though they were never stubbornly held, and he was open to conviction where a principle was not involved.

He was seldom seen away from home or his work, except when well groomed. Yet there was never anything about his dress or manner that would attract attention. Those who were familiar with his usual neat appearance enjoyed the greatly distorted cartoons of himself, more perhaps, than those who were not personally acquainted with him.

One of his characteristic poses (being tall and thin), was to sit with one leg entwined around the other.

So far as immediate relatives were concerned, "Rambler" was truly a lonely figure in this world. He had neither wife, son, daughter, mother, father, brother, sister, uncle or aunt. The death of his only child, which occurred in early infancy, followed not long afterward by that of his wife, cast a deep shadow over his inner life that time itself failed to entirely clear away. For years he made the pathway bright for thousands of readers who anxiously awaited and eagerly read his "Rambles," but little did they know of the sadness that attended him to his grave.

A portion of one clause in "Rambler's" will read as follows: "It is my request to be buried by the side of my wife in Hartford, New York." That request was complied with. Although he passed away in a foreign country, the remains were returned to his childhood home and now rest in the family plot, and are marked by a monument designed after the one that marks the resting place of our revered L. L. Langstroth.

During the two years (1900 and 1901) that "Rambler" had charge of my apiaries, he made his home on a place I owned, three miles south of where I lived, though much of his time was spent in my home. His death occurred in Cuba, but as stated, his actual home was at the place just described, and was so established when administering his will, which had been left in my possession.

All of "Rambler's" personal property left in California, other than his apiary, was bequeathed to me. The greater portion of this consisted of books, papers and photographs, pertaining to beekeeping. Six rare volumes of the books were passed on to the apiarian collection in Washington, D. C., and the remaining books as well as the papers and photographs, are now a permanent part of the special apiarian collection of the University of California, known as the "George W. York Library," and which is now in charge of the Pacific Coast Beekeepers Laboratories at Davis, California. This special collection was named several years ago in honor of the late editor of *Bees and Honey,* who had donated liberally toward it.

"Rambler's" stay in Cuba was to have been only temporary, and his plan was to return to my place and take up the work he had left. Quoting from one of his last communications, in reference to the apiary at the place where he made his home, he said: "I am hankering to raise some queens in that apiary next spring."

On meeting "Rambler" one would be impressed with his sincerity, and during all our long and intimate acquaintance, no occasion ever arose where this impression was changed in the least.

Being a total abstainer from the use of intoxicants and narcotics in every form, and with a high regard for the moral law, his influence was always for good. He was one of the exceptionally few who actually lived the Golden Rule, and never appeared to harbor the slightest thought of malice toward any one, regardless of the provocation.

Dr. E. F. Phillips, who for many years was in charge of the Apicultural Division of the Agriculture Department, in Washington, D. C., claimed that "Rambler" was the Mark Twain of American Apiculture.

I will quote from *Gleanings in Bee Culture,* in the May 1924 issue, as follows: "R. V. Murray, at one time cartoonist for *Gleanings,* who did such wonderful work in making caricatures of John H. Martin, who wrote under the nom de plume of "Rambler," in *Gleanings* from 1988 to 1903, died in Cleveland, April 12. Without question no series of articles that we have ever published were so thoroughly appreciated and enjoyed at the time, and when "Rambler" died in 1903, there was mourning throughout the beekeeping world, and, of course, Murray's cartoons stopped at that time."

It was a peculiar individual who could spend an hour in the society of "Rambler" without being permanently benefitted. Fortunate indeed were the thousands of beekeepers who have been favored with that wonderful privilege, and in whose hearts the pleasant memory of that noble character will ever be enshrined.

[Among the supplementary notes McCubbin attached to his copy of this article was the following: "John H. Martin, so far as known, was the only child of Job and Martha Goodwin Martin. His father was born August 12, 1804, and died October 6, 1883. His mother was born July 30, 1807, and died October 26, 1883. He married Miss Libbie C. Edwards, who was born March 1, 1844, and died October 29, 1881. The remains of these four persons rest in the Job Martin family plot in the cemetery at Hartford, New York."]

First Free Bridge Near Kingsburg

{*The following is the text of a letter McCubbin sent to the* Alta Advocate *on June 29, 1948, after the appearance of an article detailing the opening of a new bridge on El Monte Way. The "post script" appears to have been written at a later date.*}

The special ceremony conducted recently at the opening of the new El Monte Way bridge over the Kings River refreshed my memory concerning a rather peculiar circumstance that occurred in connection with the first bridge built across the Kings River east of Kingsburg.

One Sunday morning in September 1886, when this bridge was new, a group of us were crossing it in a surrey. We noticed where a small stream of coal oil had been spread on the floor of the bridge from one end to the other. When we reached the west end we saw where a fire had been started at the edge of the floor. Instead of igniting the floor, as was no doubt intended, the fire had run out among some trash and down the side of the grade where it had set an old log on fire, which was still smouldering.

At the time there was a toll bridge in operation where the present California State Highway 99 crosses the river alongside the main Southern Pacific Railroad tracks. This toll bridge was owned by two brothers. Suspicion for attempting the bridge's destruction naturally rested on the owners of the toll bridge, for their bridge had a practical monopoly on the travel across the river until the free bridge had been constructed a few months before.

A few days after the fire was started a group of the regular idlers were sitting in front of one of the Kingsburg saloons discussing the affair. One of the toll bridge owners was among them. Another man sitting about two feet away extended his arm out over the toll bridge man and said, "I'll bet $50 I can lay my hand right on the man who tried to burn that bridge."

The old bridge continued collecting toll into the early "nineties." The new free bridge was intended primarily to serve the residents of the 76 Country, now known as the Alta District. When the new bridge was built, Traver, and D. Dickey's little country store near the present location of Yettem, served the entire 76 Country. Now, there are some six or eight towns, large and small, in the same territory.

Post Script

For several years following the construction of the new free bridge there was no provision for crossing the deep slough just to the east of the bridge. That made fording necessary. When the river reached the moderately high stage, water in the slough would back up from below for there was no connection with the river at the upper end. When the river became very high the water in the slough would just about swim a horse.

In 1896 I crossed there with a horse and buggy when the water was extremely high. I rode the horse with my little two-year old boy in my arms. When we got to the deepest place, where the horse appeared to be swimming, instead of being scared, the little boy had a big loud laugh.

John Sutherland

John Sutherland, who was popularly known as "Jack," or rather "Old Jack," to distinguish him from his son "Jack," was a native of England. He came to California during the earlier period, probably during the fifties, for we find that he purchased a large portion of the 48,000-acre Laguna de Tache grant during the sixties. That tract was an old Spanish or Mexican grant that had been conveyed to Manuel Castro by Governor Pico, on January 10, 1846. Sutherland's ranch was located on the Kings River and intersected by the Tulare-Fresno County line.

Sutherland increased his holdings by purchasing other large bodies of land that adjoined the grant, and he and Robert McCubbin owned jointly a tract of 400 acres located in the immediate vicinity on the south side of the river. William Sutherland, a nephew who was Major Domo (Big Boss or Superintendent) for a number of years, is authority for the statement that his "Uncle Jack Sutherland paid more taxes in Fresno County than any other man, and at the same time he was a heavy taxpayer in both Tulare and San Joaquin Counties."

What was known as the "No Fence Law," enacted by the Legislature in 1874, gave the homesteader and other small land holders protection from the cattle barons and their vast herds of roving live stock. [While the "No Fence Law" did not require cattle owners to fence their lands, it made doing so a virtual necessity. Among its provisions, farmers were permitted to seize cattle trespassing on their lands, charge fees for their being held if they were reclaimed, and receive payment for damages. The law had the effect of ending California's open range and was a measure of the growing importance and political influence of farming interests.] At the time this law went into effect, Jack Sutherland owned about 12,000 head of cattle and from 4,000 to 5,000 head of horses. All this stock had been grazing far and wide at will, over the vast expanse of the San Joaquin Valley plains intermingling with the stock of other stockmen of that period. Under this new law it became necessary for the stockmen either to confine their stock on their own lands or have them herded continually.

Sutherland's land, though very extensive, would not provide sufficient feed for such vast herds as he then owned. Consequently, he marketed a big lot of them and drove 1,500 head of his horses over the John N. Thacker's big ranch on the Humboldt River in Nevada. The horses were kept on the Thacker Ranch about a year and were then driven through to the Canadian River country in Texas.

John Thacker, mentioned above, and who was a cousin of this writer, had formerly been Major Domo for Jack Sutherland. Thacker was afterwards at the head of Wells Fargo Express Company's detective force for a period of about thirty years. While serving as Major Domo for Sutherland, Thacker and his family lived about a quarter mile above Kingston, on the south side of the river, where his son Eugene was born.

Before the "No Fence Law" went into effect, Jack Sutherland made arrangements to fence 14,000 acres of his land, although this was only a portion of his vast land holdings. William Sutherland, who was Major Domo for his uncle Jack at the time, went to Stockton to purchase material with which to enclose the 14,000 acres referred to. The purchase was made from Simpson and Gray, wholesale lumber dealers of Stockton, and the invoice consisted of the following: 15,510 coast redwood posts and 413,600 feet of lumber. The posts were extra large size and of the best quality. The lumber was all Oregon pine and clear, 1½ inches thick, 8 inches wide and 24 feet long. That was perhaps the largest single order of building material ever shipped to one consumer in the San Joaquin Valley. It was shipped to the Kingsburg Switch, as the place was then called. Had it all come at once, it would have made a train load of eighty cars of the capacity of that period. No wire was used in the construction of the fence, but with the four thick, heavy boards it was a thoroughly substantial structure and one that proved to be an efficient restraint against the onslaughts of any outlaw animals that came in contact with it.

The village of Kingston, which was located on the south side of the Kings River, was headquarters for Jack Sutherland's big land holdings. These lay on both sides of the river and extended for miles in every direction from Kingston.

Kingston was a regular relay station for the Butterfield Overland Stage Company while they were operating their line of stages between St. Louis and Memphis in the East, and San Francisco on the Pacific Coast. This stage line was 2,880 miles in length and the longest continuous horse stage line ever operated in the United States.

During periods of high water, the low river bottom lands to the north of Kingston would be flooded, and at such times the stages would make a detour from Visalia, crossing at Smith's Ferry, eighteen miles above Kingston.

L. A. Whitmore had established a ferry at the site of Kingston in 1855, and his was the pioneer crossing on the lower Kings River. The little town had grown up as a result of the ferry.

Whitmore was a "squaw man" and after the order was given to round up all the Indians in that portion of California and place them on reservations, the officers came to get Whitmore's squaw. He refused to deliver her to the officers, and later placing her in a room of his residence, he took his position at the door of the room with a drawn knife to protect her. With but very little parley, the officers shot Whitmore dead where he stood. Those officers were severely censured for taking the life of Whitmore, when they could have easily overpowered him, as he had nothing but the knife with which to defend himself.

During the reign of terror of that notorious Mexican bandit, Tiburcio Vasquez, and his band of desperadoes, those bloodthirsty outlaws visited Kingston and during the evening of December 26, 1873, robbed the general merchandise store of Louis Einstein and Company and other places securing $2,500 in money and jewelry. After forcing Einstein to turn over all the cash in the store to them, they left him and his clerk lying on the floor securely bound with ropes, when they were surprised by rifle shots from the darkness outside and hastily disappeared.

About the year 1875 the Postal Department established a Star Route that left the railroad at Kingsburg and ran out through Wild Flower and Kingston to Grangeville, in Tulare County, now Kings County. E. H. Tucker secured the contract for carrying the mail and established a stage line with a daily schedule both ways, connecting the four places. The stage was a two-horse vehicle and Tucker did the driving himself at first, but later on hired a man by the name of Frank McKinney to drive. McKinney continued as driver until Tucker sold his stage line.

The road was graded up through the low lands in the river bottom to the north of Kingston, but the grade would wash out in places during high water, and in order to keep a regular schedule, provision was made to detour across the river bottom further east. A man on horseback would explore the proposed route of the detour and set up stakes on either side of the place selected, and the stage would pass between these guide stakes. In the deeper portions, the horses feet would barely touch the bottom. There was practically no current, as the water spread over a vast expanse. The thick matted roots of the wire grass prevented the horses from bogging, consequently there was little danger to the passengers, aside from the possibility of getting wet.

Following Tucker's proprietorship, the stage line was operated at different times by Pete Simpson (afterwards Constable in Kingsburg) and "Nippy" Draper, both of Kingsburg. Patronage diminished and the stage was eventually replaced by a buckboard and occasionally a road cart was the only vehicle used, for the reason that the driver seldom had a passenger. The only reason for its continued existence was to carry the mail. About 1893 this Star Route was discontinued.

Sutherland is said to have purchased his portion of the Laguna de Tache grant from a man named [Oliver H.?] Bliss. While Bliss was the owner he built a toll bridge to take the place of the old Whitmore ferry boat. That bridge was built on the old ferry site, and the place is permanently marked by some old cement pilings that were placed there when the old bridge was repaired. These pilings stand near the river bank on either side, and are about a half mile below where the Santa Fe Railroad now crosses the river.

Long after Kingston had passed into history, the ghostly remains of the old stage stable were still standing to remind the visitor of the bustling little river town, and the place where the old Butterfield stages made regular visits with their loads of overland passengers and mail. Those stages would halt just long enough for a force of men to replace the jaded stock with fresh spirited animals, while the driver remained in his seat. The lines would then be handed up to him and at the crack of his whip, the team would be off on a dash, and the weary passengers would again continue their long overland journey.

In 1937 the old Kingston stage stable was torn down and moved away. Oscar P. Noren, secured one of the long timbers of the old structure and incorporated it in a new adobe museum building on his ranch two miles north of Reedley, Fresno County.

A photostatic copy of a picture of Jack Sutherland made about 1870 has been deposited by the writer in the files of the California State Historical Association at Los Angeles.

Mrs. W. W. Hill

For this narrative about Mrs. W. W. Hill, I am indebted to Mrs. Eliza Fink, widow of Peter Fink. Mrs. Hill and Mrs. Fink were neighbors and particular friends for many years, which included the time when the two Hill babies met their untimely death as described in this article.

Mr. and Mrs. W. W. Hill were making their home in Hill's Valley, north of the location of the present town of Orange Cove, when Hill was elected Treasurer of Fresno County. His official duties would compel Hill to spend much of his time in Millerton, which at that time was the county seat of Fresno County.

The uprising of the Indians in that part of California during the early fifties was still fresh in the minds of the early settlers. Mrs. Hill was not especially timid, but the thought of being alone in that isolated settlement did give her much concern. Consequently, Hill moved his wife down to the town of Scottsburg, on the Kings River, before assuming the duties of his office.

As Mrs. Fink related to me, Mrs. Hill was a large fleshy woman, and slept so soundly it was almost impossible to awaken her. While living in Scottsburg, Mrs. Hill rolled over on her baby and crushed the life out of its little body.

They had another baby, and as a matter of precaution, they hired a young man who was a very light sleeper to sleep in an adjoining room from the one occupied by Mrs. Hill. There was only a thin board partition between the two rooms.

One night the young man thought he heard a slight commotion in Mrs. Hill's room, but not enough to be alarmed about. When Mrs. Hill awoke the next morning, she was horrified to learn that she was lying on the dead body of her infant child.

Both the Hill babies were buried in the little Scottsburg cemetery. When the cemetery was washed away, both these bodies were washed away, along with the occupants of all the other graves. Mrs. Hill spent many anxious hours wandering down each side of the river with the vain hope that she might find some indication of the remains of her two babies.

Early Day Schools

When the Smith's Ferry was in operation, there were no schools anywhere in reach for the James Smith children. John Parks Hamilton "Ham," the oldest of the Smith children, went to Centerville to board with a family and attend school there. He later went down to Kingston and did the same. That was during the 1860s.

Mrs. Julia Jacobs, nee Fink, daughter of Peter and Eliza Fink, told me that she attended a school about 1870. It was taught not far from her father's home in what is now the Alameda School District [the Alameda School was located near the southwest corner of Goodfellow and Rio Vista Avenues]. It must have been a subscription school for the Fresno County Superintendent's Office has no record of such a school.

Perhaps the first public school in what is now the Alta District was the Clarks Valley School. It was organized on August 4, 1873. The schoolhouse was located in the northwest quarter of Section 15, Township 14 South, Range 24 East [in the vicinity of the intersection of Kings Canyon Road and Cove Avenue]. One of the first trustees was John Byrd. Seventeen pupils were enrolled and the average daily attendance was eight. On July 1, 1918, the Clarks Valley School District, together with the Citrus Cove and Navelencia Districts, formed the Navelencia Union School District.

Around 1889, the country people north of Reedley were also busy. They organized the Fink School District, and erected a schoolhouse on the southeast corner on Section 10, Township 15 South, Range 23 East [the northwest corner of Adams and Frankwood Avenues].

[McCubbin recounts the history of other early day schools in his sketches on Wahtoke and the Smith's Ferry School District.]

California Fruit and Wine-Land Company

A certified copy of the articles of incorporation of the California Fruit and Wine-Land Company was filed in the office of the Secretary of State in Sacramento, on June 3, 1887. Its place of business was San Francisco, and its authorized capital stock was $1,328,000. The incorporators listed were: Robert M. Hamilton, Jacob Levi, Sr., Moses Samuel, Lippmann Sachs, John R. Jarboe, Leopold Hirsch, Nathan S. Bachman, Ephraim Simon, Solomon Sweet, James Simpson, all of San Francisco; and Louis Elkus, of Sacramento, California.

When Moses Samuel, a Russian Jew, with a German accent, was dictating the proposed name of the corporation to the stenographer, he called it "Wine-Land," when he meant "Vine-Land." The error was not detected until after the certified copy was filled and returned from the Secretary of State.

Having been personally acquainted with some of the original stockholders of this company and having personal knowledge of the activities of several others, a few items concerning these men might be in order.

Jacob Levi, Sr. was one of the homeliest men I was ever acquainted with. In 1889 he was elected Treasurer of the 76 Land and Water Company.

Moses Samuel was Vice President of the 76 Land and Water Company in 1889.

John R. Jarboe was the senior partner of the law firm of Jarboe, Harrison and Goodfellow, of San Francisco. W. S. Goodfellow was the junior partner of that firm, and in 1889 was one of the attorneys for the 76 Land and Water Company.

Robert M. Hamilton was the junior partner of the firm of Baker and Hamilton of San Francisco. They were wholesalers of hardware and farming implements. When the 76 Land and Water Company turned their irrigation system over to the Alta Irrigation District in 1890, Robert M. Hamilton was one of the stockholders of the 76 Company.

Ephraim Simon was the senior partner of Simon, Jacobs and Company that owned many thousands of acres of land in the Sand Creek and present Orange Cove territory. His partner, I. H. Jacobs ("Big Foot Jake") was president of the

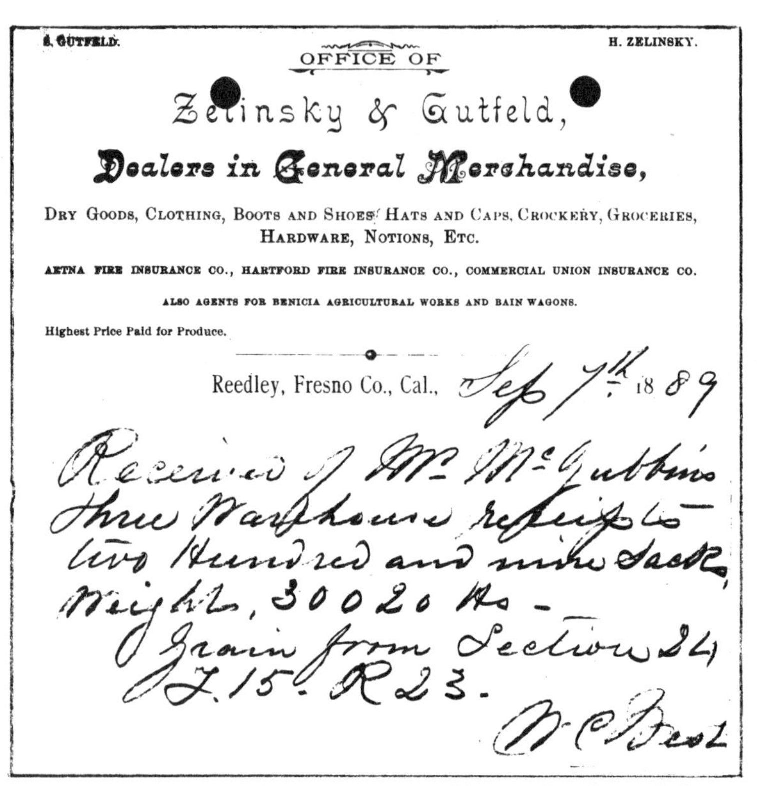

S. GUTFELD. H. ZELINSKY.

OFFICE OF

Zelinsky & Gutfeld,

Dealers in General Merchandise,

DRY GOODS, CLOTHING, BOOTS AND SHOES, HATS AND CAPS, CROCKERY, GROCERIES, HARDWARE, NOTIONS, ETC.

AETNA FIRE INSURANCE CO., HARTFORD FIRE INSURANCE CO., COMMERCIAL UNION INSURANCE CO.

ALSO AGENTS FOR BENICIA AGRICULTURAL WORKS AND BAIN WAGONS.

Highest Price Paid for Produce.

Reedley, Fresno Co., Cal., Sep 7th 1889

Received of M. McGubbins three Warehouse receipts to two Hundred and nine Sacks, Weight, 30020 lbs - Grain from Section 24 T.15 R23.

W C West

76 Land and Water Company for many years. Simon, Jacobs and Company also owned thousands of head of sheep in the San Joaquin Valley, as well as being the owners of the Merced Wollen Mills.

Solomon Sweet was the head of the S. Sweet and Company, big retail merchants of Visalia in the early days.

The California Fruit and Wine-Land Company purchased 4,000 acres of land located about four miles east of where the town of Reedley was afterwards established. The tract was two miles wide at the widest place, and five miles long from north to south. Near the middle of this tract was a natural mound, with its crown reaching about twenty-five feet high. At the time this company began operations this mound was conspicuous, standing out on the dry plains with no irrigated land for miles around. It had always fascinated me from the first time I saw it in 1886.

The California Fruit and Wine-Land Company employed as their Superintendent, W. C. West, a former employee of the Fancher Creek Nursery Company of Fresno. W. C. West had figured quite prominently in the introduction of the Smyrna Wild Capri fig into the United States. On page forty of George C. Roeding's treatise entitled, "The Smyrna Fig at Home and Abroad,"

> In the year 1886, Mr. F. Roeding, Proprietor of the Fancher Creek Nursery . . .decided to send W. C. West, then in his employ, to Smyrna for the purpose of investigating the fig industry on that spot, secure a variety of cuttings and all possible information for the successful prosecution of experimental planting.
>
> Mr. West did not reach Smyrna until October. Owing to the jealousy of the inhabitants in general and the prohibitive policy of the government in not allowing trees or cuttings of any kind to be exported, he met with some difficulties. However, with the assistance of an Englishman and a Greek, both of whom were residents of Smyrna, he ultimately succeeded in obtaining cuttings; Twenty odd

"Mount Olive" ranch, site of the California Fruit and Wine-Land Company.

> thousand of the true Lop or Commercial Fig were taken in the vicinity of Herbeyli, several thousand Wild or Capri cuttings; several hundred each of Kassaba, Bardajic and Cheker Injir were also secured in other districts.

These cuttings arrived in Fresno, May 24, 1887.

In the winter of 1887-88, active operations were begun on the 4,000-acre tract. During that year they limited their efforts to the square mile on which stood the mound mentioned above. The plan was to make that portion their show place. A fine residence was built on the top of the mound for the superintendent. Barns and implement buildings were constructed at the foot of the mound and to the southeast, while a large force of men and teams were put to work leveling and preparing ditches, etc., for planting the entire 640 acres.

When boring for water on the mound, solid granite was soon encountered. Later, efforts were made to raise water by means of hydraulic ram power at the drop in the canal. The fall was insufficient and the scheme was a failure.

Had the company secured the services of a competent landscape gardener with the plan to retain the clear view of the mound and its natural beauty and of the plantings on its slopes and the entire 640 acres, it could have been made one of the most beautiful and showy spots in the entire San Joaquin Valley. Instead of such an overall plan, the slopes of the mound were planted to olive trees that soon obstructed the beautiful view.

Apparently, this vast enterprise was never a success in any sense of the word. At the end of exactly twenty-three years, or on June 3, 1910, a certificate of amendment was filed with the Secretary of State reducing the capital stock to $5,345. A Superior Court decree of dissolution was filed with the Secretary of State on May 1, 1919.

In the meantime, the tract was subdivided into three colonies as follows:

Map of Mira Colony, including Section 16, Township 15 South, Range 24 East (640 acres) was filed in the office of the Recorder of Fresno County on May 18, 1906. [The colony was bounded by Adams, Wakefield, South and Crawford Avenues.]

Map of Springfield Colony, including Sections 20, 21 and portions of Sections

28 and 29, Township 15 South, Range 24 East (2,080 acres) was filed in the office of the Recorder of Fresno County on August 4, 1908. [The colony was generally bounded by South Avenue, Smith Mountain Ditch, Dinuba and Alta Avenues, excepting approximately 320 acres at the southwest corner.]

Map of Wakefield Colony, including Sections 4 and 9, Township 15 South, Range 24 East (1,280 acres) was filed in the office of the Recorder of Fresno County, on October 31, 1908. [The colony was bounded by American, Wakefield, Adams and Crawford Avenues.]

On account of so many Jewish names appearing among the list of the original incorporators, the wags dubbed the headquarters "Jerusalem," the Superintendent used the more dignified name of "Mount Olive." That name was really appropriate for the reason that the slopes of the mound were covered with olive trees.

[Mount Olive, still its common designation, is just north of the Mira Colony as described above.]

Example of Scientific Vineyard Improvement

{*The following article appeared in* The Fresno Morning Republican, *circa 1916.*}

The wonderful possibilities of the great San Joaquin Valley is a subject we frequently hear discussed in a prophetic way; but the need of the present, is more practical demonstrations of the actual fulfillment of these predictions.

Occasionally we find a man equal to the task, who, by taking advantage of the opportunities at hand, is actually making these demonstrations and thereby giving to the world a valuable object lesson. Lasting gratitude is due such a person, especially from those who may be following in that particular line of activity.

Experiments which have been conducted by a plain, practical farmer at Reedley, on a scale of sufficient magnitude and covering the necessary period of time to make them decisive, have thoroughly proven the possibility of materially increasing the yield of vineyards already highly productive. This object was accomplished by carefully studying out rational methods and judiciously applying the same, during various stages of each season's work.

As will be seen later on in this article, the results of the work mentioned above are apparently but little short of miraculous, the achievement of which is well worth the very best skill and training of the leading agriculturists of our government.

That these wonderful results should have been obtained by a Reedley man is but fitting and proper; as that district is noted for wonderful things. The largest raisin packing house in the world is located in that town, and no stemmer has ever been constructed on a larger scale than the one now doing duty in that plant. The vineyard containing the greatest acreage of any one in the world is near Reedley, and according to statistics, the one showing the highest yield of raisins per acre of any in the state is also located there, and four miles south of the town can be seen growing the largest tree of its age in the world [the McCubbin Gum Tree].

The Breidablik vineyard, located three miles southwest of Reedley, which comprises 350 acres, is considered one of the best pieces of property in Central California. It is owned by Matt. Mathisen, the gentleman above referred to as having secured such wonderful results from his vineyard. Since purchasing the land three years ago, he has made his home on the ranch, keeping in close touch with and taking a keen interest in all its activities.

The tract is divided as follows: Seventy acres are in Tuscan cling peaches, 263 acres are devoted to the growing of raisin grapes (of which 160 are Muscats), 58 Thompson Seedless, and 45 Sultanas, and the remaining 17 acres of the ranch have been reserved for pasture, drying yards and buildings. All the trees and vines are in full bearing, with the exception of 33 acres which were planted to Thompson Seedless grape vines during the year 1914. Ninety-nine per cent of these young vines grew and quite a number of them matured their fruit last season.

A main county road, forming a broad avenue, runs through the ranch from north to south. This avenue, as well as all margins, turning rows and ditch banks, are kept free from weeds at all times. This avenue is bordered on either side with a row of fig trees and one of these rows extends entirely around the 240 acres which lies to the west of the avenue. Three sides of this portion of the ranch faces on county roads.

The buildings, stock and implements are always in condition to consistently harmonize with the high-grade work carried on all over the ranch.

The tract is well supplied with facilities for irrigation. One of the main branches of the Alta canal system runs through the ranch, and in addition to this two immense pumping plants and one of smaller capacity have been installed for use when occasion requires.

Many substantial improvements have been added by the present owner, including a large and commodious dwelling for the foreman and his family, 75,000 first class new raisin trays, two pumping plants of immense capacity as mentioned above, ditches enlarged and levees built for the more perfect control of water while irrigating, besides many other items of less importance.

The proprietor of the Breidablik vineyard has traveled practically all over the world and is a man of wide experience and a close observer.

After taking possession of the property a careful study was made of every phase of the following subjects, both in their relation to local conditions and to each other: Pruning, cultivation, irrigation, fertilization, spraying and handling of the various matured crops. As a result of this study, intelligent consideration is given during the entire year to all the details that have been found necessary to aid in promoting the greatest growth and development of plant, tree and vine, as well as the final perfection of their products. The result of all this care has been a regular increase in quantity and a corresponding improvement in quality of crops.

This increase and improvement applies to the entire ranch but the reader's particular attention will be called to the produce of the vines.

Taking the average of the crops of raisins for the two years prior to Mr. Mathisen's coming into possession of the ranch, and using this for a comparison with those grown since, we find that the average for the years 1913, 1914, and 1915 show an increase of over 80 per cent, while the crop for 1914 alone shows an increase of over 109 per cent, or a total for that particular year of 716,000 pounds of raisins.

As this vineyard was over twenty years old when it came into the possession of the present owner, the magnificent increase in products can be attributed to no other cause than expert management.

During the drying season it is a beautiful sight to look down the rows of Muscat vines, which are half a mile long and perfectly straight, and see the wonderful crop as it lies out on the trays to dry. Lined up between alternate rows of vines, the trays lie crowded against each other. At frequent intervals, it is necessary that an extra row of trays be pressed into service. Those fancy clusters which add so much to the beauty of a tray of raisins are everywhere in evidence and a heavy per cent of the crop runs to this grade.

When the present owner took possession of this property he secured the services of Arthur D. Long as foreman. Mr. Long, whose home had been in the Reedley district since childhood, was thoroughly familiar with all details of orchard and vineyard work, and Mr. Mathisen attributes much of his success to the judgment and counsel of this gentleman.

Basing his judgment on the adaptability of the soil, Mr. Mathisen made the statement, shortly after purchasing this ranch, that he believed it possible to materially increase the product of the vineyard. Local vineyardists, however, were rather skeptical along this line. Not being content without giving his vines the very best opportunity possible, the effort was made and the record as given above has settled the question.

The success which attended the efforts put forth at the Breidablik vineyard is ample proof of the wonderful possibilities of many another tract of land in Central California. If their owners would make a thorough and systematic study of all the conditions and environments and supply the methods which might be found best adapted to the needs of each particular case, no doubt many results would be reported from time to time similar to those secured at the Breidablik vineyard.

Chapter 6

John C. McCubbin

Autobiography of John C. McCubbin

{*This version of McCubbin's autobiography has been edited to include material from several of his additional autobiographical articles.*}

I was born in Hancock County, Illinois, on September 4, 1863. My birth was sandwiched in between a brother who was eighteen months older, and twin sisters who were fourteen months younger. There were four babies in the family and the older one only thirty-two months old.

My father, Thomas B. McCubbin, and my mother, Martha McCubbin, nee Cameron, were born within two and a half miles of where I was born and raised. My grandfather, Joseph McCubbin, and wife Ellen McCubbin, nee Lipsey, and their family, moved from Green County, Kentucky, in 1834 and established their home in the eastern part of Hancock County.

John Lipsey, father-in-law of Joseph McCubbin, was making his home with the McCubbin family when they moved north. Lipsey was a native of Ireland, and served in the Revolutionary War. He lost a leg in that struggle for liberty, yet lived to be 103 years old. He died in Hancock County and is buried in the Belknap Cemetery. A bronze tablet on the walls of the Carthage court house is inscribed with the names of four veterans of the Revolutionary War buried in the county. John Lipsey is included.

In 1831, prior to Joseph McCubbin coming to Hancock County, a party headed by Pleasant McCubbin, a brother of Joseph, had come to that same locality and established homes. In that pioneer group were the following: Pleasant and Matilda Rupe McCubbin, William and Eleanor McCubbin Rupe, Levi and Barbara Winn Bloyd, and a few others. Pleasant McCubbin and Eleanor McCubbin Rupe were brother and sister, and William Rupe and Matilda Rupe McCubbin were brother and sister.

My grandfather, John Cameron, and wife Elizabeth Lee Cameron, moved from White County, Tennessee, in 1832 and established their pioneer home two and a half miles north of where the McCubbin-Bloyd settlement had been made. The McCubbin-Bloyd settlement was the first one in that part of the county, and it was two years before the county seat was established at Carthage. The Camerons came one year before Carthage was established.

An Indian scare caused the McCubbin-Bloyd settlement to be depopulated a few months after their arrival. They hurried to Beardstown, fifty miles to the east, where they remained until the scare was over.

My Schooling

Until I was eighteen, my schooling had been limited to attending an ungraded rural school four to five months each winter. In November 1881, I enrolled in the Northern Indiana Normal School and Business Institute in Valparaiso. This

The T.B. McCubbin family photographed in Selma in November 1889. L. to R., Rue McCubbin Zimmerman, Thomas Benton McCubbin, John Cameron McCubbin, Martha Cameron McCubbin, Dove McCubbin Bennett. Photograph by H. P. Gay.

school is now Valparaiso University. After two short winter terms my father took the "California Fever" and dumped the farm on my hands and moved to California. That ended my schooling and spoiled my hopes of a civil engineering course. My brother-in-law, Robert E. Zimmerman, and I farmed the land until 1885 when my father returned from California and sold the farm. We then all came to California.

[In a 1934 letter to Catherine Corboy, Secretary of the Valparaiso University Alumni Association, McCubbin writes an interesting description of his arrival at "Valpo." "Dear Miss Corboy: At the beginning of the fall term of 1881, a green country boy, who had just reached the age of eighteen, appeared on the scene at Valpo. His education consisted of what little knowledge he had acquired during the short four months annual winter terms in a small ungraded country school in Hancock County, Illinois. In imagination I now look back at that fellow and see my real self go by. As a 100 percent 'Moss Back' I made a very 'attractive' exhibit, thereby gaining the attention of other students. Of this I was fully aware, to my great discomfort . . . ."]

My Arrival in California

In April 1885, I landed at Red Bluff, Tehama County, California, where I lived until August 1886, when I moved to Traver, Tulare County. While in Traver I first conducted a paint shop. After a few months I was compelled to discontinue the painting business on account of paint poisoning. For the next few months I was employed in the local lumber yard.

I then accepted employment with the 76 Land and Water Company. I was soon promoted to the superintendent's department where I was given charge of the lands during the grain season, while Joseph Peacock, the Superintendent, concentrated his efforts on the canals and water system. The 20,000 acres of land with its numerous tenants gave me plenty to do when harvesting was in full blast. During the rest of the year I was in the office assisting the secretary.

While I was a resident of Traver, the town reached its peak of prosperity, and began its fatal decline. The population was at one time over 1,000 and in twenty years had declined until not over a half dozen families were there. But it has since staged a modest comeback. But no one who was there in 1887 is there today, nor are any of their descendants. Neither is there a vestige of a building of that period left except the old calaboose.

How I Chanced to Settle in Traver

Emerson Bloyd and his son Jefferson, and son-in-law A. E. McClanahan had

McCubbin's 1910 beeswax crop — over 1,000 pounds. Photograph taken by George Besaw at McCubbin's ranch one mile south of Reedley.

Believed to be McCubbin's honey house and apiary at his home one mile south of Reedley in 1901. McCubbin's horse, Buenos Ayres, is in the distance at the right.

ranches in the 76 Country. In 1885, they rented out their ranches and moved to Tehama County, where they rented some 2,000 acres and farmed it to wheat. My father, his brother, and I were living in Tehama County at the time. We knew the Bloyds as our families had been living as friends and neighbors since 1790. The Bloyds' very favorable description of the 76 Country prompted my father and I to drive down to Traver in a spring wagon. I remained, and later my father moved down to Traver where he purchased lots and built a house. The Bloyds all moved back to their Tulare County homes at the close of the harvest season in 1886.

The McCubbin Ranch

In March 1888, I purchased forty acres of land about seven miles to the north of Traver, which I improved. The famous McCubbin Gum Tree, which is the largest tree of its age in the world, is growing on that tract. This land had been owned by G. W. Barnes. Barnes had been the purchaser of the fourth water right sold by the 76 Company. I got that old original water right with the land. Now that same water system supplies water for 130,000 acres of land in Fresno and Tulare Counties.

Beekeeping

At the end of 1889, I resigned my position with the 76 Company and moved to Selma, Fresno County, and began my first work with bees, in partnership with my brother-in-law, Robert E. Zimmerman. At the end of the first year we dissolved the partnership and I continued the business alone. I have owned bees in the San Joaquin Valley continuously since this time, and longer than any other man did. I was never a big beekeeper, though, for my entire stock never reached 400 colonies.

My largest crop was produced in 1892, when I was producing comb honey. That crop was produced by one apiary of 206 colonies located about seven and a

REEDLEY LUMBER COMPANY

J. C. McCUBBIN, Agent.

BUILDING MATERIAL OF ALL KINDS

Doors, Window Screens, Blinds, Lime, Plaster and Cement.

Oregon Pine, Mountain Pine and Redwood Lumber.

Shingles, Shakes, Posts, Laths, Etc.
TELEPHONE, MAIN 211

Reedley, Fresno County, Cal., ... 190

J. C. McCUBBIN. F. S. KNAUER.

KNAUER & McCUBBIN

....Real Estate and Insurance....

IMPROVED AND UNIMPROVED LANDS FOR SALE IN TRACTS, FROM FIVE ACRES TO ONE THOUSAND, UNDER THE CHEAPEST IRRIGATION SYSTEM IN CALIFORNIA.

Reedley, Fresno Co., Cal. ....

J. C. McCUBBIN,
Practical Beekeeper,
REEDLEY, CAL.

Reedley, Fresno Co. Cal,, ..., 191.....

OFFICERS
PRESIDENT J. C. McCUBBIN
VICE-PRESIDENT ROBT. WATKINS
SECRETARY FRED K. HOWARD

Southern Valley Honey Producers' Co-Operative Exchange
OFFICE OF SECRETARY-MANAGER
HANFORD, CALIFORNIA

DIRECTORS
J. C. McCUBBIN, FRESNO
ROBT. WATKINS, SELMA
P. H. BALES, HANFORD
C. W. TOMPKINS, TULARE
FRED K. HOWARD, HANFORD

Letterheads from the McCubbin archive.

half miles southwest of Selma. The location was extra good, the season was a long one, and I had fed the bees over a ton of pure honey to get them in the very best condition before the regular honey flow started. My crop from that apiary, without moving, was 35,850 one-pound sections of honey. My card record kept on the rear of each hive showed the following at the end of the season: the prize colony filled 360 sections, the next best colony filled 324 sections, 22 other colonies filled from 250 to 300 sections each, 67 colonies filled between 200 and 250 sections each, and the entire apiary averaged 174 sections each.

For my honey exhibits on various occasions I have been awarded the following: a silver medal at the 1902 Pan American Exhibition at Buffalo, New York; a silver medal at the 1904 Louisiana Purchase World's Fair in St. Louis, Missouri; and two first prizes at the California State Fair. My float in the Raisin Day Parade in Fresno, in 1920, was awarded first prize. The float represented my copyrighted brand, "Unkist Honey."

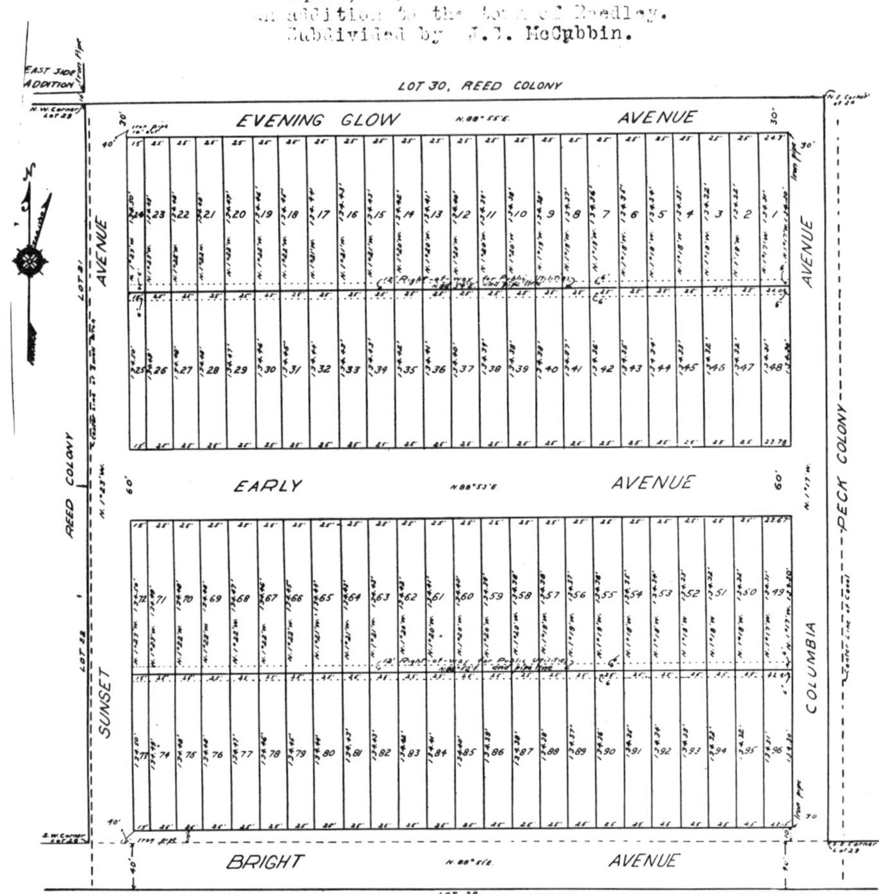

My interest in exhibiting had come from my experience in assisting the Fresno County Chamber of Commerce with their exhibit work. One year I installed and had charge of one of their citrus exhibits at the National Orange Show in San Bernardino, California.

McCubbin Colony

I bought 240 acres of land in the Windsor School District, Tulare County. After getting it all improved and set to alfalfa, I subdivided it and sold it in colony lots. It was called the McCubbin Colony. [The McCubbin Colony was in an "L" shape, north of the present Avenues 408 and 410, on both sides of Road 48.]

McCubbin Home and Morning Dawn

In December 1899 I bought a colony lot one mile south of Reedley where I made my home with my two children until 1918. In that year the property was sold and I moved to Fresno. In the spring of 1908 I planted the first Kadota fig tree in Fresno County. It still stands [1953] about thirty feet south of the southeast corner of the house. [This property was just northeast of the intersection of the present Frankwood and Floral Avenues. The old McCubbin home is still standing at that intersection.]

In addition to my colony lot home south of Reedley, I purchased a ten-acre tract just east of the town of Reedley, which I subdivided and sold in town lots. I named the tract "Morning Dawn," and put the lots on the market in 1920. The avenues I named as follows: Bright, Early, Sunrise, Sunset, and Evening Glow. [The subdivision, recorded on April 5, 1920, was bounded by Evening Glow Avenue on the north, Bright (now Duff) Avenue on the south, Sunset Avenue on the west, and Sunrise (recorded as Columbia) Avenue on the east. Running parallel to and between Evening Glow and Bright was Early Avenue.]

McCubbin in 1908. He wrote that he "had endeavored to grow an H. B. Brown moustache, but it would persist in adopting the 'wild west' style. Perhaps that was the result of the environment, and acquired while a resident of the 'wild and woolly' town of Traver."

My Family

On November 2, 1892, I married Miss Lucy Marie Terry, a school teacher living in Selma. She was born December 14, 1866, near West Fairlee, Orange County, Vermont. When six years old, she moved with her parents to Sheldon, O'Brien County, in northwest Iowa. Lucy lost her mother when she was eleven years old. Her father remarried, and when Lucy was about sixteen the family moved to Mt. Pleasant, Iowa.

Returning to O'Brien County about 1884, Lucy taught a term of school in that county. She moved with the family to Kingsburg, California, about 1886, and in the following year they moved to Selma.

During the winter of 1890-91, Lucy resumed her studies, taking those additional subjects necessary to prepare her for a teachers' examination in Tulare County. This she took and making the required grades, secured a school at

Monson, where she taught during the winter of 1891-92.

Lucy and I lived in Selma from our marriage until April 1895, when we moved to a twenty-acre tract of land three miles west of Dinuba, Tulare County. We had two children, Bruce, who was born August 3, 1894, in Selma, and Grace, who was born December 9, 1895, on the ranch were the McCubbin gum tree is growing.

Lucy passed away on December 16, 1895, when Grace was one week old. I rented the place out and boarded with the family, keeping Bruce with me. I hired different ones to take care of Grace until she was nearly three years old. I then batched it and raised the two children on my own. [In 1908, McCubbin married Lottie L. Rose, a widow from Dinuba, but they separated after three years.]

Bruce McCubbin

Bruce enrolled in the Fresno Junior College during its first and second terms. It was the first junior college in the United States. Bruce also attended the University of California, Berkeley, for one year.

When the United States declared war on Germany, Bruce resigned his position with the Union Oil Company and volunteered. He spent two and a half years in the Armed Forces, eighteen months of which were spent overseas. He was gassed at the battle Chatteau Thierry, and spent a month in the hospital while he was recovering from mustard gas burns. Back to his outfit he was in the thick of the fighting until the Armistice was signed. He then went on into Germany and was with the Army of Occupation until his outfit was sent home.

After his discharge from the Army he took a course in Expert Accounting at Woodbury College in Los Angeles, and is now a certified accountant with a good position with the Internal Revenue Department Income Tax Unit.

Bruce married Miss Margaret MacGilivray of Fresno. She came with her folks from Scotland to Fresno when she was nine years old. Bruce and Margaret were in Honolulu, Territory of Hawaii, for four years beginning in December 1938. They have one child, John Duncan McCubbin, who was born while they were in Honolulu. They lived within two and a half miles of Pearl Harbor when the Japanese made their raid on December 7, 1941. Margaret heard the shooting but didn't know what it was until it was all over. Bruce was in Maui at the time on business.

On September 4, 1943, when the Honorable James E. Murray, Senator from Montana, and co-author of the Murray-Patman small business act, came to Fresno to participate in the presentation ceremony when the Army-Navy "E" penant was awarded to the Central California War Industries, Inc., Mrs. Margaret McCubbin, Bruce's wife, was chosen to make the response for 600 employees. She was the Assistant Secretary of the corporation. The officers stated that this Fresno organization had, by delivering its war products in quantity and on time, been an outstanding one in America. That ceremony was broadcast over one of the Pacific Coast radio networks.

Grace McCubbin Cheatham

My daughter, Mrs. Grace McCubbin Cheatham, is a graduate of Domestic Science from the Lux School in San Francisco. She married Heath Spooner in 1917, and they had one child, Terry. Terry enlisted in the Navy about nine months before the Pearl Harbor raid. He was a seaman on the ill-fated *Neches,* that was torpedoed by the Japanese about a month after the Pearl Harbor raid. Fifty-six of the sailors, who were asleep at the time, were killed instantly. Terry was among the victims. The ship went down in about an hour and a quarter taking all the bodies with it.

Grace divorced Spooner and a few years later married Gilbert Cheatham. They own their own home and mattress shop on Del Mar, in San Gabriel, California.

Masonic Record

I was made a Master Mason in the Traver Lodge, U.D., in Traver, on November 17, 1888. I was its first candidate, and have been a Mason sixty-four years [as of 1953]. In 1891 I demitted from Traver Lodge, No. 294, and affiliated with Selma Lodge, No. 277. In 1901 I demitted from the Selma Lodge and affiliated with Reedley Lodge, No. 304. In 1921 I demitted from the Reedley Lodge and affiliated with Traver Lodge. This lodge had been moved from Traver to Kingsburg, located seven miles to the northwest of Traver. The lodge retained its old original name.

In November 1938, I was presented with the Masonic Veterans button. I have served in the various capacities as follows: Stewart, Senior Deacon, Secretary, Chaplain, Trustee, Junior and Senior Warden. I have never taken any of the higher degrees. My request is for a Masonic funeral, and that the casket shall not be opened for inspection by the public.

Writes Local History

I am an active member of three historical societies, one of which is the California State Historical Association. I was appointed the special representative of this association at one of the annual fiestas at the old San Gabriel Mission. [McCubbin was a charter member of the Fresno County Historical Society and its first life member. In 1922 he directed the work establishing the Society's first museum, then located at Fresno State College.]

Since 1886, I have been compiling history of the people and places in Tulare and Fresno Counties. This history has been gathered from reliable sources. I have gone to distant portions of the state to contact people who had reliable information about early day people and activities of that locality. Notes were jotted down directly from their statements. I kept a diary for twenty-five years in that locality. I also was assistant superintendent of the 76 Company, which gave me an exceptional opportunity for compiling historical data.

I have also compiled numerous historical sketches for the Hancock County, Illinois, Historical Society.

THE FRESNO BEE, TUESDAY, MAY 26, 1925.

WITH THE HISTORICAL SOCIETY :-: :-: By Buel

Illustration from the May 26, 1925, edition of The Fresno Bee *featuring members of the Fresno County Historical Society's history committee. McCubbin is shown penning "cold facts." Ironically, it is not a fact, cold or otherwise, that McCubbin was conductor of Millerton's first street car.*

Other Activities

My tabulated record shows that during the first World War, I wrote over 400 personal letters to those in our Armed Forces. During the last World War, I wrote 385 communications to our servicemen.

Since 1919 I have specialized in giving cheer and comfort to the handicapped, including the T.B. patients, the blind and other shut-ins.

To Los Angeles

I lived in Fresno County until September 20, 1928, when I moved to Los Angeles County, where I have since resided. [McCubbin died in 1957 in Los Angeles at the Hollenbeck Home for retired persons. He had lived there for many years. His sister, Rue McCubbin Zimmerman, and her husband Robert E. Zimmerman, were also residents of the Hollenbeck Home.]

A Chain of Misfortunes

The scenes described in this sketch were laid in the San Joaquin Valley, California.

On December 9, 1895, not long after our little twenty-acre farm had been cleared of its mortgage and a little five-room cottage completed, a lovely little girl was born into the family. This child was the realization of the fondest hopes of her parents, for we had a little boy nearly eighteen months old, and this little girl seemed to complete the family circle. Under such circumstances we naturally looked forward to the approaching holidays expecting them to usher in for us a full measure of Christmas cheer and New Year happiness, but from the story below it will be seen that a cruel Fate decreed otherwise.

The mother was apparently getting along all right at first, but soon developed unfavorable symptoms, and when the baby was three days old these symptoms became alarming. There were no rural telephones at that time, and I hastened off with horse and buggy, after the doctor. I drove out into an unusually heavy fog that was hurrying the close of a gloomy day on into a cheerless night of inky blackness.

This was during the pioneer period in that locality when the houses were few and far between. As I was hurrying along in utter darkness over a lonely road, I was suddenly startled by the voice of a man on horseback, and who, pretending to have lost his way in the darkness, inquired what road he was on. As I proceeded to impart the information, another man also on horseback immediately appeared from behind me. As the two closed in on me I realized that I was at the mercy of two highwaymen who had me covered with their menacing guns.

The men soon learned that they had made a mistake in the darkness, and from the few words that passed between them, I knew that their intended victim was the collector of the irrigation district! They accordingly ordered me to move on.

The official mentioned had been collecting taxes at a small town, and as he afterwards told me, had finished his work on that day, though he had to work late. There being no bank at the place, it was necessary for him to take the money to his home town. It was his custom to travel the road past my place, but on this particular occasion he had fortunately taken another road, and thereby escaped the trap laid for him, but which caught me instead.

Four days after the above experience, the soul of that wife and mother winged its flight to a better world.

During the week of my wife's fatal illness, I hired a neighbor to haul a portion of my comb honey crop to the railroad station where the bee men were grouping a car load of honey to be consigned to a commission house in Kansas City, Missouri. Financial conditions were such at that time that it was impossible to sell our crops for cash.

When the car was loaded, the honey was weighed in by a man who was also contributing a portion of the shipment, as well as acting as local agent for the commission house. This weigher's reputation for honesty was anything but complimentary.

Imagine my surprise on receiving the report from the commission house, accompanied by a small advance, to find that my statement, instead of showing 144 cases of comb honey as it should, was quite a number of cases short. My suspicions, which were shared by some of the others who were interested in the shipment, were directed toward that weigher. Our theory was that he had entered the cases that were missing from my lot on his own tally sheet. This he could have easily done, while I was not there to watch him. He knew that my wife was at the point of death, and there was no danger of my dropping in on him. When I learned of the shortage, it was too late to do anything about it, for the honey was then in Kansas City, and the advances already made to the various parties interested in the shipment.

To this chain of misfortunes there was still another one to be added. The commission house to which the honey had been consigned soon went into the hands of a receiver, and the small advance mentioned was all I ever got out of that lot of honey. It was an unusually fine lot, and the cream of my crop for that year. All of it graded "Fancy" and "No. 1".

That our suspicions of the man who weighed our honey in were well founded has since been proven. He afterwards got into a "jam" for adulterating honey and was justly punished for the act. He and his brother are now in the Federal prison at McNeils Island, where they are serving a sentence for counterfeiting.

This succession of calamities, coming as they did, at a time when we were passing through a serious financial depression, were a severe blow. But, I had good health, and with the inspiration of my children, I redoubled my efforts and carried on.

After the death of my wife, I always kept the little boy with me, but had to hire the little girl kept until she was nearly three years old. I then rented my ranch and bees out and moved to town. By batching and exercising strict economy, I was able to raise the children without the aid of a dollar from any one.

Both children being healthy and intelligent, it was but natural that an occasional childless couple should long to have one or both of them for their very own. On one occasion a wealthy but childless couple, who had become attached to the little boy, decided between themselves that they would make special overtures for him. They called to see me, and while the lady had the little fellow on her lap and they were having a jolly time together, the gentleman broached the subject. He promised to furnish me with all the bond or security that I might require, that the boy should have $20,000 when he reached the age of twenty-one, if I would let them adopt him. The cash had just been deposited in the bank. My reply was that I might not have $20 for him when he was twenty-one, but twenty million dollars would be no temptation to me. I then added that the boy's mother had given her life for his little sister and that under no circumstances would I part with either one of them.

The scene that followed that conversation was pathetic. The good lady, being

Grace McCubbin at eleven years of age, 1907.

unable to control her emotions, hugged that little motherless child more closely to her bosom as the tears coursed down her cheeks.

My little girl had unusually long and beautiful hair. When she was eleven years old it hung clear down to her knees, and it had nothing of a "stringy" nature about it, but retained its full volume almost its entire length. The wonderful head of hair was partly due to the constant care I always gave it. It was never "doped" or treated with a hair preparation of any kind.

To partially relieve this sketch of its somber hue, I will quote from a dialogue that passed between my two children when the little boy was four years old. We were riding by an alfalfa pasture where a dairy herd of beautiful Holstein cattle were grazing. The little boy, who was acting as spieler for his little sister, said: "Grace, do you see that big spotted cow over yonder?" To which she replied in the affirmative. He then said, "Well, she's a bull."

Historical Items on the McCubbin Eucalyptus Ranch

The last homestead cabin in the Alta Irrigation District was on my ranch. The

Old homestead cabin on McCubbin's ranch, looking southwest. Photograph taken in 1900 by John H. Martin. The two trees on the left are Black Mission figs, the tree on the right is a Poplar, and alfalfa is in the foreground.

cabin was built by Samuel F. Edwards, in 1877, when he filed a Preemption Claim on 160 acres described as the northeast quarter of Section 22, Township 16 South, Range 23 East [this property, located in Tulare County, is bounded by Avenue 408 on the north, Road 56 on the east, and on the south and west by the line of extension of Avenue 404 and Road 52.] A patent was issued to Edwards on September 9, 1878, and signed by Rutherford B. Hayes, President of the United States.

Edwards sold the 160 acres to G. W. Barnes, M.D., who in turn sold the forty acres where the homestead cabin was located to me in March 1888. That forty acres was described as the northwest quarter of the northeast quarter of Section 22, Township 16 South, Range 23 East [the northwest corner of the McCubbin forty acres was at the intersection of Road 52 and Avenue 408]. The McCubbin Gum Tree was planted near the north line of this tract, and about one-eighth of a mile from the old cabin. They were both at the exact same distance from the canal on the west side of the tract [east of the canal].

The fourth water right sale ever made by the 76 Land and Water Company was made to G. W. Barnes on November 1, 1884. The old water right was turned over to me when I purchased the forty acres of land. That same water right system now covers 130,000 acres of land. The system now belongs to the Alta Irrigation District.

When I purchased this land there was nothing in the way of a residence between that old cabin and the T. L. Reed home, six miles to the north. Nor was there a sign of a railroad or habitation where the town of Reedley is now located.

They were, however, starting to work on the railroad.

In 1903, that old homestead cabin with its 12 foot by 12 foot addition on its west side was moved one-half mile to the west, and relocated on the elevation in the southwest corner of Section 15 [the northeast corner of Road 48 and Avenue 408] where I then owned 200 acres of land that I had subdivided and named the McCubbin Colony.

I sold the forty acres on which the cabin stood to Carl Carlson, who later sold it to his son Elmer Carlson. In 1948 Elmer Carlson tore the old homestead cabin down and used up the old rough lumber. Thus ended the last of the old 76 Country homesteader cabins.

The John Rordon Ostrich

In 1920, the Chamber of Commerce of Selma presented the Roeding Park, in Fresno, with an ostrich. The park commissioners named the bird, "John Rordon" in honor of a leading citizen of Selma.

Three months later, "John Rordon" laid an egg.

A humorous column, in a Scotch dialect, was running in the *Fresno Republican* at the time over the name of "Scotty." That columnist scathingly criticized the park commissioners concerning their ignorance on the sex of birds, especially those of ostriches.

Close on the heels of the above incident, the American Legion held their 1920 Armistice Day celebration in Reedley. For the comic section of their parade, I made a life-sized ostrich, with a "John Rordon" sign hanging on each side and had an egg suspended beneath the beak. I was awarded first prize on my make-up.

McCubbin dressed as the John Rordon ostrich, Reedley Armistice Day Parade, 1920. Photograph by Robert A. Parker.

Friends complimented me for being able to so successfully hide my homely face and body. But, they contended that I should have also obscured my ungainly legs and big feet.

Some of My Current Activities

Thinking you might be interested in knowing how an eighty-eight year old man can occupy his time to advantage, let me mention some of my special activities [written January 15, 1952].

Eight days a month I go and help three separate groups of blind folks with their activities. Each Monday, I take my own lunch and attend what we call the Recreation Center. This is a branch of the Braille Institute of America. They have eight separate classes. Among them are the following: Handicrafts, Current Events, Choral Singing, Braille, Long-hand Writing, Dancing, Creative Writing, Sewing, Knitting, Conversational Spanish, Cooking, and Dramatics.

At the Recreation Center, the helpers' duties include meeting at the curb when the drivers land with them, then taking each one to the desired class. Then at the end of each hour, to move each one to the next class, if in a different room of the building.

At noon all have to be taken to the dining room where they eat their lunch which they have brought with them, except the coffee or milk, which is furnished free by the Institute. After lunch they are taken anywhere they desire, outside for a smoke, or for a walk, etc.

At one o'clock they are taken back to the class of their choice. At two o'clock another change of classes is made. Then at three o'clock the day's activities close, and as their drivers come for them, they are assisted to board the individual cars and station wagons and are returned to their homes.

For the 200 blind folks who attend the Recreation Center, there is plenty of work for the helpers, especially when they are changed to various classrooms or in getting them to their seats in the dining room.

There are many lady helpers who furnish their own gas and oil to bring a load of the blind folks to the Recreation Center, then help during the day, then take them back to their homes — all free of charge.

Another, though smaller group, spends each alternate Tuesday at the Thursday Evening Club house in Glendale. I also attend that class and help.

There is still another group of blind folks who spend each Thursday at the Normandy Club house in Los Angeles, where the day is spent very much as at the other two places mentioned.

The Braille Institute hires a few special teachers who are on a salary, but all of the regular helpers do their work free and bring their own lunch.

Various movie stars from Hollywood come and entertain these blind folks free. It is all informal, so they can ask questions at any point they want to and always get a pleasant answer.

In the Creative Writing class there are about fifty blind people, and among them are several who are above the ordinary good writers. Three members have sold some of their productions recently, to such publications as *The Saturday Evening Post* and the *Christian Science Monitor.* Some of the very best writers of poetry and prose come and entertain the members of the Creative Writing class, giving informal talks and reading portions of their books.

From the sports world, Man Mountain Dean and Strangler Lewis came and entertained these blind folks. Man Mountain Dean walked up and down the rows of seats where they could run their hands over him and feel what a "mountain" he really was. When he passed me I went over him also. He was wearing a very fine Shriner's button, and we talked Masonry for a minute. During the address of Man Mountain Dean, he learned that one of the blind colored ladies in the class was a daughter of his old Negro Mammy when he was a small child in Georgia.

In addition to my work with the blind folks, for about three years I had the privilege of visiting the T. B. patients at the Olive View Sanatorium in San Fernando Valley. Every two weeks I would go up there with a neighbor lady whose husband was a surgery patient in that sanatorium. There are about 1,200 patients in the Olive View Sanatorium and about that many more in smaller outside hospitals.

I never went up to Olive View Sanatorium empty handed, but always took some modest present to each of the thirty-two patients in some particular ward. It isn't convenient for me to get up there from here [Hollenbeck Home], but I occasionally send them presents and write them frequently. I am already preparing for the coming Valentine's Day.

If those elderly people who are "doing nothing, and as little of that as possible" know the real satisfaction that comes to one who is bringing cheer and comfort to the handicapped, they would look around them and see that there are many lines of activity in which their time could be well spent.

Post Script

In describing this work of bringing cheer and comfort to the handicapped, there is no thought of boasting. I am doing nothing except what is my simple duty. No one should be given a word of praise for doing their duty, under any conditions at any time.

Too many people wait until such activity becomes popular before they will engage in it. This work is not yet popular. I am the only man who attends especially to help. Another man brings a blind wife and then helps throughout the day.

The McCubbin Gum Tree

{*One of John McCubbin's greatest joys was his eucalyptus tree. Planted as a seedling on his ranch in 1889, the tree grew to a tremendous size and became a local landmark. Over the years the tree was featured in many newspaper and magazine articles — most of these articles written by McCubbin himself. McCubbin clearly enjoyed the recognition that came from being the grower of this notable tree.*

In 1962, five years after McCubbin's death, a large limb broke off the tree and fell to the ground. A subsequent inspection of the tree by park officials of Tulare County, which had assumed responsibility for its care when the land was sold three years earlier, revealed that the tree had dry rot. Having determined that the eucalyptus could not be saved, and judging it to be a hazard to visitors and passing traffic so long as it stood, the county felled the tree. After a lifetime spent working to preserve the landmarks and history of the area, it seems a perverse irony that a landmark of McCubbin's own creation should itself pass from the landscape.

McCubbin wrote the following sketch for the trade journal, Bees and Honey. *It was published in their June 1937, issue.*}

The giant Eucalyptus, growing three miles west of Dinuba, Tulare County, California, known as the "McCubbin Gum Tree," is supposed to be the largest tree of its age and kind in the world. It was planted in April 1889, and was then a small and insignificant plant, but measurements taken of it in April this year, at forty-eight years of age, showed the following gigantic proportions: Diameter at the ground, 11 feet and 7 inches. Diameter 4½ feet above the ground, 7 feet and 1 inch. It is 131 feet tall and has a bough-spread of 123 feet.

The tree belongs to that branch of the gum tree family known as Eucalyptus Viminalis, popularly called Manna Gum. A peculiar substance that exudes from the bark at certain times of the year and collects in small chunks, is supposed to resemble the manna mentioned in the Bible, hence the name.

The world renowned Luther Burbank expressed himself regarding this tree in the following words of praise:

Santa Rosa, California, April 13, 1906.

Mr. J. C. McCubbin, Reedley, California

Dear Sir: The fine picture of the most magnificent of all gum trees I have ever seen, received. I thank you heartily for this privilege. I hope, above all things, that this tree bears seed, so it may be duplicated all over California. Its seedlings will probably keep up the record of the parent tree if placed under similar circumstances.

Very truly yours, (signed) Luther Burbank.

McCubbin with children, Grace and Bruce, at the gum tree in 1900. Horse is Buenos Ayres. The gum tree was located on Avenue 408, on the south side of the road and just east of the canal running parallel to Road 52.

At the time of his death, Burbank was growing some trees from the seed of this tree.

The ground where this tree was planted was a little lower than desired, and the surface was brought up to the required elevation by the addition of a layer of about eight or ten inches of highly fertilized soil from an old sheep corral that had been located near by. Since it was planted, however, not one ounce of fertilizer has been added to the soil.

Apparently the tree reached its maximum height and outer branch contour several years ago, but the graph shows that the trunk has continued its wonderful growth at a fairly regular rate.

Standing out alone, it has always had the maximum amount of light and air privileges, and taking advantage of these conditions, its great branches have reached out farther and farther until they have attained the extensive spread of bough of 123 feet mentioned above.

While still in the nursery box, this tree suffered an injury which was inflicted under rather peculiar circumstances, but what was considered a serious injury at that time might have resulted in giving the little plant an extra good start. The 20-inch square box, containing 100 small trees, had been brought from what is now the ghost town of Traver by a neighbor, and placed in one corner of his barn, where it remained the following day. I went over at night, and groping around in the dark located the box, placed it on my shoulder and carried it home.

At the end of the journey I learned, to my great surprise and utter indignation, that I had carried a hen's nest with a fresh laid egg in it, all the way home. An ambitious biddy while prowling around had entered my "miniature forest," and deciding that the center of it would be just the proper place to establish a new home, got busy at once and began a "clearing." She uprooted all the trees that would in any way interfere with her plans, and, in doing so, thrashed the tops out of many more. The "dead and wounded" numbered over fifty per cent of the entire lot. When I surveyed the damage that old hen had caused, I longed for the opportunity to wring her head off and see her worked up into "spring chicken." Strange to say, it was one of those topless victims that has furnished the material for this sketch.

I have long since forgiven that old hen and now feel very kindly toward her memory. Her act in topping that little plant no doubt caused it to branch out lower down than it otherwise would, and thereby throw extra growth into the trunk.

To realize the immense ground girth of this tree, imagine a circle equal to it in size drawn upon the floor of a room twelve feet square. That circle would leave a space of less than three inches between it and each wall of the room.

One of the special 400-page Christmas editions of the *Timberman,* an international lumberman's journal, published in Portland, Oregon, contained an illustrated sketch, together with a graph showing the annual increase in girth of this tree, as a feature. In acknowledging receipt of the manuscript, the editor said, among other things:

McCubbin Gum Tree in 1904 at fifteen years of age.

McCubbin, daughter Grace and grandson Terry Spooner, at the gum tree in 1926.

> We consider this one of the most interesting contributions of its kind that we have ever had the pleasure to receive, and feel sure that our readers will be equally as interested in the account of this tree as we have been in reviewing the manuscript.

Several magazines have honored this tree by running its picture on their outside front cover page.

The Brooklyn Botanical Gardens of Brooklyn, New York, are using lantern slides showing views of this tree in their educational lectures.

Data covering the annual girth measurements of this tree, which are reported regularly, are kept on file in the three following places: the Forestry Service, Washington, D. C.; the California State Board of Forestry, Sacramento; and the Division of Forestry, University of California, Berkeley. These data are claimed to be the most complete of their kind in existence.

Inquiries addressed to each of the above organizations, relative to the comparative size of trees on the basis of their ages, brought replies that this was largest tree of its age that they had any knowledge of.

The tract of land on which the McCubbin Gum Tree is growing was sold a few years ago, but a clause was inserted in the conveyance reserving the tree, consequently it still belongs to its original owner.

There is a large Eucalyptus tree growing on Robertson Boulevard in the city of Los Angeles that has been given some special boasting by the local papers. A writer in one paper stated: "It is not only the largest, but the finest specimen of the eucalypti family in California." And a writer in one of the other papers claimed, "It is the noblest tree in California." This latter statement ignores entirely our Redwoods, which every one knows, or should know, are the noblest trees in the world.

Before these extravagant statements concerning the Los Angeles gum tree become too "deeply rooted" in the minds of the public, I would like to correct them. The Los Angeles gum tree is a wonderful specimen, but when compared with the McCubbin Gum Tree, the claims made for it will not stand the test. Although the McCubbin Gum Tree is ten years younger than the Los Angeles tree, it overshadows the latter in all of its dimensions. It is not only larger in every way, but its foliage, which is the crowning glory of any tree, is far more dense and beautiful than that of the Los Angeles tree.

Consider the fact that the plant from which the McCubbin Gum Tree grew was so insignificant that it narrowly escaped the rubbish heap, and that it has never had any special care. Yet in spite of these handicaps it has made the most wonderful record for rapid growth of any tree in the world. In it we see a demonstration of the truth of those immortal words of Joyce Kilmer, in which he said, "Only God can make a tree."

With its clean, smooth, light grey bole, and thick, rich olive-green foliage, the McCubbin Gum Tree makes a beautiful picture. It stands stately and grand on the south side of the road and casts a deep shadow across the highway the entire day. Swaying gently in the breeze, its long, graceful branches apparently beckon the traveler to their enchanting environment.

Having planted this tree with his own hand when the district was in its transition from desert conditions, and watched it while it was making its unparalleled growth, it is only natural that an apparent personality on its part should cause its owner to experience a feeling similar to that prompted by the ties of consanguinity.

May this young giant with its commanding presence continue its marvelous growth and retain its majestic beauty and matchless grace unimpaired for generations to come. In summer may its cool, refreshing shade always be as inviting; and in winter may the soft, delicate tints of its foliage ever be a reminder of the "Tree of Life" and eternal spring.

[When the tree was cut down in 1962, it was estimated to have been 154 feet tall, and left a stump nine and half feet in diameter.]

McCubbin at the gum tree in 1952. Photograph by John Nurmi.

Pool's Ferry Park: A Potentiality

{For many years McCubbin lobbied for a state historic park at the site of Pool's Ferry. In the following article, McCubbin sets forth the particulars of his park proposal. The proposal is preceded by a letter he sent to friend and fellow historian, Oscar Noren, on March 20, 1948, hoping to gain support for his idea.}

Letter to Oscar Noren

Dear Oscar: Herewith you will find a few of my ideas on a state park at the old Pool's Ferry site on the Kings River, about two miles north of Reedley. I don't remember whether I ever talked this matter over with you or not, but it has been in my noodle for many years.

The attached proposal is a copy of one I am also sending to Dr. Wallace Smith [Professor of History at Fresno State College and authority on San Joaquin Valley history]. I would like to have you and he go over there some day for a picnic when you would have plenty of time to go over the tract and talk over the subject of a park at that place. I may have set my stakes rather high, but for a state park I think it should be large, for we can't tell what may be needed in the future. (Some expert landscape gardener could give you some good ideas on the subject of a park there.)

I was at the dedication of the Burris Park in Kings County and it is a fine little park. I have also visited the Mooney Grove Park [in Tulare County] repeatedly. Both of these parks put together would make a very small attraction as compared with the Pool's Ferry park that I have visualized. In fact, only the big city parks could compete with it when it comes to unique and rare attractions.

I have tried to forget all about this Pool's Ferry Park proposition, but it just will not stay in the background. Instead it persists in bobbing up in my mind, so I decided to "bore" you and Dr. Smith with my ideas. I can't get the thought out of my mind that it could be made a reality if the right leader could be contacted and the idea kept before the public and persistently agitated.

Hoping this finds you well and things moving good with you despite the dry season.

Sincerely, /s/ J. C. McCubbin

Pool's Ferry Park: A Potentiality

If a state park were developed at the old Pool's Ferry site on the Kings River along the line I have in mind, I believe it would prove to be the most unique, interesting and educational small park to be found anywhere.

This park would include the west half of Section 15 and all that portion of the east half of Section 16 lying east of the Kings River. All in Township 15 South, Range 23 East. It would cover about 340 acres.

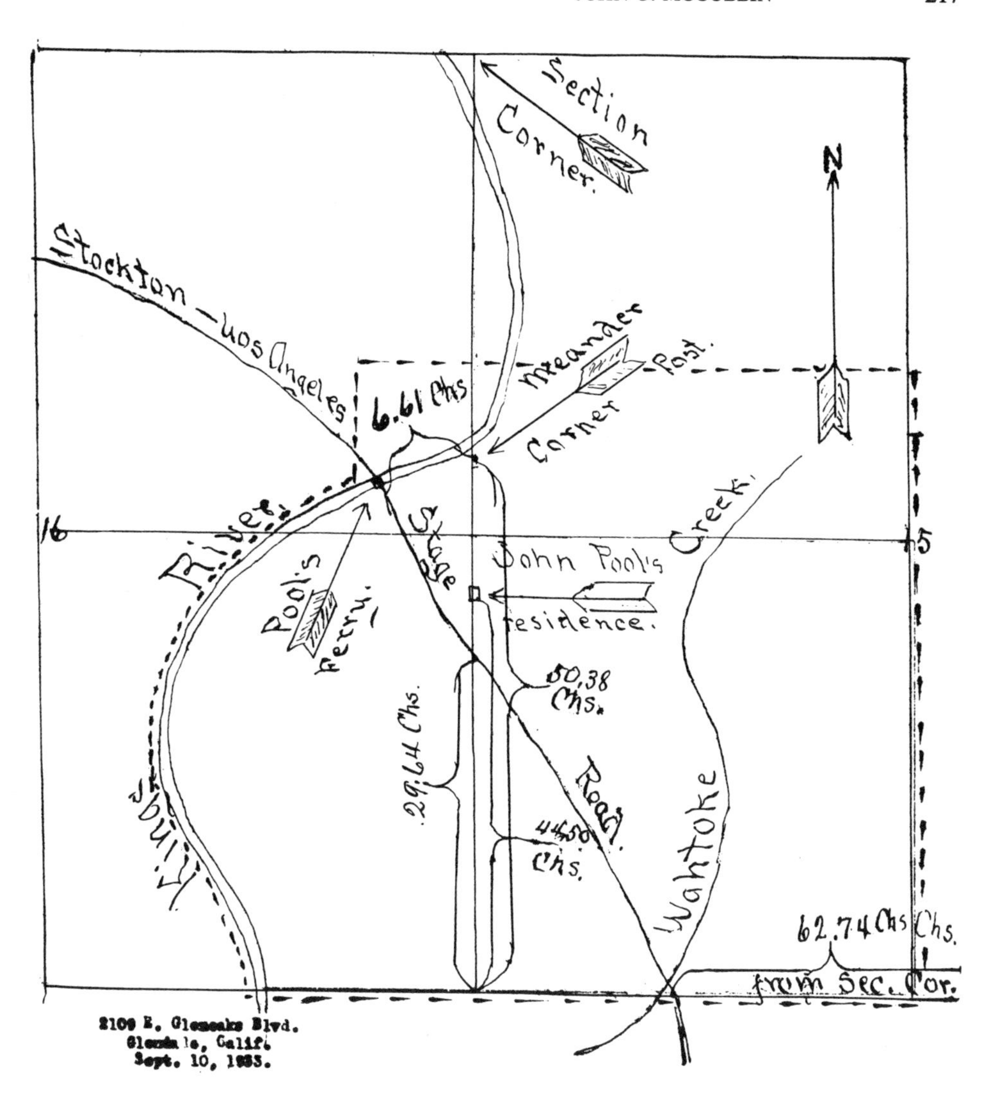

Map showing McCubbin's proposed Pool's Ferry Park. Broken line denotes area to be encompassed by park.

The topography includes a variety of surface conditions, ranging from the steep river bluff seventy feet high, to large level areas. The soil is very fertile and would lend itself to beautiful landscaping. The mile-long curve of the river that borders the tract is especially attractive for those who love boating and bathing.

The tract is now held by several different owners, all moderate in size with one exception. The exception is a rather large portion which is held by the D. N. Hershey estate. It has been in that family since the early eighties.

The historical points include the old Pool's Ferry site, and the Pool residence site. The Stockton-Los Angeles Stage Road crossed the tract from north to south. These three landmarks have been definitely located by this writer.

Pool's ferry was perhaps the first one ever operated on the Kings River. This was one of the two voting places used when Tulare County was organized in

1852. The other one being under the Charter Oak tree near St. Johns River. [See editor's note about ferry location in "Pool's Ferry."]

The large, high, level portion extending back from the river bluff on the north commands a magnificent view. From this portion the land slopes in three directions, affording excellent drainage. Over the broad neck at the northeast, gravity water could be brought in for irrigation.

The development of this park would offer almost unlimited possibilities for landscaping, including Wahtoke Creek that winds through the tract. Among the many attractions that could be developed, I'll mention only a few.

Prepare a road over the old stage road bed. Build a ferry boat patterned after the size and design of those used when Pool's was in operation. Equip it fully for operation. If necessary, build a low dam of sufficient height to afford plenty of water to accommodate the boat during low water periods.

Acquire rights-of-way from the ferry landing on the opposite side of the river over the old stage road bed to the first county highway.

Develop a vast subterranean "garden" using the hardpan for the roof. A street should run from north to south entirely through this garden to afford good ventilation. Concessions of all kinds could be located along this street.

Early day mining operations should be a demonstration, showing the use of the pan, rocker and long tom [a form of trough or sluice box used for washing gold bearing dirt]. Hydraulic could be exhibited by illustration. The mining tunnel would be a lateral with a shaft connecting it with the surface. Install an arrastra [a crude ore-crushing machine in which a horse or mule-drawn boulder would be dragged around a granite sink filled with gold ore].

There should be a Chinese restaurant with all persons connected with it in Chinese costumes of that period, including yellow and green smocks, loose flowing trousers, cloth shoes, silk coats with buttons on the top, and of course, the customary queue. Underneath this restaurant should be installed an opium den, with all the equipment, except the opium. Perhaps a substitute could be found that could be roasted over the spirit lamp that would resemble the raw, brown opium. A Chinese orchestra of that period could furnish music for the patrons of the restaurant.

Outside, and along the old stage road, could be provided a Chinese with his bamboo pole and burden baskets suspended from either end of the pole, in which all his earthly effects would be transported. With his burden he could take up the regular day trot, his step to be exactly synchronized with the spring of the pole.

Oscar Noren could furnish a group of real Indians who would demonstrate the acorn cache, the grinding of acorns in the stone mortar, and the preparing of the acorn bread. Baskets could be made — from the preparing of the material to the finished baskets. With their bows and arrows, teepees, blankets around their shoulders, papooses on their backs, etc., it would make an interesting exhibit.

A long team should be provided with not less than six animals, with all the old time equipment, including jerk line, fifth chain, stretcher, jockey stick, buck strap, etc. While the driver would ride on the wheel horse, his swamper could be along the string to make the animals jump over the chain when rounding the sharp curves, either to the right or left.

It would be very interesting, educational and convenient (if it were possible) to secure rights of way for a road to this park from the Smith's Ferry site on the east side of the Kings River. And from there over the bed of the old Stockton-Los Angeles stage road to the Pool's Ferry Park.

My first acquaintance with W. F. Chandler dates back to 1890. Long before he had made his big fortune in oil, or had entered politics, and elected State Senator, this Pool's Ferry Park "bug" was in my noodle. I had succeeded in definitely locating that important landmark, and it made quite an impression on my mind. I rang Chandler up one day and told him I had something that I would like to take up with him for about twenty or thirty minutes whenever he could spare that much time. He replied that he would be home alone that evening, that his wife was spending her vacation in San Jose. He invited me to spend the evening with him at his home.

We had a good old time visit and covered many early day subjects. When I laid my park plan before him, he told me that while he was interested like myself in such old time matters, the Legislature was really behind the times on such subjects. He told me that he had in mind the idea of acquiring a tract of land where the worst "hog wallows" were located and purchasing the land and holding it in its natural state for future generations to observe, but the Legislature was not interested. We are well aware of the measley appropriation our Legislature grudgingly gives our California State Historical Association, while other states whose historical background is very limited in comparison with our own get liberal appropriations from their legislatures.

The ideas I have expressed on this Pool's Ferry Park question are of course only in the rough, but they will serve as a basis for further consideration. You will notice that I have stressed the idea of *demonstration,* for that is my idea of the real educational value of any exhibit.

If you will make a careful study of this particular tract, I think you will find that it possesses more natural facilities for the development of a unique and interesting park then any other place in the entire San Joaquin Valley.

I realize the immense job it would be to work up this park idea, and that lots of money would be required to execute such a broad plan, but I believe the results would be well worth it.

Unkist Honey

{*John McCubbin loved a good joke, a clever pun, and bringing smiles to the faces of his friends and acquaintances. In his own words, "The mirthfulness in my makeup was always difficult to restrain." On May 31, 1921, he copyrighted the "Unkist Honey" brand to which he refers in this article, but that is pretty much*

2—376

No. 22976

UNITED STATES OF AMERICA.

DEPARTMENT OF THE INTERIOR,

PATENT OFFICE.

To wit: BE IT REMEMBERED, That on the seventh day of September, Anno Domini 1920
JOHN C. McCUBBIN,
of
Fresno, California,
deposited in this office for registration a Label, of which the following is the title:

"UNKIST HONEY,"
(for Honey)

the right whereof he claims, in conformity with the laws of the United States relating to Copyrights.

IN TESTIMONY WHEREOF I have caused the seal of the United States Patent Office to be hereunto affixed this thirty-first day of May, nineteen hundred and twenty-one, and of the Independence of the United States the one hundred and forty-fifth.

Given under my hand in the District of Columbia.

The foregoing is a copy of the record, and attached hereto is a copy of said Label.

[signature]
Acting Commissioner of Patents.

McCubbin's "Unkist Hone copyright document.

the only thing that is serious about the following, which is otherwise pure, unadulterated McCubbin-created humor.}

To Whom It May Concern, Also to the Unconcerned.
Sit Up (or Down) and TAKE NOTICE.

This to certify that the undersigned, G. O. Tewitt & G. E. T. Busy, have engaged in a general bee and honey business and have employed B. O. Nedd, alias J. C. McCubbin, as business manager.

The manager claims to have produced a very superior grade of honey which has been carefully protected from contamination and is now securely packed, where it will remain absolutely pure and in perfect condition indefinitely. This grade is to be known as "Unkist Honey."

As there are brands of California products on the market which the packers admit have been kissed and rekissed by all the suns of the Universe, including those two well known parties the "son of a gun" and the "son of a sea cook," the designation, "Unkist Honey" will suggest at once, the exceptionally sweet, charming and attractive qualities of this brand of goods.

It is further claimed by the manager, that the free use of this article will not only cure love-sickness, but that it will level the head and set it in the right direction and fix the thoughts of the victim on a real "honey" regardless of race, color, creed, sex or previous condition of heart or appetite. There are exceptions however, and those are the cases which have developed to that stage which has been described by one authority as being "an outward all-over-ish-ness and an inward insensibility," and which the Irishman, in giving his own experience, said, "there was no takin' a wink of shlape for the pleasure of the pain."

That these goods might prove to be all the manager claims for them and to aid in their protection as above referred to, he has developed a very efficient and pains-taking (as well as pains-giving) strain of bees. A home guard, composed entirely of volunteers from this strain, has been organized and thoroughly drilled for service. Their special duty (and apparent pleasure) is to remain on the *firing* line and keep things *hot.*

Woe be unto any "kissing bug" in
shape of
shiftless
shark or
shabby
shyster who
shall,
shoeless or without a
shield,
show his

shallowness by
shyly entering the
shadow or
shade of the
shed of the
shack or
shanty
sheltering the honey outfit.
Sheepishly, as if
sharing the
chagrin of some
shame-faced
sheeny or a
shrunken,
shriveled,
shaggy
shoat being
shown at the
shambles, and with hopes
shattered, he
shall
surely
shorten his stay,
shift his position,
shirk the job,
shun the place and
shed
shreds of his
chambray
shirt on the
shrubbery as he
shuffles,
shambles and
shoves his way to the friendly
shade of some
sheltering
shield.

With a
shrug of the
shoulders, he
shall
shrink, as from the close
shave of a
short

shillalah,
shudder,
shake,
shiver and
shout with a
shrill
shriek of pain from the
shock, as he
sheers off and tries to
shield his
shanks and
shins from the
shots of the
sharp un-
sheathed
shafts of "those
shocking" but
shrewd offensive defenders.

The proprietors take great pleasure in stating that they have an unlimited *lack* of confidence in their business manager and cheerfully warn the public against any and all of his extravagant statements.

Reedley, California
June 12, 1917

/s/ G. O. Tewitt
/s/ G. E. T. Busy

The McCubbin Long, Long Letter and Short, Short Letter

{The alliterative Unkist Honey article was simply the first salvo from the McCubbin arsenal of humor. The second assault on the funny bones of his friends and acquaintances was to send them his "Long, Long Letter." The letter was custom printed for McCubbin, and when pasted together, measured 1 3/8 inches high and 15 feet long. This one-line letter was truly a long, long letter. There was a 2 inch by 9 1/2 inch envelope made especially for the letter. The author's return address was listed as being in California, which he of course noted was the longest state in the Union. As with his Unkist Honey brand, the "Long, Long Letter" was copyrighted.

The "Short, Short Letter," by contrast, received short shrift, for it was merely typed by McCubbin and pasted onto the "Long, Long Letter" as a post script.}

The McCubbin Long, Long Letter

Dear Friend: I am dropping you a long line in a long envelope. You may have long longed for longer letters of greeting than the ordinary ones. If so, it is hoped that this long letter is long enough to satisfy that longing, and that you may no longer long, very long along that line. This long letter is longer no doubt, than the longest one page one line letter you have received for a long time, and longer perhaps than the longest one of any kind you will get for a long time to come. Unlike the ordinary long letters, this one is not only long at both ends and in the middle, but it is long all the way through, for the word long in its various forms, occurs 59 times. The name Long belongs to Long, but he may not be long. Although his name is Long it is not long, for it contains only four letters. Even Short's name is one letter longer than the longest Long's name you ever saw. The name of the one who composed this long letter is not Long, but it is long, for it contains eight letters. Although long it is not so long as some long names, but it is twice as long as the longest Long's name you can find. His name is also a peculiar long name for it can be "doubled" twice without making it one letter longer. Just by spelling it as follows: M-double-c-u-double-b-i-n. The picture at the head of this long letter, shows its author's long mustache (10¼ inches long, from tip to tip), as it looked long, long ago. May this long letter bring a broad smile to your face, and keep it from becoming a "long face." May the list of your friends always be long, and your life long, that you may long enjoy them. These are only a few of the items on the long list of blessings I wish for you all along throughout the year. Especially during the long six months period when the days grow longer and longer, leading up to June 21, the longest day of the year.

Sincerely, /s/ J. C. McCubbin.

[McCubbin mentions a photograph at the head of the printed version of his letter showing him with his rather large mustache. In a note attached to the photograph, McCubbin writes: "A school marm was blamed for that horrid mustache. McCubbin claims that before this one was in evidence, that one of those charming creatures said to him, 'A kiss without a mustache is like an egg without salt. Rather flat.' Willing to please, he assured her he would grow a nice, cute, little mustache. He must have been over anxious to please and put too much emphasis into the effort, for the result was neither nice, cute, nor little. All of which reminds one of the old fellow always complaining of his health who would say he was 'powerful weak.' Judging by the mustache, McCubbin must have had a 'powerful weakness' for school marms."]

The McCubbin Short, Short Letter

The names of Short and Long were misfits. Short was a long man, while Long was a short man.

Although Short's name was Short, it was not short, for Long's name was one letter shorter than the shortest Short's name you ever saw.

Short's wife was short, and her maiden nickname, "Shortie," was changed to

"Shortie Short" after she married Short.

Short's life was short and the short epitaph on his short monument was really short. Quote: Short's Corpse.

The Ghost of Shaver Lake

{There is a school of thought that says no book is complete without a ghost story. Whether Mr. McCubbin subscribed to this notion or not is unknown. Nonetheless, he did write a non-fiction "ghost story," which is reproduced here as our concluding article.}

During the open season for deer hunting in 1935, I went to Fresno County to take charge of the little store and post office at Shaver Lake. This relieved the proprietor, Bryant Ashton, who then assumed the duties of assistant to the local forest ranger during the rush season of the hunters. It proved to be a very busy season, for they checked out through that one station over 800 deer and one mountain lion.

Shaver Lake lies in the Sierra National Forest and about fifty miles east of Fresno. It is an artificial body of crystal-clear water created by the Southern California Edison Company in 1926-27. The lake has a shore line of over twenty-two miles. It has a maximum depth of 175 feet, and is the largest of their chain of Sierra Nevada mountain reservoirs.

On previous occasions when I had assisted in this same capacity of store keeper and post master, my sleeping quarters had been in a large building formerly occupied by the Shaver Lake Fishing Club. I was the sole occupant during the night. The old club house was some distance from the main group of resort buildings, with a dense forest extending about it in every direction.

Ashton assigned me again to the old vacant club house, this time with some misgivings as to my comfort. It seemed that of late, weird sounds resembling mysterious footsteps had been repeatedly heard somewhere in or about the building. The sounds came only at night, which definitely suggested the presence of a ghost.

In my childhood, my mother never allowed anyone to tell a ghost story in the presence of her children, and had carefully trained our minds against everything of a mysterious or fearful nature. Consequently, I lacked the necessary background for a belief in spooks, and made light of the rumors.

My first question was: "Will the ghost pull the covers off of me?" The nights were already becoming quite cool, for the altitude of the lake was in excess of a vertical mile. Ashton said, "No. Never pulls stunts like that. Just makes noises like footsteps. Always seven at a time, never any more, never any less. Just seven."

The number seven gave me a clue to the identity of the ghost, which I passed on to Ashton. "Don't you remember the story of Phineas Loucks, who disappeared so mysteriously back in the eighties? He left exactly seven children, four boys and three girls. Maybe it is his apparition that's haunting the lake."

My thoughts then turned from levity to serious memories, and I related the following true historical narrative of the Loucks family.

The old log cabin standing among the timber a short distance from the head of Shaver Lake, far from the road or human habitation, was built in 1887 by Phineas Loucks, who did all the work himself.

Mrs. Loucks and the children spent the long dreary winter of 1887-88 in this cabin while the husband was working down in the San Joaquin Valley, fifty miles away. That winter proved to be a severe one. The snow reached a depth of six feet on the level, imprisoning the occupants of the cabin for months.

When spring came the husband returned to his family. The following July another child was born. The mother, weakened by the rigors of the winter, passed away shortly afterwards. Her remains now rest in a lonely grave a short distance from the cabin.

The motherless children, ranging in ages from a few weeks to fifteen years, were removed to the valley and placed in the homes of relatives and friends. In the spring of 1889 the father returned to his mountain home to carry on alone.

That summer, a friend who was vacationing nearby, called to visit Phineas one day, but found no one at home. It was evident that Loucks had left with the intention of returning soon, for there was cooked food on hand, spoiling on the table, and a pot of cooked beans souring on the stove. What had kept Loucks away so long?

An immediate search was launched locally, and soon taken up by those officers and extended until finally considered hopeless. No single clue was found. The mystery surrounding the fate of Phineas Loucks is just as deep today as it was in 1889.

When Wallace Loucks, the eldest son, was grown, he married a Miss Swift whose parents had adopted one of his sisters. He purchased an eighty-acre tract of raw land a few miles east of Reedley, near the foot of Smith's Mountain. He erected buildings thereon, planted it all to fruit, grape vines and alfalfa. The soil was very fertile. Wallace was industrious and farmed his ranch faithfully until the trees and vines came into bearing. With their one year old son, they had a bright future.

But, the Loucks family trend toward tragedy came to the fore again. One beautiful Saturday afternoon, according to a previous plan, a friend drove to their ranch and took Wallace and his little family in his car and started to Fresno to spend the weekend with friends. After passing through Reedley, the machine was wrecked at a railroad crossing. Wallace was killed instantly. His wife and baby were so severely injured that they both died while being hurried back to town. They were being transported in the mail car where my nephew was clerk in charge.

The death of the mother and child occurred so nearly at the same time, there was a difference of opinion among those present as to which one actually expired first. That point was important, because it would determine who should inherit valuable ranch property.

In a long drawn out court battle it was decided that the child died first, and the inheritance moved along the following line. First, Wallace's interest passed to his wife and child jointly. Then the child's interest passed to its mother, and finally the entire estate passed from the mother to the Swifts. That valuable estate changed possession three times, wholly or in part, in less than a half hour, and by a peculiar quirk of fate, the Loucks heirs were entirely disinherited.

Following the recital of these tragic events, I told Mr. Ashton that I thought the old club house with its vacant rooms was large enough to accommodate both the ghost and me, and I went over to the old building and retired.

Just as I was getting to sleep, I heard footsteps. In my drowsiness, I was unable to count them. On the second night following this experience, the ghost walked again, but before I had gone to sleep, and I was able to count, "One, two, three, four, five, six, seven" steps. Then deathly silence followed. It sounded to me like someone mounting a flight of stairs. But, the club house was a one story building, with no stairways, and I decided that I had heard the ghost.

When I related this second experience to Ashton the next morning, he declared he would solve the mystery of that ghost. That night he took a flashlight, went into the attic, and with a box to sit on awaited the appearance of the ghost. After about an hour of tiresome vigil, he heard the ghost only a few feet away and walking across the attic where there was no floor to walk on. Turning on the light he saw the ghost at last. Real flesh and blood and very much alive. A mouse was laboriously making its way across the attic by a route which compelled it to leap over the joists to the underside of which was nailed the plyboard ceiling of the room below. There were seven joists, hence the seven steps of the ghost.

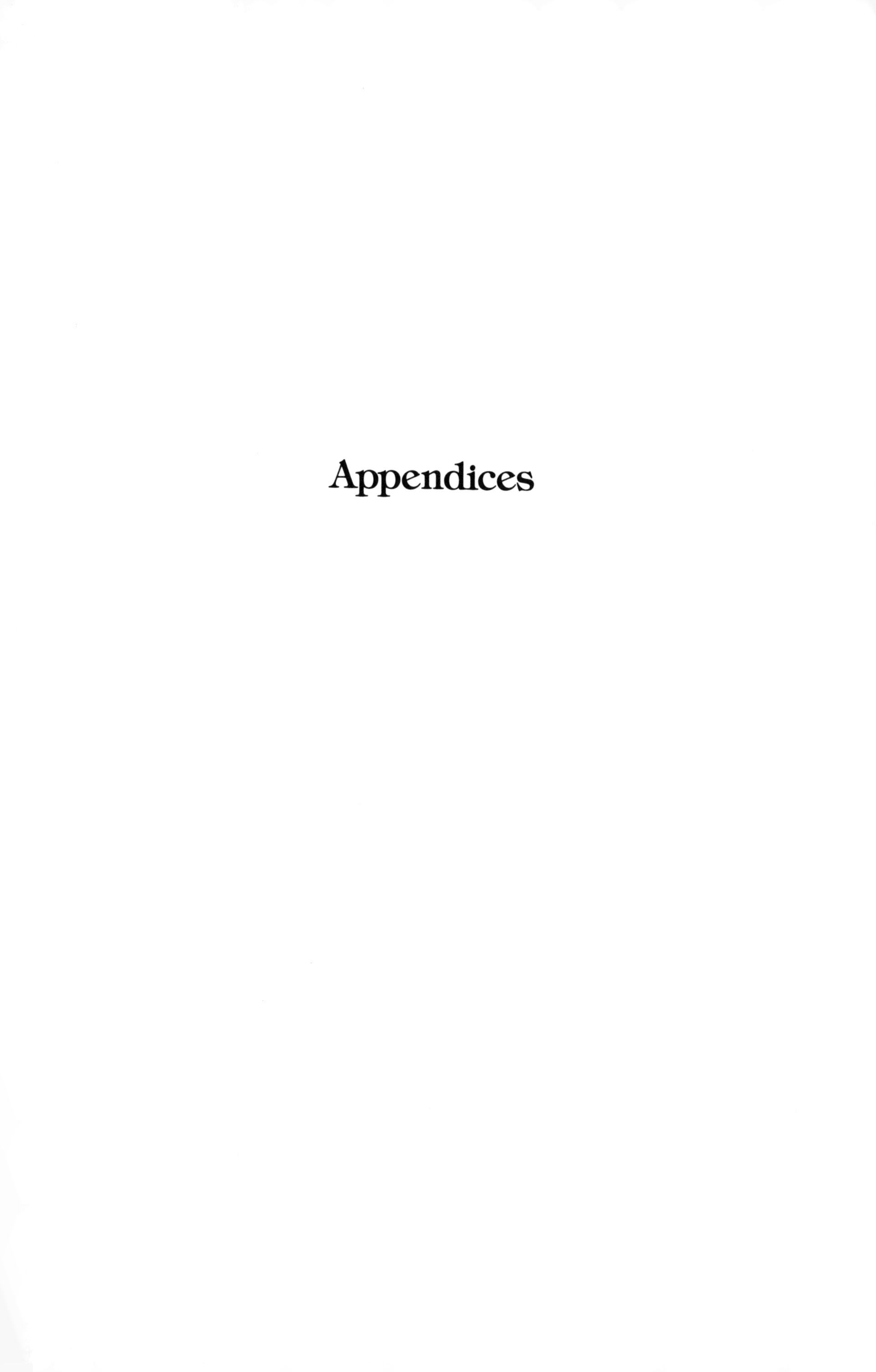

Appendices

Appendix A

The Prehistoric Trail

The various section line crossings of the old prehistoric trail were as follows.

In Township 16 South, Range 23 East, the old road crossed on a southwest course at the following points [a "chain" is equivalent to 66 feet]:

73.90 chains north on east line of Section 4
55.50 chains west on the south line of Section 4
18.40 chains north on the west line of Section 9
6.41 chains west on the south line of Section 8
30.30 chains west on the south line of Section 17
52.30 chains west on the south line of Section 20
77.40 chains north on the east line of Section 31

In Township 17 South, Range 23 East, the old road crossed on a southwest course at the following point:

53.85 chains north on the west line of Section 6.

Appendix B

A San Joaquin Valley Section of the Old Stockton-Los Angeles Stage Road

The tables herewith have been compiled from the original Government survey, and they show the section line crossings (all that were recorded) along that portion of the old Stockton-Los Angeles stage road that passed through what is now Madera, Fresno and Tulare Counties.

The items in the tables begin at a point north of the Chowchilla River, near where the southeast corner of Merced County and the southwest corner of Mariposa County connect with the north line of Madera County, and run thence in a southeasterly direction along the line of the old road to the north line of Kern County.

The section line crossing were at points described as follows [The following explanation of the very first listing may clarify the meaning of McCubbin's table: In Township 9 South, Range 18 East, the old road crossed the west line of Section 6, at a point 14.25 chains south (of the north line or top of the section). The old road was on a southeast course at this point.]:

Township 9 South, Range 18 East, M. D. B. & M.

South on west line of Section 6. At 14.25 Chs. cross old road. Course S. E.
North on east line of Section 7. At 11.00 Chs. cross old road. Course S. E.
East on north line of Section 17. At 13.25 Chs. cross old road. Course S. E.
East on south line of Section 17. At 75.00 Chs. cross old road. Course S. E.
North on east line of Section 20. At 73.50 Chs. cross old road. Course S. E.
East on south line of Section 21. At 49.75 Chs. cross old road. Course S. E.
North on east line of Section 28. At 33.50 Chs. cross old road. Course S. E.
East on south line of Section 27. At 24.50 Chs. cross old road. Course S. E.
North on east line of Section 34. At 32.75 Chs. cross old road. Course S. E.
East on south line of Section 35. At 31.00 Chs. cross old road. Course S. E.

Township 10 South, Range 18 East

South on east line of Section 2. At 70.00 Chs. cross old road. Course S. E.
West on south line of Section 1. At 61.00 Chs. cross old road. Course S. E.
South on east line of Section 12. At 65.00 Chs. cross old road. Course S. E.

Township 10 South, Range 19 East

East on south line of Section 7. At 10.00 Chs. cross old road. Course S. E.
East on south line of Section 18. At 38.13 Chs. cross old road. Course S. E.
North on east line of Section 19. At 42.50 Chs. cross old road. Course S. E.
North on south line of Section 20. At 25.00 Chs. cross old road. Course S. E.
North on east line of Section 29. At 71.00 Chs. cross old road. Course East.
North on east line of Section 28. At 50.00 Chs. cross old road. Course East.
North on east line of Section 27. At 12.50 Chs. cross old road. Course East.
North on east line of Section 26. At 17.50 Chs. cross old road. Course East.
South on east line of Section 25. At 58.50 Chs. cross old road. Course East.

Township 10 South, Range 20 East

North on east line of Section 30. At 38.50 Chs. cross old road. Course East.
North on east line of Section 29. At 22.50 Chs. cross old road. Course S. E.
West on south line of Section 28. At 20.00 Chs. cross old road. Course S. E.

Township 10 South, Range 20 East

North on east line of Section 33. At 76.50 Chs. cross old road. Course S. E.
North on east line of Section 34. At 28.50 Chs. cross old road. Course S. E.
East on south line of Section 35. At 3.50 Chs. cross old road. Course East
East on south line of Section 36. At 6.00 Chs. cross old road. Course S. E.

Township 11 South, Range 20 East

South on east line of Section 1. At 41.50 Chs. cross old road. Course S. E.

The road branched near the above point in Section 1, and after spreading apart above five miles, continued on in a general southeasterly direction for a distance of about fifty-five miles, where they came together north of the St. Johns River, a short distance southwest of the Venice Hills. These two roads were known as the "Upper" and "Lower" roads.

Upper Road

After the Upper road crossed the San Joaquin River at Jones' Ferry, in the northeast quarter of Section 7, Township 11 South, Range 21 East, at the place where the present town of Friant is located, the section line crossings were at points described as follows:

Township 11 South, Range 21 East
North on east line of Section 7. At 28.60 Chs. cross old road. Course S. E.
East on south line of Section 8. At 18.10 Chs. cross old road. Course South.
West on south line of Section 17. At 44.00 Chs. cross old road. Course S. E.
West on south line of Section 20. At 15.00 Chs. cross old road. Course South.
North on east line of Section 29. At 12.50 Chs. cross old road. Course South.
West on south line of Section 28. At 57.75 Chs. cross old road. Course S. E.
North on east line of Section 33. At 16.75 Chs. cross old road. Course S. E.
East on south line of Section 34. At 5.00 Chs. cross old road. Course S. E.

Township 12 South, Range 21 East
West on south line of Section 3. At 30.70 Chs. cross old road. Course. S. E.
North on east line of Section 10. At 57.50 Chs. cross old road. Course S. E.
West on south line of Section 11. At 25.00 Chs. cross old road. Course S. E.

A Detour: Both Roads:
West on south line of Section 11. At 47.00 Chs. cross old road. Course S. E.
North on east line of Section 14. At 73.25 Chs. cross old road. Course S. E.
North on east line of Section 14. At 60.50 Chs. cross old road. Course S. E.

Main Road
West on south line of Section 13. At 39.50 Chs. cross old road. Course S. E.
North on east line of Section 24. At 27.00 Chs. cross old road. Course S. E.

Township 12 South, Range 22 East
Cross Big Dry Creek.
East on south line of Section 19. At 15.00 Chs. cross old road. Course S. E.
West on south line of Section 29. At 71.00 Chs. cross old road. Course S. E.
East on south line of Section 33. At 29.70 Chs. cross old road. Course S. E.

Township 13 South, Range 22 East
South on east line of Section 4. At 65.15 Chs. cross old road. Course S. E.
West on south line of Section 10. At 8.30 Chs. cross old road. Course S. E.
North on east line of Section 15. At 67.70 Chs. cross old road. Course S. E.

West on south line of Section 14. At 32.67 Chs. cross old road. Course S. E.
North on east line of Section 23. At 33.34 Chs. cross old road. Course S. E.
West on south line of Section 24. At 63.1 Chs. cross old road. Course S. E.
South on east line of Section 25. At 63.00 Chs. cross old road. Course S. E.

Township 13 South, Range 23 East
East on south line of Section 30. At 4.90 Chs. cross old road. Course S. E.
North on east line of Section 31. At 14.15 Chs. cross old road. Course S. E.
West on south line of Section 32. At 15.28 Chs. cross old road. Course S. E.

Township 14 South, Range 23 East
South on east line of Section 5. At 62.80 Chs. cross old road. Course S. E.
East on south line of Section 4. At 9.14 Chs. cross old road. Course S. E.

Short Detour
East on south line of Section 4. At 18.80 Chs. cross old road. Course S. E.

Main Road
South on west line of Section 9. At 43.40 Chs. cross old road. Course S. W.

Turning to the southeast and crossing Kings River at Campbell's crossing, near the east line of section 8, the Upper Road turned again, and the recorded section line crossings were continued as follows:

North on west line of Section 16. At 43.00 Chs. cross old road. Course S. W.
North on south line of Section 17. At 9.60 Chs. cross old road. Course S. W.
North on south line of Section 20. At 17.94 Chs. cross old road. Course South.
North on west line of Section 33. At 50.00 Chs. cross old road. Course S. E.
North on south line of Section 33. At 16.31 Chs. cross old road. Course South.

Township 15 South, Range 23 East
South on west line of Section 3. At 80.54 Chs. cross old road. Course S. E.
North on west line of Section 11. At 34.18 Chs. cross old road. Course S. E.
West on south line of Section 12. At 72.16 Chs. cross old road. Course S. E.
South on east line of Section 13. At 47.83 Chs. cross old road. Course S. E.

Township 15 South, Range 24 East
East on south line of Section 18. At 52.78 Chs. cross old road. Course S. E.
North on east line of Section 19. At 62.00 Chs. cross old road. Course S. E.
North on east line of Section 20. At 12.60 Chs. cross old road. Course S. E.
West on south line of Section 21. At 11.20 Chs. cross old road. Course S. E.
North on west line of Section 27. At 77.50 Chs. cross old road. Course S. E.
North on east line of Section 27. At 7.50 Chs. cross old road. Course S. E.
North on south line of Section 26. At 71.88 Chs. cross old road. Course S. E.
North on east line of Section 35. At 5.14 Chs. cross old road. Course S. E.

Township 16 South, Range 24 East
West on south line of Section 1. At 17.45 Chs. cross old road. Course S. E.
North on east line of Section 12. At 56.72 Chs. cross old road. Course S. E.

Township 16 South, Range 25 East
East on south line of Section 7. At 40.00 Chs. cross old road. Course S. E.
North on east line of Section 18. At 23.00 Chs. cross old road. Course S. E.
West on south line of Section 17. At 64.44 Chs. cross old road. Course S. E.
West on south line of Section 20. At 13.12 Chs. cross old road. Course S. E.
North on east line of Section 29. At 55.60 Chs. cross old road. Course S. E.
West on south line of Section 28. At 43.26 Chs. cross old road. Course S. E.

Township 17 South, Range 25 East
East on north line of Section 3. At 48.00 Chs. cross old road. Course S. E.
North on east line of Section 3. At 30.63 Chs. cross old road. Course S. E.
East on north line of Section 11. At 19.40 Chs. cross old road. Course S. E.
East on south line of Section 11. At 70.35 Chs. cross old road. Course S. E.
North on east line of Section 14. At 62.50 Chs. cross old road. Course S. E.
East on south line of Section 15. At 38.7 Chs. cross old road. Course S. E.

Township 17 South, Range 26 East
West on south line of Section 19. At 37.60 Chs. cross old road. Course South.
West on south line of Section 30. At 28.40 Chs. cross old road. Course S. E.
North on east line of Section 31. At 42.80 Chs. cross old road. Course S. E.

Township 18 South, Range 26 East

The Upper Road entered this township at a point near the center of the north line of Section 5, and after passing around to the west of Venice Hills, it formed a junction with the Lower Road on the north side of St. Johns River in Section 17, near the southwest foot of the hill.

There was no record made of any section line crossings of the Upper Road in this township.

We will return to the northern junction and take up the record of the section line crossings of the Lower Road.

Lower Road

Township 11 South, Range 21 East

Beginning at the northern junction of the Upper and Lower Roads in section 1, just north of the San Joaquin River, and taking up the line of the Lower Road, we find that it started down the west side of the river, and the recorded section line crossings were as follows:

Township 11 South, Range 20 East
East on south line of Section 12. At 16.25 Chs. cross old road. Course S.W.
South on east line of Section 14. At 37.50 Chs. cross old road. Course S. W.
West on south line of Section 14. At 21.60 Chs. cross old road. Course S.W.

After crossing the San Joaquin River at Brackman's crossing, in the northwest quarter of section 24, the road turned down the river, and the recorded section line crossings continued as follows:

Township 12 South, Range 20 East
North on east line of Section 2. At 31.75 Chs. cross old road. Course S. E.
West on south line of Section 1. At 60.00 Chs. cross old road. Course S. E.
North on east line of Section 12. At 30.70 Chs. cross old road. Course S. E.

Township 12 South, Range 21 East
East on south line of Section 7. At 43.70 Chs. cross old road. Course S.E.
North on west line of Section 17. At 34.00 Chs. cross old road. Course S. E.
West on south line of Section 17. At 58.50 Chs. cross old road. Course S. E.
North on east line of Section 20. At 15.75 Chs. cross old road. Course S. E.

Cross Big Dry Creek near S. W. corner Section 21.

North on east line of Section 28. At 26.90 Chs. cross old road. Course S. E.
West on south line of Section 27. At 50.27 Chs. cross old road. Course S. E.
North on east line of Section 34. At 38.50 Chs. cross old road. Course S. E.

Township 13 South, Range 22 East
South on west line of Section 6. At 62.15 Chs. cross old road. Course S. E.
West on south line of Section 6. At 64.75 Chs. cross old road. Course S. E.
North on east line of Section 18. At 51.00 Chs. cross old road. Course S. E.
North on east line of Section 32. At 41.40 Chs. cross old road. Course S. E.
East on south line of Section 33. At 17.78 Chs. cross old road. Course S. E.

Township 14 South, Range 22 East
West on south line of Section 4. At 29.50 Chs. cross old road. Course S. E.
North on east line of Section 9. At 2.30 Chs. cross old road. Course S. E.
West on south line of Section 10. At 77.63 Chs. cross old road. Course S. E.
West on south line of Section 15. At 43.16 Chs. cross old road. Course S. E.
West on south line of Section 22. At 10.80 Chs. cross old road. Course S. E.

In Sections 15 and 22, the road passed through what is now the town of Sanger.

East on south line of Section 26. At 21.80 Chs. cross old road. Course S. E.
East on south line of Section 35. At 52.46 Chs. cross old road. Course S. E.

Township 15 South, Range 22 East
North on east line of Section 2. At 51.72 Chs. cross old road. Course S. E.
South on east line of Section 1. At 75.84 Chs. cross old road. Course S. E.

Township 15 South, Range 23 East
East on north line of Section 7. At 19.57 Chs. cross old road. Course S. E.
North on east line of Section 7. At 59.73 Chs. cross old road. Course S. E.
West on south line of Section 8. At 2.80 Chs. cross old road. Course S. E.

North on west line of Section 16. At 78.80 Chs. cross old road. Course S. E.

Cross Kings River at John Pool's Ferry, at a point about ten chains in a northwesterly direction from the quarter corner on the east line of section 16 and continuing the recorded section line crossings were as follows:

North on east line of Section 16. At 29.64 Chs. cross old road. Course South.
West on south line of Section 27. At 46.65 Chs. cross old road. Course South.

In Section 27 the road passed through what is now the town of Reedley. Near the center of Section 34 the road passed Smith's Ferry.

Township 16 South, Range 23 East

South on east line of Section 3. At 15.00 Chs. cross old road. Course S. E.
West on south line of Section 2. At 18.65 Chs. cross old road. Course S. E.
North on west line of Section 12. At 63.50 Chs. cross old road. Course S. E.

Cross Kennedy Slough in the west half of Section 12.

West on the south line of Section 12. At 30.85 Chs. cross old road. Course S. E.

Township 16 South, Range 24 East

North on east line of Section 30. At 58.10 Chs. cross old road. Course S. E.
West on south line of Section 29. At 43.16 Chs. cross old road. Course S. E.
North on east line of Section 32. At 52.16 Chs. cross old road. Course S. E.
North on east line of Section 33. At 1.24 Chs. cross old road. Course S. E.

Cross Fourth Standard Line.

Township 17 South, Range 24 East

West on south line of Section 3. At 29.75 Chs. cross old road. Course S. E.
North on east line of Section 10. At 54.40 Chs. cross old road. Course S. E.
North on east line of Section 11. At 30.00 Chs. cross old road. Course S. E.
West on south line of Section 12. At 45.00 Chs. cross old road. Course S. E.
West on south line of Section 24. At 10.20 Chs. cross old road. Course S. E.
South on east line of Section 25. At 20.00 Chs. cross old road. Course S. E.

Township 17 South, Range 25 East

East on south line of Section 30. At 39.00 Chs. cross old road. Course S. E.
North on east line of Section 31. At 14.35 Chs. cross old road. Course S. E.
East on south line of Section 32. At 12.00 Chs. cross old road. Course S. E.

Township 18 South, Range 25 East

The Visalia detour branched off in Section 5, this Township, and after passing through the town, ran in an easterly direction a distance of about four miles, where it formed a junction with the main road. The recorded section line crossings of this detour, will be found on a separate table.

South on east line of Section 5. At 72.00 Chs. cross old road. Course S. E.
West on south line of Section 4. At 66.20 Chs. cross old road. Course S. E.
North on east line of Section 9. At 62.00 Chs. cross old road. Course East

South on east line of Section 11. At 38.00 Chs. cross old road. Course East.
South on east line of Section 12. At 74.00 Chs. cross old road. Course East.

Township 18 South, Range 26 East

West on south line of Section 7. At 70.60 Chs. cross old road. Course S. E.

The Lower Road formed a junction with the Upper Road in Section 17. After forming this southern junction, the road ran in an easterly direction, passing between the "Election Tree" and the foot of the hill, and then followed around the base of the hill in a northeasterly direction, a short distance, and turning toward the southeast. The recorded section line crossings continued as follows:

North on west line of Section 16. At 28.85 Chs. cross old road. Course S. E.

Crossed St. John's River.

East on south line of Section 16. At 5.95 Chs. cross old road. Course South.
North on east line of Section 20. At 67.70 Chs. cross old road. Course S. W.

Cross Kaweah River at Woodsville, the original county seat of Tulare County in Section 20.

East on south line of Section 30. At 29.80 Chs. cross old road. Course S. W.
East on south line of Section 31. At 27.40 Chs. cross old road. Course S. E.

The Visalia detour formed a junction in the western part of the above Section 31.

Township 19 South, Range 26 East

North on east line of Section 6. At 57.24 Chs. cross old road. Course S. E.
North on south line of Section 5. At 53.80 Chs. cross old road. Course S. E.
West on south line of Section 9. At 69.53 Chs. cross old road. Course S. E.
West on south line of Section 16. At 26.70 Chs. cross old road. Course S. E.
West on south line of Section 22. At 40.60 Chs. cross old road. Course S. E.
North on east line of Section 27. At 17.80 Chs. cross old road. Course S. E.
West on south line of Section 2. At 64.17 Chs. cross old road. Course S. E.
East on south line of Section 35. At 71.60 Chs. cross old road. Course S. E.

Township 20 South, Range 26 East

South on west line of Section 1. At 15.71 Chs. cross old road. Course S. E.

In the above Section 1, the old road skirted along the west side of what is now the town of Lindsay.

West on the south line of Section 12. At 3.00 Chs. cross old road. Course S. E.

Township 20 South, Range 27 East

East on south line of Section 18. At 39.96 Chs. cross old road. Course S. E.
East on south line of Section 19. At 76.21 Chs. cross old road. Course S. E.
North on east line of Section 30. At 72.35 Chs. cross old road. Course S. E.
West on south line of Section 29. At 44.71 Chs. cross old road. Course S. E.
East on south line of Section 33. At 38.75 Chs. cross old road. Course S. E.

Cross Fifth Standard Line.

Township 21 South, Range 27 East
East on north line of Section 4. At 38.75 Chs. cross old road. Course S. E.
West on south line of Section 4. At 3.00 Chs. cross old road. Course S. E.
South on west line of Section 10. At 7.00 Chs. cross old road. Course S. E.
West on south line of Section 10. At 45.00 Chs. cross old road. Course S. E.
South on east line of Section 15. At 59.00 Chs. cross old road. Course S. E.
West on south line of Section 14. At 66.00 Chs. cross old road. Course S. E.
West on south line of Section 23. At 10.50 Chs. cross old road. Course S. E.
South on west line of Section 25. At 5.34 Chs. cross old road. Course S. E.
West on south line of Section 25. At 48.50 Chs. cross old road. Course South.
East on south line of Section 36. At 73.22 Chs. cross old road. Course S. E.

In the above Sections 25 and 36, the road passed through what is now the town of Porterville.

Township 22 South, Range 26 East

The place now known as Plano, in Section 1, was originally called Vandalia, and was located on the old stage road.

There were no field notes made by the man who made the original Government survey, showing any of the section line crossings of the old road, but its location was roughly lined out on the township plat, which shows that it ran through Sections 1, 7, 8, 17, 16, 22, 27, 34, and 35.

Township 23 South, Range 28 East
North on west line of Section 11. At 9.2 Chs. cross old road. Course S. W.
West on north line of Section 15. At 2.82 Chs. cross old road. Course South.
East on south line of Section 15. At 5.66 Chs. cross old road. Course South.
North on east line of Section 22. At 18.53 Chs. cross old road. Course S. E.
West on south line of Section 23. At 55.04 Chs. cross old road. Course South.
West on south line of Section 26. At 50.00 Chs. cross old road. Course South.
East on south line of Section 35. At 32.50 Chs. cross old road. Course South.

Township 24 South, Range 28 East
West on south line of Section 2. At 63.16 Chs. cross old road. Course South.
North on west line of Section 11. At 30.00 Chs. cross old road. Course S. W.
West on north line of Section 15. At 9.73 Chs. cross old road. Course South.
West on south line of Section 14. At 68.80 Chs. cross old road. Course South.
West on south line of Section 23. At 74.28 Chs. cross old road. Course South.
North on east line of Section 27. At 72.00 Chs. cross old road. Course S. W.
West on north line of Section 34. At 19.07 Chs. cross old road. Course South.

The old road crossed the Tulare-Kern County line from the above Section 34.

Visalia Detour from the Stockton-Los Angeles Stage Road

This road branched off from the "Lower Road" somewhere near the center of

Section 5, in the township described below, and the recorded section crossings were as follows:

Township 18 South, Range 25 East
West on south line of Section 5. At 18.00 Chs. cross detour. Course S. E.
South on east line of Section 8. At 23.00 Chs. cross detour. Course S. E.
West on south line of Section 9. At 23.00 Chs. cross detour. Course S. E.
South on west line of Section 15. At 8.50 Chs. cross detour. Course S. E.
North on east line of Section 15. At 2.50 Chs. cross detour. Course East.
North on west line of Section 24. At 25.50 Chs. cross detour. Course S. W.
North on west line of Section 23. At 7.50 Chs. cross detour. Course West.
East on south line of Section 22. At 45.50 Chs. cross detour. Course S. W.
East on south line of Section 21. At 69.00 Chs. cross detour. Course N. W.
Also:
East on south line of Section 21. At 23.00 Chs. cross detour. Course S. W.
North on east line of Section 29. At 53.00 Chs. cross detour. Course S. W.
West on south line of Section 29. At 67.00 Chs. cross detour. Course S. W.

The above point was in Visalia.

Returning to the main road, the detour went south out of town, then turning east, traversed Sections 32, 33, 34, 35 and 36. On this return, only two section line crossings were noted by the surveyor. They were as follows:

North on east line of Section 35. At 53.00 chains, cross detour. Course East.
North on east line of Section 36. At 48.50 chains, cross detour. Course East.

Appendix C

Traver Business Directory, 1887

{*McCubbin states in another place that this is a partial list, and that no attempt was made to list common laborers.*}

Alexander, C. F., Hotel and saloon
Anthony, Al., Butcher
Apperson, Mrs. A. E., City milk route
Applegate, W. J., Bookkeeper
Baker, Chas., Liveryman stable
Baker, Eph., Liveryman stable
Baker, P. Y., Real Estate
Bare, John, Road overseer
Bare, Jacob, Teamster
Bare, Mrs. Jacob, Milliner
Bare, Chris, Restaurant
Barris, Emery, Contractor
Bennett, Fred, Clerk
Bennett, Geo., Millwright
Bennett, Warren C., Druggist
Bissett, David, Bartender
Blakemore, W. B., Constable
Bledsoe, J. W., Photographer
Blum, Jacob, Clerk
Bobo, J. J., Druggist
Bookwalter, Dr. ________, Physician

Boone, J. T., Nurseryman
Boone N. I., Dentist
Boone, W. P., Nurseryman
Bowhay, Jasper Newton, Butcher
Bowman, Dan., Saloonkeeper
Boyd, Calvin, Drayman
Boyd, Geo. W., Druggist
Boyd, C. John, Clerk
Boyd, Jas. A., Sr., Merchant
Boyd, Jas. A., Jr., Merchant
Brown, ________ , The painter
Brownstone, Henry, Merchant
Burke, Harry A., Saloonkeeper
Cahn, Gus., Clerk
Cahn, Nathan, Clerk
Cannon, ________ , Bookkeeper
Carman, Al., Street sprinkler
Cassady, James, Butcher
Cassady, Mrs. James, Boarding house
Chase, Story, Carpenter
Cogley, C. C., Confectionery
Cole, Jas. R., Blacksmith
Cole, John S., Blacksmith
Cook, Sam. R., Carpenter
Cornwell, Chas. W., Teamster
Cosby Bros., Merchants
Coughran, Mrs. Belle, 76 Hotel
Curtis, C. C., Photographer
Dahle, John, Shoemaker
Davidson, C. A., Saloonkeeper
DeBelville, [D. T.], Reverend
Deming, Byron, Restaurant
Deming, Wm., Saloon keeper
Dewey, Fred. V., Traver *Advocate*
Dixon, W. O., Bookkeeper
Doody, James, Saloonkeeper
Dopkins, Geo. M., Carpenter
Dougherty, Pat., Sack piler
Drake, Chas., Blacksmith
Drake, John, Blacksmith
Duffy, J. B., Blacksmith
Dunlap, Ed., Barber
Durgin, N., Clerk
Earl, Sumner Fremont, Secretary, 76 Land and Water Company
Egenhoff, [David], Mariposa Hotel
Ellert, John A., Painter
Elliott, Judd., Druggist
Everton, Alfred, Feed yard
Frey, Samuel, Miller
Frisch, Chas., Restaurant
Fuller, Frank, "Boston"
Fullerton, Geo., Carpenter
Gass, Benjamin, City milk route
Gebhart, E. M., Physician
Gilstrap, James M., Dentist
Gleason, Ed. E., Saloonkeeper
Gordon, Lincoln, Machinest
Gramley, Uriah M., Teamster
Greene, Sam K., Machine Shop
Greenberg, Wolfie, Merchant
Greenwood, Geo., Sack piler
Gribble, Chas., Clerk
Grosbauer, ________ , Bartender
Gumm, Doug., Upholsterer
Gutfeld, Chas., Clerk
Haas, [Gus?], Restaurant
Hackney, Joseph E., Physician
Haden, Mrs. C. B., Millinery
Haden, H. T., Real Estate
Haden, John, Blacksmith
Haines, W. D., Jeweler
Hall, Geo., Carpenter
Hall, Homer, Contractor
Hall, The painter
Heidt, Jes
Hellman, Henry, Liveryman
Hemming, Wm., Painter
Henderson, Wm., Liveryman
Hirschfeld, Louie, Merchant
Hollenback, Perry, Carpenter
Holzhouser, L. J., Miller
Howard, Wade N., Clerk
Hughes, Bert. L., Bookkeeper
Hunsaker, [Archibald S.], Reverend
Hunsaker, J. L., Clerk
Hurd, John, Driver of Milk Wagon

Hurst, Harry, Carpenter
Jacobs, Henry, Merchant
Jesus, Mexican Tamale vender
Johnson, Bart, Carpenter
Jones, Jack, Butcher
Jordan, Thos. J., Liveryman and Traver and Visalia Stageline
Jurgens, Peter, Secretary, Traver Warehouse and Business Association
Kelsey, ________ , Carpenter
Kempter, T. B., Harnessmaker
Kimble, J. A., Machine Shop
Lee, ________ , Barber
Lewis, Henry, Wagonmaker
Linn, Fred., Saloonkeeper
Littlefield, Fred. A., Liveryman
Lobb, Geo., Carpenter
Loggins, W. E., Carpenter
Long, Joseph, Painter
Lowenberg, Solomon, Clerk
Mallock, Dan., Bartender
Mathews, John, Big rancher living in town
Mason, Frank, Clerk
McClanahan, A. E., Real Estate
McCord, Doug. H., Butcher
McCubbin, J. C., Painter
McCubbin, T. B., Carpenter
McCulloch, R. S., Harnessmaker
McDonald, Alex., Blacksmith
McElfercy, Peter, Painter
Michaels, Geo., Saloonkeeper
Miles, Ed., Foreman, 76 warehouse
Morris, Geo. W., Blacksmith
Morton, Ed., Well borer
Morton, Lee W., Well borer
Mugler, Al. M., Merchant
Murray, Mike., Bartender
Nelson, Wm. D., Manager, Traver Warehouse and Business Association
Newby, Ellsworth, Principal, Traver School
Paz, Cessaya, Barber
Peacock, Joseph, Supt., 76 Land and Water Company
Peacock, Harry R., Feed Yard and Restaurant
Phelps, O. B., Warehouseman
Pierce, Al. L., Painter
Pillsbury, Joseph D., Carpenter
Poncelot, ________ , Blacksmith
Putinton, J. K., Blacksmith
Ray, Samuel, Barber
Raymer, John W., S.P.R.R. Agent
Rebar, G., Jeweler
Redding, Jack, Carpenter
Rieffel, ________ , Baker
Rieffel, Eugene, Barber
Rockwell, Anson J., Millwright
Rockwell, Lorenzo A., Druggist and Post Man
Roes, Louis, Saloon keeper
Ross, William E., Real Estate
Rucker, J. P., Washington Hotel
Ruggles, Lyman B., President, Traver Warehouse and Business Association
Russell, Wm. E., Night Watchman
Scott, S. H., Clerk
Seligman, Emil, Merchant
Semorile, L., Clerk
Shelton, Robert C., Cigars and Confection
Shoemaker, C. H., Carpenter
Spangler, Lafayette, Restaurant
Spears, M. Cisero, Drayman
Spinks, "Budd", At one time the Proprietor of the Traver Hotel built by L. Semorile
Starring, Harry F., Traver *Tidings*
Storr, Fran, Machinist
Strannon, Geo., Blacksmith
Sweet, Richard, Clerk
Tadlock, Wm. L., Drayman
Theal, S., Carpenter
Thym, F., Bookkeeper

Tuxbury, Wm. D., Capitalist
Tyer, Dan., Harnessmaster
Watson, Thos. H., Merchant
Weathers, Jennie, Seamstress
Weathers, Lucy, Clerk
Weaver, Geo. H., Merchant
Weaver, Carrie J., School teacher
Weddle, E. S., Undertaker
Weddle, Thel., Carpenter
West, H. D., Justice of the Peace
Wheeler, Joe., Saloonkeeper
Wiley, Simeon, Teamster
Williams, Geo. C., Carpenter
Wilson, Oscar P. Jr., Clerk
Wilson, Oscar P. Sr., Miller
Wilson, R. M., Miller
Winnes, Harry F., Contractor
Wolff, S., Merchant
Woolery, Henry, Dance Hall and Saloon
Wright, O. S., Carpenter

Chinatown

Tin San, "Mayor," Employment office and gambling house
Tong Toong Sing, Merchant
Sam Lung, Laundry
Lee Toy, Laundry
Ah Sow, Labor contractor

Appendix D

Directory of the 76 Country
Now Known as the Alta District
Also Including Portions of What is Now Kings County

Those who are listed below made Traver their trading point and delivered their crops at that place. About ninety per cent of them came to the above territory after January 1, 1883.

Abbott, M. O.
Abbott, O. L.
Abbott, S. B.
Adams, Ambrose
Agee, J. Newt.
Alcorn, Joseph
Allen, Frank
Allison, Jasper
Allison, Joseph
Allison, W. P.
Anderson, Geo. B.
Anderson, Joseph E.
Archer, A. J.
Archer, J. W.
Archer, W. H.
Arnold, J. D.
Arnold, J. H.
Ashurst, G. C.
Aull, John
Bailey, Wm. A.
Baker, Thos. N.
Barlow, Charles
Barnes, E.
Barnes, G. W.
Barnett, Z. T.
Barris, David
Barris, W. S.
Bates, Thos.
Beaty, W. C.
Becknell, J. C.
Belt, Geor. M.
Benadom, F. A.
Benadom, Wm. O.

Bingham, Ozias S.
Bland, Edward
Blench, C. C.
Bloyd, Benjamin
Bloyd, Emerson
Bloyd, L. Jefferson
Bloyd, Leander J.
Blunt, A. W.
Boone, L. L.
Bownman, Joel
Boyd, Alex.
Boyd, Thos.
Brewer, Ole Skeen
Brown, T. J.
Bump, A. J.
Burum, G. G.
Burum, H. H.
Burum, P. F.
Burum, W. H.
Caesar, James
Caesar, John
Caesar, Thomas
Calloway, Henry
Campbell, J. E.
Campbell, Nathan
Campbell, T. H.
Carpenter, W. H.
Carrington, W. R.
Cederberg, Swan S.
Chamberlain, L. A.
Clark, Amaziah W.
Clark, E. W.
Clark, James M.
Clark, L. A.
Clark, Sam. C.
Clarke, Dell
Collins, O. A.
Cook, David T.
Coombs, W. J.
Cornwell, E. H.
Coy, Milt. M.
Crane, G. W.
Cravens, Josh.
Crow, L. W.
Curle, Ralph S.
Curtin, Matt. W.
Curtis, W. I.
Dawson, John W.
Deiss, G. W.
Dickey, D.
Dittman, Geor. W.
Dopkins, Dewitt H.
Doyle, S.
Dudney, ______
Dye, Mose
Easterhouse, L.
Eder, Theo.
Eliott, C. W.
England, S. D.
England, Wm.
Engle, Henry W.
Ensley, Lyman H.
Evenberg, Wm.
Field, Richard
Fisher, S. C.
Flourney, W. V.
Fox, John
Fraser, Abner
Fraser, A. R.
Fraser, J. H.
Fraser, J. W.
Fraser, Lark L.
Fraser, R. J.
Freman, Capt. Robert
Furman, A. C.
Gare, J. W.
Garton, W. Z.
Gass, Benjamin
Giddings, C. Frement.
Giddings, E. E.
Giddings, W. R.
Gilbert, D. E.
Glasebrook, J. R.
Gobin, Arthur
Golden, John
Greene, Clark
Gregg, L. W.
Gregg, S. H.

Griggs, J. D.
Hackett, Jesse
Hackett, John
Hackett, Oscar
Haden, Cammy B.
Hamilton, R. E.
Harden, James H.
Hart, Fred W.
Hayward, D. C.
Heimroth, Anton
Heins, Wm. L.
Helm, Samuel C.
Hicks, Stephen
Hill, Charles
Hill, John
Hill, Stark
Hilliard, F. M.
Hogan, Joseph W.
Holmes, E. W.
Hoover, Pres.
Hopkins, W. S.
House, Joseph A.
House, Thomas
Housley, J. C. "Dad"
Hubbard, Wm.
Hudson, J. H.
Hunter, C. B.
Hunter, W. G.
Hurst, James
Hurst, Wm. H.
Ingram, Geo.
Jack, "Cub"
Jack, Milt. M.
Jack, Wilbourn
Jaynes, Henry
Johnson, J. H.
Johnson, Thomas
Johnson, T. V.
Jordan, John
Keller, ________
Kendall, W. A.
Kennedy, Robert
Kerr, ________
Kieley, Michael
King, Bishop
King, Robberson Jeff.
Lahann, Henry
Lee, James
Lee, Wellington
Lemmon, G. T.
Levey, A. F.
Lewis, Rev. Joshua "Pap"
Macomber, J. A.
Magee, Ben
Mall, Peter
March, John C.
Marrs, James
Mathews, Harry S.
Mau, Charles
McCanne, Thos. B.
McClanahan, Allen E.
McFarland, C. Z
McFarland, Charles
McQuiddy, J. T.
Meisenheimer, D. S.
Meisenheimer, Moses
Merritt, E. P.
Merritt, F. M.
Metcalf, G. W.
Miller, A. O.
Miller, Boss W.
Miller, W. A.
Miller, W. K.
Milsap, M.
Moore, ________
Morgan, R. F.
Morgan, T. M.
Morris, C. E.
Murray, M. J.
Nance, Geo. W.
Nance, J. E.
Neil, James Polk
Neil, Wm. R.
Nemway, D. W.
Noel, F. W.
Ogle, Barton
Ogle, Emmett
Overman, E. M.

Palmar, J. R.
Pest, L. S.
Pest, Park
Pinnell, C. W.
Pintler, Jarred
Polander, J. H.
Poole, A. F.
Poole, J. H.
Purtyman, Dan.
Randall, J. E.
Ray, Frank
Reed, Thomas Law
Rhodes, Daniel
Rhodes, John
Rice, I. R.
Ringold, A. M.
Roark, ______
Robinson, B. S.
Robinson, G. A.
Roes, Henry
Ruggles, John D.
Russell, J. C.
Ruth, Wm.
Sanford, Robert P.
Saunders, E. W.
Saville, Joseph
Scoggins, A. J.
Scoggins, Byron
Scott, M. V.
Segrue, Patrick
Shannon, Sam.
Sharp, C. B.
Shaw, James
Shipe, James W.
Shipe, John W.
Sibley, James
Simpson, Al. T.
Simpson, Robert
Slocumb, C. J.
Slocumb, J. A.
Slocumb, J. C.
Smith, Albert K.
Smith, Crosby
Smith, D. M.
Smith, S. E.
Smith, Wm. "Flap Jack"
Snow, Benjamin
Snyder, W.
Spafford, Vick.
Spangler, Dan.
Sproat, Lorin S.
Stamgood, R.
Stirewalt, M. S.
Street, Joseph
Streuer, August
Swain, T. H.
Thomas, W. P.
Thompson, J. D.
Thompson, Mort. G.
Thompson, W.
Thornton, John
Tomlinson, G. W.
Tout, Ben. F.
Tout, Elias
Tout, John
Tout, Perry
Tracy, Thomas
Tucker, I. B.
Turner, C. M.
Tutt, H. C.
Tyner, Thos.
Underdown, Jesse
Vanney, J. D.
Vaughn, D. V.
Vineyard, W. T.
Vose, Warren
Wakefield, Atwood F.
Walsh, R.
West, Milt M.
Williams, C. H.
Williams, Fount.
Williams, J. H.
Williams, W. A. "Bee"
Williams, W. W.
Wilson, O. S.
Wooton, William
Worsley, A.
Wright, Joseph
Young, D. W.
Young, J. S.

Index

Page numbers in italics refer to maps, illustrations or photographs.